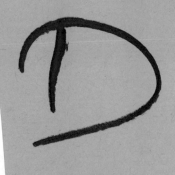

ARNOLD'S
POETIC LANDSCAPES

ARNOLD'S

POETIC
LANDSCAPES

The description does not adorn
or decorate the thought; it is
part of it; they have so grown
into each other that they seem
not welded together, but
indivisible and twin-born.—Swinburne

ALAN ROPER

THE JOHNS HOPKINS PRESS, BALTIMORE

"An English Landscape," the wood engraving reproduced on the dust jacket and title page, is from a painting by John Constable.

To My Wife

Contents

The epigraph is taken from Swinburne's review of Arnold's volume of *New Poems* (1867), although Swinburne by no means restricts himself to the contents of that volume. I take his observation to represent the goal rather than, as Swinburne believed, the consistent achievement of Arnold's poems. To my knowledge, no attempt has been made in the hundred years since Swinburne wrote his essay to apply the value standard of his observation in a full-length study of Arnold's poems. Evaluation of Arnold as a landscape poet has been discharged in essays and asides, or in the subordinate terms of studies proposing different primary goals. Such an evaluation is the primary goal of this study, although I have occasionally rested in the kind of descriptive elucidation of meanings to which, in recent years, the landscapes of Arnold's poems have been quite frequently submitted.

In my attempt to bring some measure of coherence and readability to this study I have been greatly assisted by Professor Earl Miner of the University of California at Los Angeles, who read the complete draft and made many suggestions for its improvement.

Santa Monica, California   A. R.
May, 1968

Unless otherwise stated, the place of publication is London.

Where a date or part of a date for a letter is conjectural, it is shown in square brackets. Quotations from the poems follow the text of *The Poetical Works of Matthew Arnold,* ed. C. B. Tinker and H. F. Lowry (1950) .

Frequently cited works are referred to in the notes by the following abbreviations:

Allott:	*The Poems of Matthew Arnold,* ed. Kenneth Allott (1965)
Clough Letters:	*The Letters of Matthew Arnold to Arthur Hugh Clough,* ed. Howard Foster Lowry (1932)
Commentary:	C. B. Tinker and H. F. Lowry, *The Poetry of Matthew Arnold: A Commentary* (1940)
Complete Prose:	*The Complete Prose Works of Matthew Arnold,* ed. R. H. Super (Ann Arbor, 1960–)
Culler:	A. Dwight Culler, *Imaginative Reason: The Poetry of Matthew Arnold* (New Haven, 1966)
Works:	*The Works of Matthew Arnold,* ed. George W. E. Russell, Edition de Luxe, 15 vols. (1903–4)

ARNOLD'S
POETIC LANDSCAPES

I F IT HAD BEEN WRITTEN shortly after it was first projected, this study would have been called *Arnold's Poetic Landscape.* In making the small change to *landscapes,* I have marked
what was for me a large change in critical position. I began with a
conviction that the most important thing about landscape in
Arnold's poetry was the occurrence in different pieces of the same
features with similar meanings. Such occurrences suggested to me
that, at some level of his consciousness, Arnold pictured a more or
less fixed symbolic landscape which he used to represent his ideas
about Victorian life and the human condition. For the benefit of
my students and myself I was prepared to draw a map of Arnold
land from sea to coast, to river, plain and town, to foothills and
glade, mountain top, sun, moon, and stars. Each feature was labeled
with one or more usually moral meanings ascertained from explicit
glosses in separate poems. Individual poems were then charted on
this map as a partial or complete ascent or descent from plain to
mountain or summit to sea. It was when I tried to expand the
brief readings which such a map supplied into reasonably full explications that I realized its inadequacy and, from one point of
view, its fallaciousness.

To note the interesting recurrence of landscape features from
poem to poem was no new venture in Arnold criticism. To go no
earlier, such recurrences are frequently remarked in Louis Bonnerot's critical biography, *Matthew Arnold: Poète* (Paris, 1947),
and in the chapter on Arnold in E. D. H. Johnson's *The Alien*

Vision in Victorian Poetry (Princeton, 1952). For Paull F. Baum they are so obvious as to make their exposition supererogatory;[1] but, ignoring his proleptic dismissal of their endeavors, most critics of Arnold since 1961 have attended at least to some extent to the matter of landscape. The many differences between expositions of the Arnoldian landscape apparently result from the critics' selection of different key poems for glosses upon various features. Whether or not, for example, we find the glade and its variants in sequestered chapel or tomb to be wholly desirable for Arnoldian man will depend on how we balance its two main qualities of escape and detachment and on whether we invoke *The New Sirens* and *Stanzas from the Grande Chartreuse* or *Resignation* and *Lines Written in Kensington Gardens*. The value or meaning of the sea emerges differently in *The Forsaken Merman, Dover Beach,* and *To Marguerite—Continued. In Utrumque Paratus* exemplifies that ascent to the mountain top could lead either to unhappy isolation or to proximity to "truth." The moon and the stars, and sometimes the sun, are frequently associated with purpose and clarity of vision; their blotting out by cloud, as in *Mycerinus* or *Empedocles on Etna,* a loss of clarity. But in *Dover Beach* the moon illuminates only "a world which seems," while dreams and wistful delusions are several times accompanied by moonlight in *Tristram and Iseult*. The most consistent feature is the burning plain and the hot city upon it, as it nearly always expresses some variation upon the unpleasant life battle of the mid-nineteenth century. Interestingly, the plain and city are usually presented with only brief description or in the form of brief metaphor; they almost never evoke the expansive response prompted by glade or river. There are occasions, moreover—in *The Strayed Reveller* and *The Forsaken Merman*—when the town is by no means as unpleasant as is, say, Bokhara.

Unquestionably, Arnold worked again and again with areas of what is recognizably the same landscape, and a composite map may be drawn by extrapolating features from different poems. The enigmas of *The Hayswater Boat* further suggest that on at least one occasion Arnold gave that landscape a private—because wholly unexplicit—meaning. But *The Hayswater Boat* was never reprinted by Arnold, and perhaps its suppression should caution us against using

[1] Paull F. Baum, *Ten Studies in the Poetry of Matthew Arnold* (Durham, N.C., 1958), p. 30: "Those readers [of *Resignation*] who look for allegory and symbol will find them easily in the river of life, the dusty road, the noisy town, the sea of life, and so on."

on other poems the only method by which *The Hayswater Boat* can be made to yield a full meaning: applying to each of its features—the weird domes, the twin brooks—meanings overtly associated with similar features in other poems. If we rest content with such a reading, we imply a conviction that *The Hayswater Boat* works to an extent Arnold apparently thought it did not. The value of the composite landscape to a critic primarily interested in the meaning of individual poems is that it can sharpen his awareness of possible significances he might otherwise have missed. A. Dwight Culler's reading of *Sohrab and Rustum* is a fine example of an exposition which benefits greatly from the critic's awareness that landscape features rarely operate in Arnold's poems as mere decorative backdrop, but are again and again the source and correlative of a mood and a representation of a kind of life.[2]

But a map of Arnold land is usually most satisfactory as a contribution to *oeuvre* criticism. That is to say, however much a composite map may draw upon individual poems for contours and features, it has, as a complete map, no direct reference back to any individual poem. It charts a total *oeuvre*, whose literary status is different from the individual poems it comprises. That it is so emerges clearly from J. Hillis Miller's interesting reading of Arnold in *The Disappearance of God* (Cambridge, Mass., 1963). In his analysis of Arnold's sensibility, drawing, of course, not only on landscape motifs, Professor Miller quotes widely from both the verse and prose. But the sources of his quotations are usually identified by page references to Arnold's collected works: such citation does not encourage a consideration of the work drawn upon at that point. Quotations no longer exist as contributory parts of individual poems and essays; their contribution is entirely to a construct of the total sensibility responsible for individual works. Even that last phrase—a sensibility responsible for individual works—is misleading in its implication that we can return to the sources and apply to individual works the lessons of the *oeuvre*. We cannot. *Oeuvre* criticism does not justify itself by the extent to which it stimulates a reading of particular works in the light of its propositions. A total sensibility is not a literary fact; it expresses itself, part here, variant there, in the separate literary facts of created works.[3]

[2] Culler, pp. 209–14.

[3] "Though the distinguishing traits of an author's genius may be present in each of his creations, just as every work bears the mark of its age, those traits are usually recognized only with difficulty in a single work," *Disappearance of God*,

Obviously, any one part may be expressed quite completely in any one work, and Professor Miller's analysis of that part will overlap considerably with an analysis of the work in which it is expressed. The boundaries between critical modes must not be drawn too firmly. But where analysis of a work justifies itself either by the completeness with which it accounts for the work or the extent to which it stimulates other readers to a full response, Professor Miller's reference to any one work only justifies itself when the part he has discussed is related to the total sensibility.

Professor Miller's reading of Arnold constitutes a pure and self-denying appreciation of what can be accomplished by *oeuvre* criticism. It is pure because it does not contaminate the exposition of a sensibility with readings of particular works. It is self-denying because it does not indulge itself with evaluation of individual works. Professor Miller plainly recognizes that an evaluation derived from his reading must judge the adequacy of the total sensibility as a response to the givens of the age. *Oeuvre* criticism, in fact, concerns itself with what works, or, more usually, parts of works, mean. It does not concern itself with how successfully those meanings are generated within individual works. But *oeuvre* criticism is not always practiced so purely. Most often it accompanies readings of particular works as, among other things, a recognition that a study of one author ought to be more than a set of wholly separate explications. Such a combination, fruitful of insights though it be, raises problems over the proper application of generalizations about landscape and thought to particular works. These are problems both of elucidation and evaluation.

Professor Culler's estimate of *The Scholar-Gipsy* as "Arnold's finest poem" depends upon his belief that Arnold for once succeeded in poising his life, succeeded, that is, in finding a total poetic embodiment of his recurrent expression of nostalgia for a lost innocence in the glade, fretful despair at the empty bustle of mature life in the cities of the plain, and final hope for spiritual amelioration through culture.[4] The estimate is a non sequitur because it applies the value standards of *oeuvre* criticism to a particular work. There

---

pp. vii–viii. Miller, it is true, begins his Preface by describing the single work, the total *oeuvre* and the whole age as "like three concentric circles," the outer providing the inner with ambiance or "atmosphere." He goes on to describe free critical movement between each of the circles, but does not explain how this is accomplished, and does not provide an example of it in his discussion of Arnold.

[4] Culler, pp. 193–94.

is no reason why Arnold's "best" poem should not be located almost
entirely in the glade, as are *Stanzas from the Grande Chartreuse*
and *Lines Written in Kensington Gardens,* provided it justifies its
use of landscape as the proper place in which to express an adequate response to the "facts" confronted by the poem. But if Professor Culler's evaluation is suspect, the elucidation on which it
depends is at times incredible. I shall argue more fully in a later
chapter my reasons for challenging Professor Culler's association of
the Tyrian trader and through him of the Scholar Gipsy with the
Bhagavad-Gita, Arnold's Joubert, and the burden of *Culture and
Anarchy* because he sails across the sea from the eastern Mediter-
ranean. At present it may be sufficient to take a smaller point in his
elucidation: the assumption that the cities of the plain figure meaningfully in the poem. Neither city nor plain is mentioned, but the
reflections on modern life in lines 141–230 are of a kind often accompanied in Arnold by an image of, say, a desert town. There is
no such accompaniment in *The Scholar-Gipsy* and Professor Culler
is forced to supply it by the impressionistic affirmation that "the
language [of the reflections] is as arid and barren as the world from
which it comes." Such impressionism needs support, and Professor
Culler finds it in the speaker's exhortation to the Scholar to

> plunge deeper in the bowering wood!
> Averse, as Dido did with gesture stern
> From her false friend's approach in Hades turn.

Part of the aptness of the simile for Professor Culler is explained
"because the scene is Hades, the Hades in which the poet himself is
located."[5] He means, if I understand him, that Arnold's burning
plain is as hot as Hades. But Arnold's allusion to Virgil is much
more precise: the "bowering wood" of the Cumnor Hills into
which the Scholar must plunge is a close translation of the *nemus
umbriferum* into which Dido fled when Aeneas accosted her in the
fields of mourning.[6] The speaker, at this point in the poem, is
"located" in Hades as Aeneas was, because he realizes that he lives,
while the Scholar is dead, and that in apostrophizing the Scholar he
is conversing with an inhabitant of the underworld. In order to
make the individual work correspond fully with a composite and

[5] Culler, pp. 186, 189.
[6] *Aeneid,* VI, 440–76.

meaningful landscape, Professor Culler gives to reflection a landscape feature it lacks, while his reading of the Tyrian trader simile gives to landscape a series of reflections it does not establish for itself.

The attribution to individual works of readings drawn from elsewhere in the *oeuvre* need not be as questionable as Professor Culler's analysis of the latter part of *The Scholar-Gipsy*. When it is, another reader may easily say "I do not believe this to be so." A more specious consequence of combining the *oeuvre* approach with separate explications in the study of an author like Arnold is the assumption, to quote myself, that the landscape "proposes a quest which is completely analogous to the programme of life drawn up in the later essays."[7] "Completely" is very comprehensive, a tacit license to "find" in poem after poem a system of ethical relationships between landscape features: the sequestered glade is a pleasing distraction from the hard but morally necessary ascent to the summit of truth. Sometimes it is so: *The New Sirens*; sometimes it is not: *Lines Written in Kensington Gardens*. Most of Arnold's best poems in fact record a saddened sense of what is; moral issues are present, if at all, as a strong and also saddened awareness of how difficult it is to ascertain and hold to what ought to be. Moreover, the search for ethical relationships leads easily, if not inevitably, to an explication which addresses itself to the unfolding of meaning rather than the process by which meaning is generated. Any poem worth considering creates its meaning as it proceeds by, in Arnold's case, the combination of reflection and description, the repetition with differences of key terms, images, motifs. The process cannot be identical in two poems; if it were, there would be not two poems, but one. *Thyrsis*, for example, is interestingly similar to *The Scholar-Gipsy*; but it is importantly different. *Thyrsis* uses the same geographical site as the earlier poem, but it uses it in a way which makes a different poetic landscape. By attending to the way in which different landscapes are made from the same geographical site we can judge the adequacy of each poem's response to and use of descriptive detail, and we can judge the effectiveness in each poem with which the human condition is rendered by poising realms of change and permanence.

[7] Alan H. Roper, "The Moral Landscape of Arnold's Poetry," *Publications of the Modern Language Association*, LXXVII (1962), 289–96.

Such judgments will be aesthetic and holist, answering the questions "how does the poem work, how are reflection and description united, is their combination convincing?" Aesthetic judgments find common ground with moral judgments of the kind involved in Arnold's own criterion of an adequate criticism of life principally in matters of probability: is the literal identity of a scene neglected in the interests of investing that scene with meaning? Does *Thyrsis* establish its signal tree as a convincing mediator between the Cumnor world of mortality and the immortal world of the old Sicilian pastoral? Is a Victorian respect for the positive facts of landscape and experience convincingly combined with an equally Victorian emphasis upon higher (and sometimes transcendent) truths?

The last question concerned Arnold in the early letters to Clough, where he answered it by expressing a preference for the "natural" over the "allegorical."[8] The Clough letters, in fact, frequently address themselves in various ways to the aesthetic and holist issues raised in the preceding paragraph. Increasingly, Arnold wrote to Clough and others of the moral concerns which were to form the center of his later, public criticism, and it is those concerns which have usually dominated discussions of Arnold's private and public views of criticism and poetry. I have therefore found it necessary to preface a consideration of Arnold's poems with a review of his poetic theory which emphasizes his interest in the relation of part to whole, of matter to manner, of "composition, in the painter's sense," and satisfactory "evolution" in poetry.[9] While such a review necessarily finds most of its evidence in the Clough letters, its emphasis also increases awareness of how the critic of moral profundity and the discriminator of touchstones continued to include in his public essays, if incidentally, the aesthetic concern with poetic wholeness of the earlier letters to Clough.

Arnold's pronouncements on poetry rarely continue for long at a wholly theoretic level; they are usually accompanied by examples, even if, notoriously, the examples are not analysed in a manner to satisfy twentieth-century critical expectations. What the pronouncements and examples show is that Arnold had a developed sense of different ways in which poetry may incorporate landscape description. Although, unsurprisingly, his discriminations are very different from the kind we have been taught to make by recent critics

[8] *Clough Letters*, p. 60.
[9] *Clough Letters*, p. 139; *Works*, IV, 358.

of landscape poetry, it is evident, when he turns to matters of appropriate diction or poetic evolution, that he is responding to poetic facts which still interest us. By adapting Arnold's own criteria, adding others of more recent definition, and applying them to some poems Arnold wrote, spoke of, or glanced at, I have tried to describe some of the ways in which poetry makes use of landscape, some of the varieties of landscape poetry. My wish is to establish a context for a more extensive discussion of Arnold's poems, a context which will be primarily critical rather than historical. I wish, that is, to avoid repeating the considerable and careful research which has been made into, say, Arnold's echoes of the Romantic poets and the qualities he does or does not share with other Victorian poets. I hope to accomplish this by choosing some Augustan landscape poems for detailed analysis and treating the Romantic poets only by summary recall of critical positions which are now familiar.

Although my primary object is a critical description of some ways in which landscape poetry has been written, I have found that analysis of Thomson, Gray, and Collins provides terms more immediately appropriate to Arnold than could be derived from a similar analysis of the Romantic poets. The reason is no doubt partly historical: very generally, the Augustans and Victorians share a strongly objective sense of nature and landscape as something to be reflected upon, examined for evidence of transcendent truth, or used as the correlative of a mood. What, in general, they do not share is a Romantic conviction that behind the objective phenomena known to the senses there are truths or realities apprehensible by an exercise of the imagination which eliminates the distinction between subjective observer and observed object. In some ways, it is true, the Victorians were unlucky inheritors of disparate elements from the Augustan and Romantic traditions. They share the Augustan separateness of subject and object, but are not sustained by the Augustan habit of finding in nature a system of social relationships relevant to the social preoccupations of man. The habit is denied them because they share the Romantic belief that the "truths" of nature are relevant for the individual observer as individual, not as representative member of society. Arnold, especially, scans nature with Augustan eyes in search of something like Romantic "truths," but having lost the secret of the Romantic way of finding them.[10] The characteristic melancholy of his poetry

[10] This "Victorian" disjunction is phrased somewhat differently by Herbert R.

marks the unavoidable failure of such an endeavor. The result of this disparate inheritance was the familiar picture of Victorian man alone in an alien universe, unable to follow the Augustan in finding lessons in nature for the social and urban life of man and equally unable to follow the Romantics in asserting or assuming the social life of man to be irrelevant to the lessons of nature, except when nature taught that society should respect individual dignity. The major poetic document of this simultaneous desire and failure to unite nature and human society is, of course, *Empedocles on Etna*.

All poets of landscape must face the problem of uniting natural description with human significance if they wish to write something more than country contentments in verse. The proposition sounds simplistic, but all of its terms permit multiple possibilities. There are as large variations in the naturalism of the description as there are in the humanity of the significance. Such varieties admit equally wide possibilities in the manner of achieving unity. It is true that poets of one age will normally be more like each other than like poets of another age, and that the poems of one writer will be more like each other than like those of other writers. Such similarities encourage the listing of typical qualities: a use of metaphor and symbol or of simile and analogy as means to unite description and significance. If drawn up with reasonable accuracy, such lists have value in indicating what questions it might be initially helpful to ask of a particular work.[11] But the work's particularity quickly asserts itself in any thorough analysis. It is in this sense that the

---

Coursen, Jr., " 'The Moon Lies Fair': The Poetry of Matthew Arnold," *Studies in English Literature,* IV (1964), 569–81: "In that he can be placed 'between two traditions,' Arnold might be called the representative Victorian poet; he is Romantic in his use of the symbolic landscape, Modern in his finding there only negation" (p. 581).

[11] A critical response to these issues is also conditioned by the extent to which a critic is primarily interested in poetry or in poems. The relationship between description and reflection may be analysed as it emerges in a particular passage or image, as, for the purposes of analysis, a primarily local quality. Or that local relationship between description and reflection may be analysed in terms of its contribution to the whole complex of meaning which is the poem. Ideally, perhaps, if not economically, a critic should distribute his attention equally between the part as part and as contributor to the whole. But such an ideal supposes readers of limitless patience and critics of catholic talents. In addressing myself primarily, but not, I hope, exclusively, to qualities of poems, I do not wish to imply that I find unhelpful or unrewarding the criticism of those who are able, as I am not, to address themselves primarily, but not necessarily exclusively, to qualities of poetry. An interesting example of "poetry" criticism concerning itself with reflective-descriptive verse is Patricia Meyer Spacks's *The Poetry of Vision: Five Eighteenth-Century Poets* (Cambridge, Mass., 1967).

landscape of one poem is inevitably different from the landscape of another using, perhaps, the same geographical site or tending to find a similar significance in the natural descriptions.

But critical respect for the individuality of poems need not result in wholly separate, unrelated readings. The raising by different poems of similar if not identical issues of landscape and reflective matter and their poetic embodiment indicates the usefulness of grouping works for the purpose of comparison. It is only necessary to adopt groupings which bring together whole poems rather than their parts. A grouping according to leading ideas, landscape motifs, or recurrent characters necessitates, if rigorously pursued, distributing the discussion of all but the shortest and simplest poems over several parts of a study and thus interfering with an attempt to show how a single poem brings together idea, landscape, and characters into a particular whole. A grouping by genre, which Arnold came to prefer for his own poems, must cope with his highly idiosyncratic classification of poems which, although some may involve an element of narrative or drama, are nearly all lyrical, meditative and elegiac.[12] An arrangement by date of composition, in so far as it can be determined, while appropriate to Kenneth Allott's fine edition, not only suggests no obvious divisions, it also separates poems which plainly ask to be considered together.

I have decided to use the contents of Arnold's first two volumes for the major groups, excepting from them only *Empedocles on Etna* for the separate treatment it deserves and *Stanzas in Memory of the Author of 'Obermann'* for the obvious comparison with *Obermann Once More*. The poems in both 1849 and 1852 are apparently arranged to permit the playing of one against another and the variation of recurrent concerns (the law and the poet in 1849, a European itinerary of sage and lover in 1852) which make for an overall unity in each volume. Not only *Empedocles on Etna* but also the Cumnor poems deserve separate treatment, and a further advantage of comparing *The Scholar-Gipsy* and *Thyrsis* is that their different use of landscape evidently comes, in part, from a change in Arnold's view of the proper matter and tone of poetry during the decade that separates their composition. This often discussed change is further exemplified in a final grouping of poems published, with the exception of '*Obermann*,' after 1852.

[12] The best use of a genre group is certainly Culler's discussion of Arnold's "formal" elegies on dead men or pets (pp. 232–86). But there is no other genre group which lends itself so rewardingly to critical study.

While these divisions raise problems to replace those they apparently settle (whether, for example, the contents of the early volumes should be respected to the extent of preferring their readings to Arnold's later revisions), they carry for me the recommendation of permitting comparison between poems without blurring the individuality of particular works. They express, in fact, my conviction that however similar Arnold's various descriptions of forest and mountain, sea and stream may be, his works contain from one (and, I believe, the most important) point of view as many poetic landscapes as there are poems to unite, each in its own way, significance with description.

IN THE LAST PARAGRAPH of the preface to his *Poems* of 1853 Arnold recalls Goethe's distinction between the two kinds of dilettante poet: "he who neglects the indispensable mechanical part, and thinks he has done enough if he shows spirituality and feeling; and he who seeks to arrive at poetry merely by mechanism, in which he can acquire an artisan's readiness, and is without soul and matter."[1] Arnold's characteristic gloom about the *"unpoetry-lessness"*[2] of his times emerges in his assumption that the poets of his day are perforce dilettantes of Goethe's second class. But they need not therefore, he insists, be dilettantes of the first class. Indeed, it is their duty to the poets who will come after to transmit "the practice of poetry, with its boundaries and wholesome regulative laws,"[3] undamaged by the kind of aesthetic caprice which is gratified by "occasional bursts of fine writing, and with a shower of isolated thoughts and images"[4] to the neglect of that *"Architectonicè . . .* which creates, forms, and constitutes."[5]

i

Just over four years after the 1853 preface, in the preface to *Merope,* Arnold found "boundaries and wholesome regulative laws"

[1] *Complete Prose,* I, 15.
[2] *Clough Letters,* p. 126; Dec. 14, 1852.
[3] *Complete Prose,* I, 15.
[4] *Complete Prose,* I, 7.
[5] *Complete Prose,* I, 9.

in prosodic mastery, and expressed himself in a variation upon the rivers which flow through so many of his poems and letters:

Powerful thought and emotion, flowing in strongly marked channels, make a stronger impression [than "variety and the widest possible range"]: this is the main reason why a metrical form is a more effective vehicle for them than prose: in prose there is more freedom, but, in the metrical form, the very limit gives a sense [of] precision and emphasis. This sense of emphatic distinctness in our impressions rises, as the thought and emotion swell higher and higher without overflowing their boundaries, to a lofty sense of the mastery of the human spirit over its own stormiest agitations. . . . What has been said explains, I think, the reason of the effectiveness of the severe forms of Greek tragedy, with its strongly marked boundaries, with its recurrence, even in the most agitating situations, of mutually replying masses of metrical arrangement. Sometimes the agitation becomes overwhelming, and the correspondence is for a time lost, the torrent of feeling flows for a space without check: this disorder amid the general order produces a powerful effect; but the balance is restored before the tragedy closes: the final sentiment in the mind must be one not of trouble, but of acquiescence.[6]

It is sometimes, and properly, pointed out that the prefaces to the 1853 edition and to *Merope* are occasional pieces, having as their primary purpose the justification, implicit in the first preface, explicit in the second, of Arnold's poetic practice in *Sohrab and Rustum* and *Merope*. In the prefaces, the poem, and the play, it is Greek precedent which Arnold would invoke, and the overt classicism leads to propositions about the relationship between form and content reminiscent of the *concordia discors* of the ancients and neoclassicists. "Disorder amid the general order," like the observation which precedes the quotation from the *Merope* preface that men demand on the one hand variety, on the other concentration, may bring to mind the opening lines of *Windsor Forest*, with their "order in variety."

It would be a mistake, I believe, to lay total emphasis on the occasional nature of these prefaces, and to conclude that their relevance is limited to the works they introduce or would vindicate. What Arnold says of the final acquiescence, banished trouble, and restored balance of Greek tragedy describes not only, if most clearly, the closing lines of *Sohrab and Rustum*, but the frequently celebrated codas of so many of his poems, of *The Scholar-Gipsy*, *The Buried Life*, *Empedocles on Etna*. It is critically pointless to spec-

[6] *Complete Prose*, I, 58–59.

ulate whether the codas were influenced by Arnold's sense of Greek
tragedy or whether his theoretical formula for Greek tragedy was
colored, in part at least, by his prior poetic practice. What matters
is the consonance between the two. And it matters because it indicates the validity, if not necessarily the value, of considering
Arnold's practical poetics, in part at least, in terms of his critical
theory.

The validity of such an endeavor has sometimes been challenged.
Few would now condone the labor of sacrificing *Empedocles on
Etna* to the greater glory of *Sohrab and Rustum* to which the 1853
preface largely addresses itself. It has been pointed out that the
1853 preface's exclusive concern with narrative and dramatic poetry
limits its relevance for the output of "a poet whose principal
achievements are meditative lyrics."[7] Perhaps even more striking
than the disjunction between Arnold's practice and the theory of
the 1853 preface is Arnold's return upon himself in his inaugural
lecture as Professor of Poetry at Oxford, delivered in 1857 and published with the title *On the Modern Element in Literature* more
than eleven years later.[8] In the lecture Arnold questions the status
of Virgil as an adequate interpreter of his age, the golden age of
Rome, because his work, while not morbid, is suffused with a sweet
melancholy. Lucretius falls even farther short of the high goal of
adequacy because he is "overstrained, gloom-weighted, morbid."
"How," Arnold asks of Lucretius, "can a man adequately interpret
the activity of his age when he is not in sympathy with it?"[9] Inevitably, the question and the strictures on Virgil and Lucretius recall the melancholy alienation of Arnold's own poetry, which, by
his own standard and in his sense of the word, is similarly inadequate. When we think of Arnold's long-projected but never completed play about Lucretius, and of the ennui, which, it is clear
from the 1853 preface, attracted him to the subject of Empedocles,
it is impossible to believe that Arnold was unaware of the appropriateness of his remarks to his own poetry, peopled as it is with
figures as disenchanted as he felt Lucretius to be.

Like the 1853 preface, then, the inaugural lecture has a negative
appropriateness to Arnold's poetry: it points to ways in which he
(presumably) found his poems unsatisfactory. In fact, the bulk of

[7] Melvin L. Plotinsky, "Help for Pain: The Narrative Verse of Matthew Arnold,"
Victorian Poetry, II (1964), 168.
[8] *Complete Prose*, I, 225–26.
[9] *Complete Prose*, I, 33–35.

Arnold's comments on his poetry, chiefly contained in his letters to Clough, is almost uniformly given up to critical self-flagellation—in striking contrast (even when proper allowance has been made for the difference in audience) to the generally satisfied comments about his essays which he addressed to his mother and, occasionally, to his sisters. His engaging agreement with Clough that *The New Sirens* "is exactly a mumble"[10] swells into an admission to his sister Jane that he has "got absolutely to dislike" the whole volume of 1849 in which *The New Sirens* appeared.[11] The "mumble" of *The New Sirens* undergoes metamorphosis a few years later in an assurance to Clough that if he ever republishes *Tristram and Iseult* he will "try to make it more intelligible. . . . The whole affair is by no means thoroughly successful."[12] Even *Sohrab and Rustum*, in the writing of which he reported great satisfaction to Clough, his mother, and his sister Jane,[13] he came to like less when he had written it out, apparently because he felt it unsatisfactory in "composition, in the painter's sense."[14]

Arnold's fullest and most interesting extant stricture on his poems comes in a letter to Jane Arnold:

Fret not yourself to make my poems square in all their parts, but like what you can my darling. The true reason why parts suit you while others do not is that my poems are fragments—*i.e.* that I am fragments, while you are a whole; the whole effect of my poems is quite vague & indeterminate—this is their weakness; a person therefore who endeavored to make them accord would only lose his labor; and a person who has any inward completeness can at best only like parts of them; in fact such a person stands firmly and knows what he is about while the poems stagger weakly & are at their wits end. I shall do better some day I hope—meanwhile change nothing, resign nothing that you have in deference to me or my oracles; & do not plague yourself to find a consistent meaning for these last, which in fact they do not possess through my weakness.[15]

[10] *Clough Letters*, p. 107.
[11] *Unpublished Letters of Matthew Arnold*, ed. Arnold Whitridge (New Haven, 1923), p. 14.
[12] *Clough Letters*, p. 136; May 1, 1853. Clough agreed, and utilized his favorite stricture by describing the poem as "a sort of faint musical mumble" in a review he wrote for the *North American Review* of July, 1853 (*Selected Prose Works of Arthur Hugh Clough*, ed. Buckner B. Trawick [University, Alabama, 1964], p. 158).
[13] *Clough Letters*, p. 136; *Works*, XIII, 38, 39.
[14] *Clough Letters*, p. 139; Aug. 8 [1853].
[15] *Unpublished Letters of Matthew Arnold*, ed. Whitridge, pp. 18–19; [1853?].

Since the chief task I propose for myself in this study is to determine degrees of wholeness and coherence in Arnold's poems, this judgment by the poet himself is not heartening. I hope it will emerge, however, that the kind of coherence which interests me is not the kind which Arnold seems here to have in mind. I say "seems" because Arnold does not express himself with full clarity: there is a no doubt suggestive impalpability about this presumably unstudied observation which recalls the formal criticism of his later career. The initial talk of parts and fragments promises the application of some neoclassical or Coleridgean theory of literary holism. But this expectation is quickly checked by an explanation in terms of authorial psychology and quite lost, I think, by the concluding reference to consistent meaning. That his poems are fragments because he is fragments suggests that Arnold is here thinking of philosophic content, and reflecting on the tendency of some of his longer poems to raise philosophic issues which are left unresolved or obscure. Many of Arnold's poems are from one (very limited) point of view hesitant attempts to become

a complete magister vitae as the poetry of the ancients did: by including, as theirs did, religion with poetry, instead of existing as poetry only. . . . The language, style and general proceedings of a poetry which has such an immense task to perform, must be very plain direct and severe: and it must not lose itself in parts and episodes and ornamental work, but must press forwards to the whole.[16]

It is tempting to gloss this remark in terms of John Crowe Ransom's distinction between essential meaning and local texture.[17] But where for Professor Ransom texture and meaning together make ontology and wholeness, for Arnold the *whole* is (verbally at least) comprised in the *complete* "magister vitae," the paraphrasable content, while the parts are so many potential distractions from the expression and apprehension of the whole. Such a doctrine irresistibly prompts an enquiry into just what is meant by the parts of a poem. Arnold is quite clear about it, at least in the "magister vitae" letter. Modern critics, he complains, "still think that the object of poetry is to produce exquisite bits and images—such as Shelley's *clouds shepherded by the slow unwilling wind,* and Keats passim: whereas modern poetry can only subsist by its *contents*:

[16] *Clough Letters,* p. 124; Oct. 28, 1852.
[17] John Crowe Ransom, *The World's Body* (New York, 1938), pp. 347–49.

by becoming a complete magister vitae." To achieve this end poetry should shun the exuberant expression, the rich imagery of the Elizabethans, which Keats and Shelley misguidedly endeavored to reproduce, and strive instead for "great plainness of speech." And there we have it: all those magic casements and domes of many-colored glass are so many beautiful distractions from the bald contents.

Both the "magister vitae" letter to Clough and the "fragments" letter to Jane Arnold were written before the volume of 1853 for which Arnold wrote the preface that constitutes his first published criticism. It is evident that the two letters constitute tentative formulations of the position he sets out more fully in the preface. What we have in the preface is a redefinition of "consistent meaning" and the attachment to contents which makes for wholeness in terms appropriate to narrative and dramatic poetry. Keats's *Isabella,* we learn, "is a perfect treasure-house of graceful and felicitous words and images," but "the action, the story," excellent in itself (as we know from Boccaccio's handling), is so feebly conceived, "so loosely constructed, that the effect produced by it, in and for itself, is absolutely null."[18] The kind of effect Arnold requires and which Keats fails to provide is identified a little later in an account of what a modern poet may learn from judicious study of the ancients. "He will learn from them how unspeakably superior is the effect of the one moral impression left by a great action treated as a whole, to the effect produced by the most striking single thought or by the happiest image."[19] The *"Architectonicè,"* then, which "creates, forms, and constitutes," finds its proper vehicle in the action and its teleological value in a moral impression. Single thoughts, however profound, rich imagery, and abundant illustration are no more than "attractive accessories of a poetical work."[20] It is unquestionably a highly rhetorical view of poetry and recalls Aristotle's distinction between the substance of the action in bare outline and the interpolation of illustrative episodic matter. But Aristotle's brief, indeed almost enigmatic, remark becomes in Arnold's fuller statement highly questionable. It would seem that these "attractive accessories of a poetical work" are themselves poetical, since they were pre-eminently the special gift of Shakespeare, but they were not, we find, "his fundamental excellences *as a poet.*"

[18] *Complete Prose,* I, 10.
[19] *Complete Prose,* I, 12.
[20] *Complete Prose,* I, 9.

If Arnold's italics are truly meaningful, they imply that those attractive accessories of imagery and illustration are not excellences (if excellences they be) which Shakespeare possessed by virtue of being a poet, but excellences which came to him from some other and unspecified aspect of his character. A knotty point, but the sword of Goethe is at hand: "what distinguishes the artist from the mere amateur, says Goethe, is *Architectonicè.*" It is plain that there is considerable juggling with the terms *poet, artist, amateur* and, a few pages later, *dilettante*: poets and artists excel in the architectonic ability to treat a great action as a whole; they may also (although it is apparently not essential that they should) excel in the happy talent of amateurs and dilettantes to throw off single profound thoughts and rich images. The confusion, and it is a confusion, comes from the attempt to convert a difference in degree into a difference in kind, an attempt signaled by the employment of different nouns: poet and amateur, instead of the same noun with different adjectives: great and minor poet.

As he was later to admit so disarmingly and with such rhetorical effectiveness, Arnold's was not a systematic mind.[21] He endorsed Joubert's dictum that it is better to use the received sense of words when discussing intellectual matters, to avoid specialist jargon and recondite meaning; to use, as far as possible, popular words in order to reach a wide audience.[22] This view, which so obviously informs his public criticism, has a counterpart in the terms in which Arnold expresses himself in the private criticism of his early letters. His own remark in *Last Words on Translating Homer,* "criticism is so apt in general to be vague and impalpable,"[23] comes again and again as irresistibly to mind in reading the letters to Clough as it does in reading, say, *The Study of Poetry.* But it is recalled by the letters not because they fail to tackle practical poetic issues but because, in tackling them, they rarely proceed to a point at which one can say confidently "Arnold here means this and not that." The consequence is that the task of interpretation is so taxing as to prompt a doubt of its usefulness. But such a doubt should be

[21] The admission is most successfully used in *Culture and Anarchy* to bait Frederic Harrison, but variations occur throughout his essays as part of his persuasive stock-in-trade. See, e.g., "it is the very simplicity of our [i.e. my] understanding that incapacitates us for the difficult style of the philosophers, and drives us to the use of the most ordinary phraseology," *God and the Bible, Works,* VIII, 136.

[22] *Complete Prose,* III, 194–96.

[23] *Complete Prose,* I, 195.

banished. The letters were written during Arnold's most productive period as a poet: roughly the seven years from 1847 to 1853. Even when Arnold overtly addresses himself to some aspect of Clough's poetry, it is evident that he is arguing out, as much for his own benefit as for Clough's, matters relevant to poems he had himself written or was working on. Exasperatingly fragmentary and inconclusive as his comments often are, they constitute, not a poetic, it is true, but reflections upon poetics. To put their value no higher, they are evidence that Arnold was thinking hard and theoretically during his period of major creativity. In undertaking the necessary task of elaborating upon these letters, it is principally necessary to beware of assuming that separately or as a whole they constitute a directly and fully relevant theoretical counterpart to his poetic practice. At the very least, Arnold was as incident as any poet to mistaking the nature of what he had done.

In his letters to Clough, Arnold concerns himself in a variety of ways with four main aspects of poetry: composition, content, description, and style. Sometimes he concentrates upon one aspect to the exclusion or disparagement of another; sometimes he seeks to determine the relationship between two or more aspects. But nearly all his comments share an attempt to define poetic wholeness and to identify practices hostile to such wholeness. It is, we have seen, an attempt which recurs in the 1853 preface. Indeed, the preoccupations of these early letters reappear in various guises throughout the public literary criticism of his later career. Description, at which he only glances in the early years, is most fully considered under the heading of "natural magic" in the lectures on Celtic literature and the essay on Maurice de Guérin. Content becomes successively the "magister vitae," "moral profundity," and, finally, "criticism of life." Style reappears in the lectures on translating Homer and is apparently the aspect which underlies those notorious touchstones. Composition "in the painter's sense" appears briefly in *Celtic Literature,* but the association in the 1853 preface of its variant, *architectonicé,* with moral impression is discernible throughout Arnold's usual assumption that poetic wholeness comes principally from a unity of moral effect attainable only by a man who is himself whole and harmonious. At this point begins the overlap between Arnold's literary and social criticism.

ii

But before that point, before attempting to describe literary holism in terms either of Romantic expressionism or Aristotelean affectivism,[24] Arnold's references to composition in the Clough letters point to an attempt to isolate the structural relationships between the components of a literary work. In the letters written before 1850 this attempt led Arnold to stress the how rather than the what of poetic content.

I often think that even a slight gift of poetical expression which in a common person might have developed itself easily and naturally, is overlaid and crushed in a profound thinker so as to be of no use to him to help him to express himself.—The trying to go into and to the bottom of an object instead of grouping *objects* is as fatal to the sensuousness of poetry as the mere painting, (for, *in Poetry,* this is not *grouping*) is to its airy and rapidly moving life.
'Not deep the Poet sees, but wide':—think of this as you gaze from the Cumner Hill toward Cirencester and Cheltenham.

Earlier in the same letter Arnold expressed the disjunction between form and content even more sharply:

Many persons with far lower gifts than yours yet seem to find their natural mode of expression in poetry, and tho: the contents may not be very valuable they appeal with justice from the judgement of the mere thinker to the world's general appreciation of naturalness—i.e.—an absolute propriety—of form, as the sole *necessary* of Poetry as such: whereas the greatest wealth and depth of matter is merely a superfluity in the Poet *as such.*[25]

The critic of "high seriousness," "moral profundity," and "criticism of life" is almost unrecognizable here. The dictum that form, not content, is the normative quality of poetry is superficially similar to the dictum of the 1853 preface that *architectonicé* is normative. But a change in Arnold's views is clearly marked in the preface by his associating architectonics exclusively with action and the evalua-

[24] "Expressionism" is used in the sense given it by M. H. Abrams in his discussion of Romantic poetics, which accounts for poetry by "an efficient cause—the impulse within the poet of feelings and desires seeking expression," in *The Mirror and the Lamp* (New York, 1953), p. 22. My reference to Aristotelean affectivism is based on the discussion of "The Affective Fallacy" by W. K. Wimsatt, Jr. and Monroe C. Beardsley, *The Verbal Icon* (Lexington, Ky., 1954), pp. 21–39.
[25] *Clough Letters,* pp. 98–99; [early Feb., 1849].

tion of action in terms of moral effect. It is not only that Arnold moved from a structural to a didactic view of poetry,[26] but also that he endeavored to reunite the matter and manner he had earlier treated as separable.

The first quotation in the preceding paragraph is particularly important because it is clear, if implicit, that Arnold is concerned with poetry as landscape poetry. The implication emerges in the rejection of "mere painting" as antithetical to the grouping of objects in poetry. The verbal equivalent of "mere painting" is, in Pope's phrase, "pure description," and Arnold's preoccupation here with natural description is evidenced by his not strikingly apt quotation from *Resignation* and his application of it to the panorama from the Cumnor hills. When standing on "Cumner Hill," Clough must suspend his habit of focusing upon one object in the view before him trying to invest it with moral significance. Instead, he must concentrate on seeing the various objects comprised by the view as composed into a whole, as existing to each other in a formal relationship of mass and color (and, perhaps too, a relationship of moral or human significance, for Arnold the critic, like Arnold the poet, was never an unadulterated aesthete).

The analogy between poetry and painting, with all its suggestive fallacies, dogged Arnold throughout his career. In seeking to define the nature of Celtic literary genius, Arnold thought it helpful to adduce a parallel with English painting.

Reynolds and Turner are painters of genius, who can doubt it? but take a European jury, the only competent jury in these cases, and see if you can get a verdict giving them the rank of masters, as this rank is given to Raphael and Correggio, or to Albert Dürer and Rubens. And observe. . . . [that] they fall short in *architectonicé,* in the highest power of composition. . . . Their defect, therefore, is on the side of art, of plastic art. And they succeed in magic, in beauty, in grace, in expressing almost the inexpressible: here is the charm of Reynolds's children and Turner's seas.[27]

[26] As has been suggested by M. G. Sundell, "The Intellectual Background and Structure of Arnold's *Tristram and Iseult," Victorian Poetry,* I (1963), 274–76.
[27] *Complete Prose,* III, 354–55. Compare the later remark in *Literature and Science:* "Fit details strictly combined, in view of a large general result nobly conceived; that is just the beautiful *symmetria prisca* of the Greeks, and it is just where we English fail, where all our [plastic and architectural] art fails. Striking ideas we have; but that high symmetry which . . . combines them, we seldom or never have" *Works,* IV, 346.

The literary distinction which this analogy most clearly serves to illustrate is given in the preceding lecture.

The Celt has not produced great poetical works, he has only produced poetry with an air of greatness investing it all, and sometimes giving, moreover, to short pieces, or to passages, lines, and snatches of long pieces, singular beauty and power. . . . But the true art, the *architectonicé* which shapes great works, such as the *Agamemnon* or the *Divine Comedy,* comes only after a steady, deep-searching survey, a firm conception of the facts of human life, which the Celt has not patience for. So he runs off into technic, where he employs the utmost elaboration, and attains astonishing skill; but in the contents of his poetry you have only so much interpretation of the world as the first dash of a quick, strong perception, and then sentiment, infinite sentiment, can bring you.[28]

The genesis of architectonic ability in "a firm conception of the facts of human life" looks back to the 1853 preface as clearly as it looks forward to a "criticism of life" in *The Study of Poetry.* The formula in *Celtic Literature,* the distinction between *architectonicé* and technic as different, if by no means commensurate qualities of poetry, is more satisfactory than the confused linguistic juggling in the 1853 preface of art and dilettantism. But it is clear that Arnold's praise of the Celt, however qualified, is exactly for the production of those glorious bits and pieces which so disturbed him in 1853. The coincidence of this, unfortunately fragmentary, "natural magic" in Celtic literature and those "attractive accessories of a poetical work" so sternly reproved in 1853 is further indicated by Arnold's proceeding to illustrate natural magic by quotations from Keats and Shakespeare[29] those principal exemplars in 1853 of "exquisite bits and images."

Some time in 1848, apparently, Clough recommended that Arnold read Keats's letters. Arnold did so, and responded with one of his most frequently quoted outbursts:

What a brute you were to tell me to read Keats' Letters. However it is over now: and reflexion resumes her power over agitation. . . . I recommend you to follow up these letters with the Laocoön of Lessing: it is not quite satisfactory, and a little mare's nesty—but very searching.[30]

[28] *Complete Prose,* III, 345.
[29] *Complete Prose,* III, 377–80.
[30] *Clough Letters,* pp. 96–97; [after Sept., 1848].

It is not altogether clear to which poisonous Keatsian doctrine Lessing is supposed to be the antidote. The charge against Keats, "the harm he has done in English Poetry," is that, like Browning, his desire for "movement and fulness" leads only to a "confused multitudinousness" because he does not "begin with an Idea of the world."[31] This looks like an early and opaque version of the later distinction between *architectonicé* and technic, although "idea of the world" is by no means as tied to specifically moral content. One may guess (and one can only guess, I think) that Arnold is principally disturbed by the Keatsian doctrines of the camelion poet and negative capability, of the life of sensations. What seems to trouble Arnold about this doctrine is that a zestful concentration upon the manifold of sensory experience does not lead directly to that steadiness and wholeness of vision for which he praised Sophocles in a sonnet probably addressed to Clough and written very shortly before the outburst against Keats's letters. In a letter to Clough just before that outburst he quotes from his sonnet praising Sophocles and deposes that "the difference between Herodotus and Sophocles is that the former sought over all the world's surface for that interest the latter found within man."[32] This searching of the world's surface sounds like the "dawdling" with the "painted shell" of the universe which Arnold had already found so "fatiguing" in Tennyson.[33]

If it is true that Arnold opposes both what he understood as Tennysonian descriptiveness and Keats's imaginative entrance into manifold experience to a Sophoclean wholeness and steadiness, it still remains to determine in what sense Lessing, however mare's nesty, can be held to check "that desire of fulness without respect of the means" which Arnold had already detected in himself.[34] The *Laokoon* largely concerns itself with the analogy between poetry and painting which intrigued Arnold, although Lessing insists more firmly on the dangers and inadequacies of the analogy than Arnold was ever to do except, perhaps, in his late verse *Epilogue to Lessing's Laocoön*. Lessing is concerned with both sides of the analogy, with the dangers of the dumb poem theory of painting and the speaking picture theory of poetry. His principal

[31] *Clough Letters,* p. 97.
[32] *Clough Letters,* p. 90; [Aug.-Sept., 1848].
[33] *Clough Letters,* p. 63; [mid-Dec., 1847].
[34] *Clough Letters,* p. 97; [after Sept., 1848].

distinction between the two forms rests upon the insistence that painting has a largely spatial, poetry a largely temporal existence.

If it be true that painting employs wholly different signs or means of imitation from poetry,—the one using forms and colors in space, the other articulate sounds in time,—and if signs must unquestionably stand in convenient relation with the thing signified, then signs arranged side by side can represent only objects existing side by side, or whose parts so exist, while consecutive signs can express only objects which succeed each other, or whose parts succeed each other, in time.

Objects which exist side by side, or whose parts so exist, are called bodies. Consequently bodies with their visible properties are the peculiar subjects of painting.

Objects which succeed each other, or whose parts succeed each other in time, are actions. Consequently actions are the peculiar subjects of poetry. . . .

Actions . . . cannot exist independently, but must always be joined to certain agents. In so far as those agents are bodies or are regarded as such, poetry describes also bodies, but only indirectly through actions. . . .

Poetry, in its progressive imitations, can use but a single attribute of bodies, and must choose that one which gives the most vivid picture of the body as exercised in this particular action.[35]

By the time of his verse *Epilogue* in the mid-1860's, Arnold had certainly taken Lessing's distinction:

'Behold,' I said, 'the painter's sphere!
The limits of his art appear.
The passing group, the summer-morn,
The grass, the elms, that blossom'd thorn—
Those cattle couch'd, or, as they rise,
Their shining flanks, their liquid eyes—
These, or much greater things, but caught
Like these, and in one aspect brought!
In outward semblance he must give
A moment's life of things that live.'   (ll. 49–58)

The poet, on the other hand,

'must life's *movement* tell!
The thread which binds it all in one,

---

[35] *Laocoon,* trans. Ellen Frothingham (Boston, 1893), pp. 91–92 (section XVI).

> And not its separate parts alone.
> The *movement* he must tell of life,
> Its pain and pleasure, rest and strife;
> His eye must travel down, at full,
> The long, unpausing spectacle.
>
> . . . .
>
> 'The cattle rising from the grass
> His thought must follow where they pass.'   (ll. 140–46, 153–54)

The reference is explicit in the *Epilogue,* but there seems also to be a *Laokoon* note in a passage already quoted from the Clough letters: "The trying to go into and to the bottom of an object instead of grouping *objects* is as fatal to the sensuousness of poetry as the mere painting, (for, *in Poetry,* this is not *grouping*) is to its airy and rapidly moving life." The castigation of "mere painting," enumerative description presumably, as inimical to poetic movement is certainly Lessingesque, but the proferred alternative of "grouping objects" suggests that Arnold was reluctant to follow Lessing in a total separation of poetry and painting.

iii

One reason for this reluctance (and perhaps part of the mare's nest Arnold discovered in the *Laokoon*) may be that Lessing's weakness is to tie his theory of poetry too firmly, not just to one poetic genre, but to one representative of that genre: the *Iliad.* If poetry should imitate only actions, and if actions are defined as the succession of bodies or parts of bodies in time, what then becomes of landscape poetry, where the matter imitated consists to a large extent of the succession of bodies in space? Johnson had asked the same question and concluded, of poems like *Windsor Forest,* that "as the scenes, which they must exhibit successively, are all subsisting at the same time, the order in which they are shown must by necessity be arbitrary."[36] Lessing's landscape example was Von Haller's *Alps,* to which he granted a vividness of pictorial detail while denying it a satisfactory "conception of the whole," for "if that is to become more vivid, none of the separate details must stand in undue prominence. . . . Our imagination must be able to embrace them all with equal rapidity in order to form from them

---

[36] *Lives of the Poets,* ed. G. Birkbeck Hill (Oxford, 1905), III, 225. For a similar remark about Thomson's *Seasons* see *Lives,* III, 299–300.

in an instant that one harmonious whole which the eye takes in at a glance."[37] Arnold's version of the doctrine is that "when you adopt this or that form you must sacrifice much to the ensemble, and that form in return for admirable effects demands immense sacrifices."[38] In fact, picturable detail in a poem of some length does not by itself lead to wholeness of composition. What should a poet do? If he describes a blasted oak at the beginning of his poem, a knot of banditti at the end, and a craggy alp in the middle, any wholeness of composition which a reader may think he detects belongs to the Rosa-ish painting into which he has tacitly converted the poem and not to the poem itself. " 'When a poetaster,' says Horace, 'can do nothing else, he falls to describing a grove, an altar, a brook winding through pleasant meadows, a rushing river, or a rainbow.' . . . Pope, when a man, looked back with contempt on the descriptive efforts of his poetic childhood. . . . A merely descriptive poem he declared to be a feast made up of sauces."[39] But no poet worth considering ever invited his readers to such a meal.

Landscape poetry which is worth considering is so either because it embodies an interpretation of the landscape which it describes or because it uses the description of landscape to interpret something else. Both modes are capable of many variations, but they have in common that it is the interpretation and not the descriptive details which brings (or fails to bring) wholeness of composition to the poem as poem. Hence, presumably, Arnold's insistence that it is necessary to "begin with an Idea of the world in order not to be prevailed over by the world's multitudinousness." One of Arnold's more interesting attempts to distinguish the two modes of landscape poetry roughly defined above occurs in a paragraph of his essay on Maurice de Guérin. Although Arnold speaks generally of poetry, it is clear from his examples that he is, as usual, principally concerned with poetry which makes use of landscape to present man's relationship with the world, with the circumstances in which he passes his life. Like practically all of his criticism, his discussion is too brief, unelaborated, almost aphoristic to be applied directly and fruitfully to particular poems. Its value lies in its suggestiveness, in its potential translatability into terms appropriate to practical analysis. "Poetry," he says, "interprets in two ways."

---

[37] *Laocoon*, trans. Frothingham, p. 104 (section XVII).
[38] *Clough Letters*, p. 81; [May 24, 1848].
[39] *Laocoon*, trans. Frothingham, pp. 107–8 (section XVII).

It interprets by expressing with magical felicity the physiognomy and movement of the outward world, and it interprets by expressing, with inspired conviction, the ideas and laws of the inward world of man's moral and spiritual nature. In other words, poetry is interpretative both by having *natural magic* in it, and by having *moral profundity*. In both ways it illuminates man; it gives him a satisfying sense of reality; it reconciles him with himself and the universe. . . . Great poets unite in themselves the faculty of both kinds of interpretation, the naturalistic and the moral. But it is observable that in the poets who unite both kinds, the latter (the moral) usually ends by making itself the master. In Shakespeare the two kinds seem wonderfully to balance one another; but even in him the balance leans; his expression tends to become too little sensuous and simple, too much intellectualised. The same thing may be yet more strongly affirmed of Lucretius and of Wordsworth. In Shelley there is not a balance of the two gifts, nor even a co-existence of them, but there is a passionate straining after them both . . . whatever he achieves, he in general fails to achieve natural magic in his expression. . . . But in Keats and Guérin, in whom the faculty of naturalistic interpretation is overpoweringly predominant, the natural magic is perfect; when they speak of the world they speak like Adam naming by divine inspiration the creatures; their expression corresponds with the things's essential reality.[40]

It was presumably in this Adamic sense that Arnold found the *Ode to Autumn* pure poetry of natural description,[41] for he links the poem in *Celtic Literature* with Wordsworth's *Solitary Reaper* and Shakespeare's account of the daffodil in *The Winter's Tale* as examples of natural magic.[42]

The discussion in the Guérin essay is not concerned with the compositional aspects of poems, and one must assume that Arnold felt both kinds of interpretation could yield integrity. It is true that, for him, natural magic too often resulted in technic to the exclusion of *architectonicé,* in the production of glorious fragments. But moral profundity in itself could also be destructive of composition. Such at least seems the burden of his complaint to his sister Jane that "more and more I feel bent against the modern English habit (too much encouraged by Wordsworth) of using poetry as a channel for thinking aloud, instead of making anything."[43] To

[40] *Complete Prose,* III, 33–34.
[41] *Works,* X, 188.
[42] *Complete Prose,* III, 376.
[43] *Unpublished Letters of Matthew Arnold,* ed. Whitridge, p. 17.

judge from his strictures, Arnold felt that Clough was among those who had been so encouraged. He balances Clough's endeavor "to *solve* the Universe" with Tennyson's "dawdling with its painted shell" as equally unsatisfactory, and advances the solution of an attempt "to *re-construct* the Universe," admitting that that, too, is unsatisfactory, but insisting upon it as the necessary, if imperfect, end of "the poetic office."[44] A few months later he writes to his much-abused friend: "but you know you are a mere d—d depth hunter in poetry. . . . You might write a speech in Phèdre . . . but you could not write Phèdre."[45] If, as seems likely, it is justifiable to find in depth-hunting an early form of moral profundity, then the inward interpretation is as incident to the production of un-composed fragments as the outward. With such scepticism about the ability of the poetic modes he recognized to produce the poetic end he desired, it is not surprising to find Arnold exclaiming that "you may often hear my sinews cracking under the effort to unite mat-ter."[46] The difficulties of composition still weighed upon him ten years later, as he confessed to his sister Jane:

What a temptation there is, if you cannot bear anything not *very good,* to transfer your operations to a region where form is every-thing. Perfection of a certain kind may there be attained, or at least approached, without knocking yourself to pieces, but to attain or approach perfection in the region of thought and feeling, and to unite this with perfection of form, demands not merely an effort and a labour, but an actual tearing of oneself to pieces, which one does not readily consent to.[47]

iv

Despite the creative pains, Arnold seems never to have been strongly attracted by the temptation he describes. "What is Keats?" he once demanded of the patient Clough; and answered, "a style and form seeker." It is apparent from the same letter, that "form" is here a virtual synonym for "style": "it is true about form. . . . On the other hand, there are two offices of Poetry—one to add to one's store of thoughts and feelings—another to compose and elevate the mind by a sustained tone, numerous allusions, and a grand style."

[44] *Clough Letters,* p. 63; [mid-Dec., 1847].
[45] *Clough Letters,* p. 81; [May 24, 1848].
[46] *Clough Letters,* p. 65; [Dec., 1847–early 1848].
[47] *Works,* XIII, 95–96; Sept. 6, 1858.

He goes on to describe style as "the expression of the nobility of the poet's character, as the matter is the expression of the richness of his mind."[48] In a letter written a few weeks earlier, matter—"a superfluity in the Poet *as such*"—is glossed as form of conception, while style is form of expression; and no doubt we have yet another attempt to define what he eventually called moral profundity and natural magic. "Form of Conception . . . is generally developed late: but this lower form, of expression, is found from the beginning amongst all born poets, even feeble thinkers, and in an unpoetical age: as Collins, Green[e] and fifty more, in England only."[49]

Without doubt the aspect of Arnold's criticism which has most troubled later readers (and apparently his contemporaries) is his preoccupation with style, especially as it finally emerges into the touchstones doctrine. Arnold once wrote that "few people have any real care to analyse closely in their criticism; they merely employ criticism as a means for heaping all praise on what they like, and all blame on what they dislike."[50] More than most critical undertakings, discussion of style is resistant to sustained close analysis. Again and again it reaches the dead end of mere assertion: this style is good or inadequate. It will reach this point all the more quickly if, instead of engaging in the rhetorical analysis of local effect, it premises, as Arnold so often did, some variation on the axiom that style expresses the man. No doubt it does, but if the interest is "to analyse closely," it scarcely helps to say so.

To observe the gradual crystallization of Arnold's views on style is to become aware of how thoroughly his position denies the relevance of close rhetorical analysis. Arnold's total position, in fact, involves the unstated belief that as soon as a man's style becomes amenable to rhetorical analysis it ceases to be adequate, because the manner of expression must be detachable from the matter in order to be capable of separate scrutiny. For Arnold, unimpeachably, the stylistic manner should be determined wholly by the matter to be expressed. To learn and reproduce another man's style, something quite possible for a sensitive writer to do, is to involve oneself in a literary decadence. By contrast,

[48] *Clough Letters*, pp. 100–101; [about Mar. 1, 1849].
[49] *Clough Letters*, p. 99; [early Feb., 1849].
[50] *Complete Prose*, III, 380.

the strength of the German literature consists of this—that having no national models from whence to get an idea of *style* as half the work, they were thrown upon themselves, and driven to make the fulness of the content of a work atone for deficiencies of form. Even Goethe at the end of his life has not the inversions, the taking tourmenté style we admire in the Latins, in some of the Greeks, and in the great French and English authors. And had Shakespeare and Milton lived in the atmosphere of modern feeling, had they had the multitude of new thoughts and feelings to deal with a modern has, I think it likely the style of each would have been far less *curious* and exquisite. For in a *man* style is the saying in the best way *what you have to say*. The *what you have to say* depends on your age. In the 17th century it was *a smaller harvest than now,* and sooner to be reaped: and therefore to its reaper was left time to stow it more finely and curiously. Still more was this the case in the ancient world. The poet's matter being *the hitherto experience of the world, and his own,* increases with every century.[51]

We have in this letter of, at the latest, the beginning of 1848, a full and clear anticipation of his objection in the 1853 preface to Keats and Shelley on the grounds of an inappropriate attempt to reproduce Elizabethan richness and abundance.

Arnold's preference for a "very plain direct and severe" style comes evidently from a feeling that anything less—or, perhaps, more—too readily distracts from both the matter and the sense of the whole. A few years later, when lecturing on the grand style simple of Homer and the grand style severe of Milton,[52] Arnold, while unstinting in his admiration of Milton, unhesitatingly accords the palm to the simple style of Homer, partly, although not entirely, because it cannot be copied. "The severe [style] is much more imitable, and this a little spoils its charm." The plainness and lucidity of the simple style give way to the severe style when the lines are packed with allusive meaning, so packed that the meaning cannot come out in straightforward observation and description. It seems that for Arnold, where the simple style is so wedded to the matter it expresses that any failure in matter is immediately evident, the "taking tourmenté style" of severity is always in danger of becoming an end in itself, of continuing to function with the show of sublimity when its matter is in fact impoverished. "A kind of semblance of this style keeps Young going, one may say, through all the nine parts of that most indifferent

[51] *Clough Letters,* pp. 64–65; [Dec., 1847-early 1848].
[52] *Complete Prose,* I, 188–91.

production, the *Night Thoughts*." "What leagues of lumbering movement!" Arnold later exclaimed of "the so-called Miltonic blank verse of Thomson, Cowper, Wordsworth." "What desperate endeavours, as in Wordsworth's

And at the 'Hoop' alighted, famous inn,

to render a platitude endurable by making it pompous!"[53]

The danger, then, of the severe grand style, as of the richly exuberant Elizabethan imagery, is that it can easily become a mere rhetorical trick distracting from the fundamental task of rendering the thing in itself. So stated, it is apparent that Arnold's requirements for verse style are very close to his requirements for prose. There are differences, of course. Shortly after completing his first venture into published prose, the 1853 preface, he wrote to Clough:

How difficult it is to write prose: and why? because of the *articulations of the discourse:* one leaps these over in Poetry—places one thought cheek by jowl with another without introducing them and leaves them—but in prose this will not do. It is of course not right in poetry either—but we all do it.[54]

The differences between verse and prose, the suggestive consequences of an elliptic syntax, are more fundamental than Arnold's final sentence here allows, and it is of note that Arnold blurs the very distinction he has set up. For, in general, when he is not reflecting upon matters of tone, authorial attitude and audience reaction, Arnold's comments on the desiderata of prose consistently stress the value of rendering object or concept precisely, without indulging in the intoxicating pleasures of word-spinning. Such is the basis of his life-long disparagement of Macaulay, of which the following remark is characteristic:

Already, in the *Essay on Milton,* the style of Macaulay is, indeed, that which we know so well. A style to dazzle, to gain admirers everywhere, to attract imitators in multitude! A style brilliant, metallic, exterior; making strong points, alternating invective with eulogy, wrapping in a robe of rhetoric the thing it represents; not, with the soft play of life, following and rendering the thing's very

---

[53] *Works, X,* 255. For a similar judgment on this line from the *Prelude* see *Complete Prose,* I, 187.

[54] *Clough Letters,* p. 144; Oct. 10 [1853]. Compare: "Ruskin's new volume of *Modern Painters. . . .* [is] full of excellent *aperçus,* as usual, but the man and character too febrile, irritable, and weak to allow him to possess the *ordo concatenatioque veri,*" *Works,* XIII, 67; March 31, 1856.

form and pressure. For, indeed, in rendering things in this fashion, Macaulay's gift did not lie.[55]

The requirements of prose and poetry are so close in Arnold because prose is the proper medium of the critical power. And although "the critical power is of lower rank than the creative," it, nonetheless, through its unremitting endeavor "to see the object as in itself it really is . . . tends, at last, to make an intellectual situation of which the creative power can profitably avail itself."[56] The verbal similarity between "critical power" and the "criticism of life" which he came finally to require of poetry itself points to the contiguity of prose and poetry in Arnold's thought as much as the prosaic nature of his late verses evidences his final inability to discriminate between the two modes. When, in *The Literary Influence of Academies,* he supported with examples his distinction between a provincial and an urbane or central prose, the most striking feature of the prose examples he finds provincial is their highly imaginative use of extended metaphor; they are richly and excitingly metaphoric: "barborously rich and overloaded," Arnold calls them. The urbane French prose he quotes in contrast is characterized by a paucity of metaphor, by a plain and simple diction.[57] Ironically enough, perhaps the two most admired, because most moving passages of Arnold's own prose are the closing paragraphs of *The Function of Criticism* and the preface to *Essays in Criticism.* The first with its extended metaphor of the wilderness and promised land is decidedly provincial by Arnoldian standards, and the second, with its famous apostrophe to Oxford, certainly strays from the center of urbane prose.

It is sometimes pointed out that the notorious poetic touchstones have about all of them a strain of melancholy, and are consequently evidence of an unduly personal estimate by Arnold, the melancholy man. The observation is true, but unfair because it fails to add that the touchstones share two other qualities of at least equal note. They all direct their attention to fundamental and largely unchanging questions of human existence, to death, pain, suffering, love of God. These questions are the great conceptions of Longinus

[55] *Works,* X, 228. The disparagement of Macaulay should be compared with the remark already quoted from the essay on Maurice de Guérin in which Keats and Guérin are credited with an "expression [which] corresponds with the thing's essential reality," *Complete Prose,* III, 34.
[56] *Complete Prose,* III, 260–61.
[57] *Complete Prose,* III, 245–48.

and are exemplary evidence that Arnold's rendering of Aristotle's *spoudaioteron*—of more weight—as "high seriousness"[58] comes, presumably indirectly, by way of the Longinian sublime. The second quality shared by the touchstones is their directness, simplicity, and generally unelaborate use of metaphor: Shakespeare, it will be remembered, is represented by "absent thee from felicity awhile." The more characteristic Shakespearean metaphor, at once richly developed and strikingly compressed,[59] Arnold thought—surely rightly—an unsafe model for practicing writers, because it is dangerously imitable but not instructive:

It may be imitated and exaggerated, it cannot be learned or applied as an art. He is above all suggestive; more valuable, therefore, to young writers as men than as artists. But clearness of arrangement, rigour of development, simplicity of style,—these may to a certain extent be learned; and these may, I am convinced, be learned best from the ancients, who, although infinitely less suggestive than Shakespeare, are thus, to the artist, more instructive.[60]

In Shakespeare himself the rich elaborateness of style corresponded to, was the appropriate expression of, a rich "fertility of thought."[61] But his "taking tourmenté style" was, like Milton's, susceptible to imitation by a writer who lacked the needed complexity of conception. The result for Arnold is an inevitable discrepancy between manner and matter and a consequent loss of the inevitability which comes from integrity.

v

It is this assumption which in part underlies his Romantic insistence that in landscape poetry especially the eye should be on the object. In itself, in the form in which it has so often been invoked by subsequent critics, the criterion of the eye on the object yields a not very compelling standard of value. Why should a poet so com-

---

[58] *Works*, IV, 16–17, 24. See John Shepard Eells, Jr., *The Touchstones of Matthew Arnold* (New York, 1955), pp. 230–31: ". . . if high seriousness is pseudo-Aristotelian, the grand style may be termed neo-Longinian" (p. 231). High seriousness seems also to be "neo-Longinian."
[59] In the initial schedule of touchstones in *The Study of Poetry*, Hamlet's request is coupled with a few lines from Henry IV's soliloquy on sleep which are more richly metaphorical; but "absent thee from felicity awhile" is the line which recurs later in the essay as a widely applicable touchstone, *Works*, IV, 14. 31.
[60] *Complete Prose*, I, 12. It will be recalled that the disparagement of Macaulay's prose includes the charge that it is likely "to attract imitators in multitude," *Works*, X, 228.
[61] *Complete Prose*, I, 11.

pose? What is to be gained beyond accuracy of physical representation? For Arnold it evidently achieved avoidance of the mere functioning of style by rote, whose occurrence signals the desire to say something rather than the having something to say. In his distinction between four ways of handling nature he first illustrates "the conventional way of handling nature, [when] the eye is not on the object; what that means we all know, we have only to think of our eighteenth-century poetry:—

'As when the moon, refulgent lamp of night'—

to call up any number of instances."[62] He once told his mother that in *Thyrsis* "the images are all from actual observation, on which point there is an excellent remark in Wordsworth's notes, collected by Miss Fenwick. The cuckoo on the wet June morning I heard in the garden at Woodford."[63] Since a large proportion of the notes Wordsworth dictated to Isabella Fenwick concerned the occasions of his poems, there are several which could qualify as the one Arnold had in mind. But the most likely is the note to *An Evening Walk,* in which, after remarking that "there is not an image in it which I have not observed," he added of one image that "I date from it my consciousness of the infinite variety of natural appearances which had been unnoticed by the poets of any age or country, so far as I was acquainted with them; and I made a resolution to supply, in some degree, the deficiency."[64] Wordsworth's "excellent remark," in fact, simply affirms the importance of the eye on the object, a procedure which, in itself, led only to what Arnold called "the faithful way of handling nature," a way abundantly exemplified in German poetry and inferior to the addition of "radiance" to fidelity in the Greek way and the addition of "magic" in the Celtic way.[65] The faithful way is nonetheless superior to the conventional way, and its admittedly modest aims no doubt underlie in part Arnold's scrupulous care to achieve an accurate oriental setting for *Sohrab and Rustum* and *The Sick King in Bokhara,* while the notes for his projected play about Lucretius include under the heading of " 'Italy—vegetation' . . . details of trees, vines, and gardens."[66]

[62] *Complete Prose,* III, 377.
[63] *Works,* XIV, 83; April 7, 1866.
[64] *Poetical Works,* ed. E. de Selincourt, I (Oxford, 1940), 318–19.
[65] *Complete Prose,* III, 377–78.
[66] *Commentary,* pp. 76–80, 85–88, 344. Compare the observation to W. E. Forster: generally speaking, the history, topography & natural history of Merope are

Botanical accuracy, whether practiced in the Cumnor hills or on Mount Etna, is not in itself conducive to poetic integrity. If anything, patient enumerative detail is likely to work against the wholeness or composition of the poem in which it occurs and not only because, in Lessing's terms, it involves a disparity between the necessarily temporal representation of spatially perceived objects. More important is the fact that the terms needed for accurate delineation are rarely capable of carrying other than physical significance. An "orange and pale violet evening-sky" is, as the prelude to an epiphany, no more significant than a sky which is purple and pale yellow.[67] There is no point in doubting that Arnold saw a sky just as he described it, principally because it scarcely matters that he did. Herein lies the danger of composing with the eye on the object: it too readily leads to the kind of description in a poem which has full significance only outside the poem, in the poet's originating experience. The advantage of keeping the eye off the object and on a stock diction is that a stock diction is often rich in epithets of established significance which the poet can re-use in ways which not only describe but compose his landscape into significance.

Such a composed significance often involves, especially in the kind of landscape poetry Arnold writes, the problem of uniting description and reflection. Arnold, in fact, rarely concerns himself directly with this problem. He prefers, instead, to speak of composition in the painter's sense of grouping objects, or to seek *architectonicé* in unity of action and effect, or to insist, very generally, that the adoption of a particular form involves the poet in great sacrifice (presumably of possibly relevant matter and effects) for the sake of the ensemble. But he also spoke of the difficulty of "uniting matter" and complained about "the modern English habit . . . of using poetry as a channel for thinking aloud, instead of making anything." He once told Clough that "if one loved what was beautiful and interesting in itself *passionately* enough, one would produce what was excellent without troubling oneself with religious dogmas at all. As it is, we are *warm* only when dealing with these last—and what is frigid is always bad."[68] The disjunction between

faithful—that is so far as anything about Greece from one who has not seen it can be faithful," *Unpublished Letters of Matthew Arnold*, ed. Whitridge, p. 36; Jan. 11, 1858.
[67] *Thyrsis*, l. 159. Although the line's context certainly requires two colors in the sky, one to represent day, one to represent night, the spectrum provides a variety of possible combinations.
[68] *Clough Letters*, p. 143; Sept. 6 [1853].

dogma and what is "beautiful and interesting in itself" apparently underlies a confession over ten years later to Grant Duff:

One is from time to time seized and irresistibly carried along by a temptation to treat political, or religious, or social matters, directly [in, presumably, essays]; but after yielding to such a temptation I always feel myself recoiling again, and disposed to touch them only so far as they can be touched through poetry.[69]

Arnold does not indicate how far a poetic treatment differs from a direct treatment, any more than he indicates in the early letter to Clough just what he thinks has to be sacrificed to the ensemble.

vi

For all this characteristic impalpability, this avoidance of theoretical utterance with a direct and obvious practical application, nothing is more evident than Arnold's almost lifelong endeavor to define the nature of poetic integrity. He praised Clough for "a lovely aperçu" about *"sequence"* in the review Clough wrote of Arnold's first two volumes and the poems of Alexander Smith.[70] "We do not find," Clough wrote of Smith's *Life-Drama,* "that happy, unimpeded sequence which is the charm of really good writers."[71]

There are frequent fine lines, occasional beautiful passages; but the tenor of the narrative is impeded and obstructed to the last degree, not only by accumulations of imagery, but by episode, and episode within episode, of the most embarrassing form.[72]

The obvious coincidence with the view Arnold expressed in the 1853 preface, a few months after Clough's article appeared, is reinforced by Clough's identifying the malign source of this incoherence as the "extravagant love for Elizabethan phraseology" to which Keats and Shelley had earlier succumbed.[73] Sequence, clear sequaciousness, is manifestly conducive to the kind of integrity which fulfills Coleridge's requirement that a poem contain within itself the reason why it is so and not otherwise. A variation upon the

[69] *Works,* XIII, 308; May 24, 1864.
[70] *Clough Letters,* p. 144; Oct. 10 [1853].
[71] *Selected Prose Works of Arthur Hugh Clough,* ed. Trawick, p. 167.
[72] *Ibid.,* p. 147.
[73] *Ibid.,* p. 166.

desideratum of sequence occurs as late as Arnold's lecture on Emerson:

> Gray holds his high rank as a poet, not merely by the beauty and grace of passages in his poems; not merely by a diction generally pure in an age of impure diction: he holds it, above all, by the power and skill with which the evolution of his poems is conducted. Here is his grand superiority to Collins, whose diction in his best poem, the 'Ode to Evening,' is purer than Gray's; but then the 'Ode to Evening' is like a river which loses itself in the sand, whereas Gray's best poems have an evolution sure and satisfying.[74]

A practical consideration of landscape poetry, including Arnold's, may properly concern itself with this distinction between Gray and Collins, as well as the 1853 preface's stress upon "clearness of arrangement, rigour of development, simplicity of style." When these remarks are given a context in the observations scattered throughout Arnold's letters and prefaces, it is evident that, to put it no higher, he endeavored to find theoretical formulas for (especially landscape) poetry which, if their primary attention is to problems of poetic composition, are often translatable into terms appropriate to a reader's attempt to articulate his response. The remark in the Emerson lecture recognizes that there are aspects of poetry which are primarily integrative and others whose contribution is primarily to that maximum felicity of the parts required by Coleridge. When Arnold is particularly impalpable, it is usually because in his manifold attempts to define the relationship between part and whole he from time to time stressed one or the other unduly: the *architectonicé* of 1853 unduly stresses wholeness as much as the touchstones of 1880 unduly encourage a fragmenting concentration on the parts.[75] But this weakness is small when set beside the total sense we gain of views of poetry which are neither rigorously and exclusively holistic nor irritatingly innocent of any awareness that a poem is a made thing and one thing. Somewhere in his scattered observations there is nearly always a remark, a suggestive term or phrase, relevant to most of the critical issues which may be raised about landscape poetry.

[74] *Works*, IV, 358.
[75] Arnold did remember to add that "the greatness of the great poets, the power of their criticism of life, is that their virtue is sustained," *Works*, IV, 25. But it is not clear whether he means they sustained it through many productions or whether, in accordance with the Longinian requirement, they sustained it throughout individual works.

THE GROUPING, PRINCIPALLY BY GENRE, which Arnold adopted for the later editions of his poems is less confusing than Wordsworth's occasional and psychological categories. But it nonetheless involves at times some extension of generic limits. In what sense, for example, is the *Epilogue to Lessing's Laocoön* a lyric poem? This verse *causerie,* or *entretien* perhaps, with its faint reminiscences of a Horatian *sermo* is as close in spirit as it is in time to the critical essays of the 1860's. Occasionally, the conversation issues in notes, as it were, for recognizably lyric poems:

> 'Sometimes a momentary gleam
> They catch of the mysterious stream [of life];
> Sometimes, a second's space, their ear
> The murmur of its waves doth hear.
> That transient glimpse in song they say,
> But not as painter can pourtray.'   (ll. 177–82)

What in song the poets say might be *The Buried Life* or *The River* of *Faded Leaves;* it might well be *Dover Beach,* but it would not be, with luck, *Epilogue to Lessing's Laocoön.*

i

The *Epilogue* is a poor poem, and some of the reasons for its inadequacy emerge in the few lines quoted above. They prompt the speculation with what organ Arnold would have his poet hear if it is not his ear. The pleonasm clearly results from a groping for rhyme, as it also does in the following couplet, where the awkward inversion of "in song they say" manifestly exists for the sake of a rhyme with "pourtray." As it happens, the awful exigencies of the octosyllabic couplet are most obviously straitening in the first thirty-five lines of the poem, the majority of which Arnold rather unfairly assigns to the anonymous friend who serves as interlocutor or *adversarius*. Pragmatically considered, the English octosyllabic couplet works best when it is used for humorous effect. Arnold matched the grave assurance of Marvell or Milton in *Resignation*. But in the *Epilogue* the adoption of a frequently matter-of-fact tone, presumably to capture the note of *causerie*, leads all too often into an unfortunate reminiscence of *Hudibras*:

> One morn as through Hyde Park we walk'd,
> My friend and I, by chance we talk'd
> Of Lessing's famed Laocoön;
> And after we awhile had gone
> In Lessing's track, and tried to see
> What painting is, what poetry—
> Diverging to another thought,
> 'Ah,' cries my friend, 'but who hath taught
> Why music and the other arts
> Oftener perform aright their parts
> Than poetry? why she, than they,
> Fewer fine successes can display?
>
> 'For 'tis so, surely! Even in Greece,
> Where best the poet framed his piece,
> Even in that Phœbus-guarded ground
> Pausanias on his travels found
> Good poems, if he look'd, more rare
> (Though many) than good statues were—
> For these, in truth, were everywhere.'   (ll. 1–19)

The unfortunate friend, with his tortured syntax, his Arnoldian "ah," his poetic "hath" and "Phœbus-guarded," his informal parentheses, this, one hopes, is a conversational chimera that never lived. But if Arnold is uncharitable to his friend, he is no less harsh on himself as narrator. Of an infelicitous passage from the Prioress's Tale in Wordsworth's version Arnold once temperately observed that, compared with Chaucer's original, "the charm is departed."[1] It could be said of the opening of the *Epilogue* that charm is never achieved, even though the first couplet at least seems to be an attempted verse equivalent to the *"charm,"* the "sinuous, easy, unpolemical mode of proceeding," he told his mother he had achieved in prose.[2] Arnold has found to express his matter not a diction but congeries of dictions: formal and informal, inverted and straightforward, poetic and matter-of-fact, banal shading into bathetic. The uncertainty and confusion, the inability to find a proper and consistent manner for his matter, result, unquestionably, from the difficulty of maintaining a serious but unelevated tone in the jog and jingle of octosyllabics.

Stylistic inadequacies, so manifest in the opening lines because so thickly exemplified, recur more or less obtrusively throughout the poem as constant evidence that Arnold has failed to conceive the poem whole, has failed to find an appropriate tone and a diction. Such integrity as the piece possesses thus derives from the relationship between the description of landscape and the reflections in and upon it. The *Epilogue* is instructively typical of many of Arnold's poems because much of it is reflection in landscape rather than experience of it, because it endeavors to convert the spatially observed scene into a temporal record by means of physical movement through the scene, and because the description of an actual landscape is extended into generalized landscape metaphors that convey part of the reflections. The typicality should not be stressed too strongly, however. The relationship between scene and reflection is principally rhetorical, and such is not the case with the important poems of the early years. The landscape matter is ordered to suit the requirements of the argument instead of having a narrative or imaginative interest of its own which the argument expatiates upon. The roughly southward stroll across Hyde **Park** pauses at three points: the pastoral fields, the Serpentine bridge, and Rotten Row. The fields provide a static scene, a tableau appropriate to a painting (ll. 36–60). A painter restricted to such unpromising materials as a "blossom'd thorn" and cattle with "liquid eyes" unsurprisingly succeeds in providing only an "outward semblance." On the Serpentine bridge the visual record of cows and trees is replaced by the sound of wind and water and, with the aid of a glimpse of Westminster Abbey, the sound of church music:

[1] *The Study of Poetry, Works,* IV, 23.
[2] *Works,* XIII, 266, 321; Oct. 29, 1863, and Dec. 7, 1864.

"*Miserere, Domine!*" (ll. 61–106). (It is of note that the immediate surroundings in Hyde Park have to be extended to include the Abbey. The wind about the bridge is a rustling breeze, the water "light-plashing," both thus evidencing a levity which makes them inappropriate analogies for what Arnold thought the properly melancholy sound of humanity. The inclusion of the Abbey, then, facilitates a movement reminiscent of *Dover Beach,* in which the opening visual tranquility is broken by the sound of waves bringing "the eternal note of sadness in.") The church music expresses the "inmost heart," and substitutes depth of feeling for the painter's "outward semblance." The final stand by Rotten Row, with its view of "the human tide," brings us, climactically, to "the poet's sphere," the representation of "life's *movement*" (ll. 107–62). It is here that Arnold's command of the landscape exempla to his discourse is weakest, and it is weakest because, while the pastoral scene and the church music really are exemplary, the bustle in Rotten Row is more properly seen as an analogy for what Arnold means by "life's *movement.*" For Arnold is not primarily concerned with a Lessingesque distinction between the spatially composed bodies of painting and the temporally articulated actions of poetry. The movement which interests him and which constitutes, he feels, the poet's most challenging problem is not the physical movement of action, but the temporal movement of vicissitudinous experience and the psychological movement from pain to pleasure.

> 'He must life's *movement* tell!
> The thread which binds it all in one,
> And not its separate parts alone.
> The *movement* he must tell of life,
> Its pain and pleasure, rest and strife;
> His eye must travel down, at full,
> The long, unpausing spectacle;
> With faithful unrelaxing force
> Attend it from its primal source,
> From change to change and year to year
> Attend it of its mid career
> Attend it to the last repose
> And solemn silence of its close.' (ll 140–52)

The poetry which results from such a preoccupation is not an *Iliad,* unless it be an Iliad of woes; it is a *Resignation.* But Arnold, tied to his landscape, illustrates his proposition by a supposedly significant variation upon the painter's matter:

'The cattle rising from the grass
His thought must follow where they pass.'   (ll. 153–54)

And what then? In what way does his seeing the cows watered, milked and bedded represent "the long, unpausing spectacle" of human life? Nor is it clear how it helps to "follow through the crowd" the musician's "penitent with anguish bow'd" (ll. 155–56). Music is as temporally existent as poetry, and, to hold to Arnold's own criterion of emotion, the musician is no more restricted than the poet to "the feeling of the moment" (l. 132). If Arnold had not observed this in his own example of Beethoven, he could have found it spelled out in *Alexander's Feast*. The difference between music and poetry is not one of movement but, to stress the obvious, between the non-mimetic and the mimetic, a difference most apparent, perhaps, in the periodic attempts to circumvent musical limitations, if limitations they be, by means of program music.

The failure of the descriptive detail here to do the work required of it by the argument is evidence of a conceptual cloudiness and an accompanying imprecision in the use of landscape as objective example and as metaphoric matter. The opening account of the occasion, the walk in Hyde Park, is followed immediately by an ambulatory metaphor: "after we awhile had gone / In Lessing's track . . . / Diverging to another thought" (ll. 4–7). The proximity of literal and metaphorical walking suggests a possibly meaningful connection between the two: the physical course across the park providing a close analogy for the figurative course of the discussion. But in these opening lines there is no such analogy and the otherwise innocuously local metaphor is rendered distracting precisely because the analogical possibility is not realized. No doubt this commonplace little metaphor is a minor oversight, a virtually dead metaphor revivified by its context to no purpose. But one of the demands we make of the artist who imitates in words is that he evidence the kind of sensitivity for his verbal medium which issues in the meaningful revivification of dead metaphors. Especially may we ask this of a poet like Arnold, so many of whose landscapes are based upon metaphoric commonplaces superimposed upon existing or at least fully realized sites and explored for significances beyond the commonplace. At his best, Arnold can give us something like the closing lines of *Sohrab and Rustum*: the imaginative renewal of cliché. But when he is not at his best, and sometimes when he is close to it, Arnold provides us with cliché which remains obstinately cliché through all his attempts at imaginative renewal.

Something of this kind occurs in the closing section of the *Epilogue,* whose delineation of the poet's matter and the temptations he faces is dominated by one of Arnold's favorite metaphors: the life stream. The metaphor, used here to convey the emotional movement of life, is prepared for in the Abbey section by a reference to "the stream of music" (and if Arnold had paused upon the implications of this phrase he might not a little later have limited the musician to "the feeling of the moment"). The emotional associations of the musical stream (ll. 82–85) are picked up in "the human tide," "the stream of life" in Rotten Row (ll. 108–12), the "eddying, motley throng / That sparkles in the sun along" (ll. 157–58). With the eddying throng Arnold is ready for the full presentation of the life stream. It is not the best of images to elaborate upon, and it always gave Arnold trouble. The problem is to maintain a conceptual clarity in the tenor consistent with the physical detail of the vehicle. In the *Epilogue* Arnold wants the stream to be the manifold of human experience, the poet's raw material, confused and confusing: a motley throng. In telling the movement of this stream, the poet is to render "not its separate parts alone" (which, one suspects, Arnold thought Keats and Browning guilty of doing) but, with a troubling mixture of metaphors, "the thread which binds it all in one" (ll. 140–42). It is not a happy variant. We may accept that "thread" suggests the continuity of movement rather than its eddying to and fro, and thus a "general life" uniting particular lives. But a thread which binds instead of threads suggests a bundle of sticks rather than Carlyle's organic filaments. The perception of unity, in whatever shape, comes to the poet not from participation in but sympathetic contemplation of the manifold of life. Don't get your feet wet, Arnold warns the would-be poet.

> 'Many, many are the souls
> Life's movement fascinates, controls;
> It draws them on, they cannot save
> Their feet from its alluring wave;
> They cannot leave it, they must go
> With its unconquerable flow.'
> (ll. 163–68)

So it is now a stream of necessity. But the consequences of wallowing in or on its waters are very curious. The inability to leave the unconquerable flow leads, maddeningly, to leaving it.

'But ah! how few, of all that try
This mighty march, do aught but die!
For ill-endow'd for such a way,
Ill-stor'd in strength, in wits, are they.
They faint, they stagger to and fro,
And wandering from the stream they go;
In pain, in terror, in distress,
They see, all round, a wilderness.'   (ll. 169–76)

Careful scrutiny reveals that the errant *they* are the few and not the "all that try" (for a poet so dedicated to simplicity of expression Arnold was too frequently capable of confused syntax). Having put ashore the weak few who are not swept along by the irresistible current, Arnold banishes them to a wilderness, presumably because they have now left life and habitation. In such surroundings their intermittent consolation is an occasional glimpse of the gleam and murmur of the life stream, a Pisgah sight which they embody in a poem, and it is to this category, one feels, Arnold would assign most of his own early poetry. But there is yet another few to be placed in this landscape, a happy few, who

'the life-stream's shore
With safe unwandering feet explore;
Untired its movement bright attend,
Follow its windings to the end.'   (ll. 189–92)

To what end, one wonders? No doubt the customary end of life streams, a marine death. But while this may do very well when the stream represents the life of a single man, its relevance is by no means clear to a stream representative of multitudinous human life, all those people from Rotten Row splashing about happily or sorrowfully. Such a stream ought, like Tennyson's brook, to go on forever, unless, and this seems not to be the case here, it terminates in an ocean of eschatology.

It is perhaps unfair to enquire so curiously into the qualities of a poem which most would surely agree to call poor.[3] But some

[3] G. Robert Stange has recently offered a more sympathetic reading of the *Epilogue* than mine in his *Matthew Arnold: The Poet as Humanist* (Princeton, New Jersey, 1967), pp. 86–97.

legitimate gains may result. The life-stream passage presents a characteristically Arnoldian desideratum for the poet: detached observation of life without total withdrawal from it. Because the terms of this formula imply spatial relationships, it may be appropriately (if not always felicitously) embodied in landscape, preeminently a matter of spatially related objects. The awkward contrivances of the life-stream passage further exemplify the practical consequences of the difficulty Arnold confessed to finding in the unification of thought and feeling. Even in his best work Arnold was prone to sacrifice clarity of thought in the tenor to the pursuit of emotions prompted by his landscape vehicle. In a poem as argument-centered as the *Epilogue,* such a disintegration of thought and feeling, tenor and vehicle, is crucially damaging.

It would be unfair to call the *Epilogue* prosaic; Arnold never botched his prose in this way. But the way in which the landscape is used to illustrate by example or analogy a theoretical discourse is more reminiscent of his later essays than his earlier poems. It is true that the landscape matter has a certain coherence of its own: the walk across the park, the three stops, the gradual emergence of the final landscape metaphor out of the descriptions of the actual landscape. But the patness with which each stop yields the required aesthetic example or analogy makes it clear that the landscape arrangement is contrived to suit the needs of argument. To use an Arnoldian criterion, the poem lacks "naturalness—i.e.,—an absolute propriety—of form" because it is principally the product of "the mere thinker."[4] The difference between the late mode of the *Epilogue* and the handling of landscape in much of the early poetry can be seen by placing the *Epilogue* beside another piece associated with Hyde Park, the *Lines Written in Kensington Gardens,* published in 1852 and probably written not long before.[5]

ii

Kensington Gardens is a superficially simple little poem consisting of eleven octosyllabic quatrains, the first nine of which describe the life of nature in a "lone, open glade" in comparison with the life of man in the busy city around, while the last two quatrains apply this description to a moral lesson couched in the form of a petition

---

[4] *Clough Letters,* p. 98; [early Feb., 1849].
[5] See Allott, p. 254, for a discussion of the date.

to the "calm soul of all things." Perhaps because the rhyme scheme of the quatrain is less demanding than that of the couplet, the diction of the poem is more successfully assured than it is in the *Epilogue*. There are few forced inversions, the syntax has a sustained clarity rare for Arnold even in poems of this length, and the tone, while it skirts the sentimental in its references to children and the portentous in its exclamations and exhortations, never goes unbearably beyond the limits. The poem's diction is generally satisfactory—adequate, in Arnold's sense—although it never achieves the memorable felicity of Arnold's best poems, and must consequently be valued below them.

That it should nonetheless be valued highly is a result of its generally adequate expression and its assured integrity of landscape detail and reflection. Like *Dover Beach,* the poem makes of its landscape setting a metaphor or analogy for a kind of life at the same time that it renders with literal exactness the mood and thoughts prompted by such a setting. Like *Dover Beach* again, although less obviously and clearly, it achieves integrity by the controlled evolution of literal landscape into metaphor. We begin, then, with the place itself:

In this lone, open glade I lie,
Screen'd by deep boughs on either hand;
And at its end, to stay the eye,
Those black-crown'd, red-boled pine-trees stand!

Birds here make song, each bird has his,
Across the girdling city's hum.
How green under the boughs it is!
How thick the tremulous sheep-cries come!

Sometimes a child will cross the glade
To take his nurse his broken toy;
Sometimes a thrush flit overhead
Deep in her unknown day's employ.

Here at my feet what wonders pass,
What endless, active life is here!
What blowing daisies, fragrant grass!
An air-stirr'd forest, fresh and clear.   (ll. 1–16)

The initial placing of the speaker is conveyed in terms both precise and suggestive. The "lone" is almost a transferred epithet applied to the glade because the speaker is himself alone; loneness is scarcely a quality one would immediately associate with a popular London park. The first line, then, commences the association of the speaker's feelings with his surroundings. Although the glade is open, the speaker looks into it toward the end closed by trees, and since he is also blinkered by trees on either side, his concentration is wholly upon the glade, its life and significance. The speaker, in fact, closes off the glade by turning his back to the open end; he becomes, as it were, the fourth side of the glade, a part of it and therefore able to attribute his own isolation to the whole of which he is part. Although the last line of the first stanza offers descriptive details not greatly significant beyond themselves, it is literally proper that the eye, stayed by trees, should rest upon them and record their appearance. Moreover, and importantly, the two compound adjectives and the compound noun load the line with heavy stresses and slow down the octosyllabic to a tempo appropriate to the calm and unhurried delineation which follows. The 1852 reading of the fifth line: "The birds sing sweetly in these trees," made for a smoother transition from the pine trees than the later reading, for which we have to supply the connection between trees and singing birds. In either case, the stanza concentrates upon the sounds heard if not necessarily originating in the glade, for the third line's glance at the grass prepares for the cries of sheep that feed on it. It is noteworthy that the city noise, later to be presented as shattering, is only a (presumably pleasant) hum. At this point the noise is dissociated from the actual "uproar" it expresses and is one of the constituents of the glade's peace. The sound of animal life gives place in the third stanza to the sight of it. An occasional child crossing the glade to his nurse, who is presumably outside the charmed ground, is the only other human being who enters the circle of the speaker's observation. The thrushes which share the third stanza with the children have in their "unknown day's employ" a significance which is immediately applied in the turning to the vegetable life on the floor of the glade. The grass and flowers both epitomize the freshness and clearness of the glade and partake of its "endless, active life." The innocence of this activity as well as of the thrushes' employment is implied by the occasional appearance of children engaged upon simple and harmless pursuits.

The significance of the glade in itself is now complete, as is the relation of the speaker to his setting. He is of it, the fourth side, but he does not partake of the life within; the sounds, the thrushes and the children come, the daisies blow without concern for his presence. It is the achieved Arnoldian harmony with nature, modest, mundane, unmystical, unquestioning.

For the poem to proceed, for the glade's significance to widen, there must be movement or reference away from it. But Arnold does not, as he so easily might have done, immediately evoke in harsher form the girdling city. Instead, he offers a stanza which at first sight gratuitously transports us out of London altogether: he finds in the grass at his feet

An air-stirr'd forest, fresh and clear.

Scarce fresher is the mountain-sod
Where the tired angler lies, stretch'd out,
And, eased of basket and of rod,
Counts his day's spoil, the spotted trout.   (ll. 16–20)

The stanza actually performs three important functions in the poem. It provides a human and adult counterpart to the innocent and peaceful activity within the glade of the life in the grass, the thrushes and the children, and it accordingly prepares the way for the following stanzas' account of "the huge world" 's loss of peace and "impious uproar." The posture of the angler, identical with that of the speaker in the glade, is an idyllic picture of a life fully integrated, where happy labor and contented rest succeed each other in the same peaceful surroundings, unlike the life of the speaker, who can achieve only an inferior integrity by withdrawing to the glade from the scene of his far from happy labor: "I, on men's impious uproar hurl'd." The final value is that the stanza makes plain by the easy association of glade and country that the glade is the countryside in little, *rus in urbe*.

The observant but inactive harmony of the speaker with the glade is given perspective by the angler who is in harmony with his surroundings in both labor and rest. The point of this perspective is then drawn out in four stanzas which record the speaker's alien responsibilities and his consequent separateness from the glade:

In the huge world, which roars hard by,
Be others happy if they can!
But in my helpless cradle I
Was breathed on by the rural Pan.

I, on men's impious uproar hurl'd,
Think often, as I hear them rave,
That peace has left the upper world
And now keeps only in the grave.

Yet here is peace for ever new!
When I who watch them am away,
Still all things in this glade go through
The changes of their quiet day.

Then to their happy rest they pass!
The flowers upclose, the birds are fed,
The night comes down upon the grass,
The child sleeps warmly in his bed.   (ll. 21–36)

The conventional primitivism, the opposition between the peaceful
and innocent life of the country and the discordant impiety of
urban existence, finds its equally conventional extension into the
opposition between childhood and maturity. The children who
alone of human beings enter the speaker's glade can do so because
they possess the qualities apportioned to the infant Arnold in
Laleham. A year or two before *Kensington Gardens* was probably
written Arnold recorded for his mother his nostalgia on revisiting
the location of his "helpless cradle."

It was nearly dark when I left the Weybridge Station, but I could
make out the wide sheet of the gray Thames gleaming through the
general dusk as I came out on Chertsey Bridge. I never go along
that shelving gravelly road up towards Laleham without interest,
from Chertsey Lock to the turn where the drunken man lay. To-
day, after morning church, I went up to Pentonhook, and found the
stream with the old volume, width, shine, rapid fulness, 'kempshott,'
and swans, unchanged and unequalled, to my partial and remembering eyes at least.[6]

It is such unexceptional sentiments as these which underlie the
poem's brief reference to his infancy. But if the reference is "explained" biographically by the sentiments, it can be accounted for
poetically only by observing its relevance to the children of the
glade, who must, like the animal and vegetable life of the glade, be
put safely to rest at nightfall. The glade has as one of its important
aspects an innocent and constantly renewed activity readily avail-

[6] *Works*, XIII, 3; Jan. 2, 1848.

able only to a child, because a child, like the flowers, accepts unquestioningly. To visit the glade, to adopt its mood and become a part of it, is to revisit or recreate in spirit one's own idyllic childhood. And if the view of childhood seems now unduly naive, it is at least a naivety which Arnold shares with Wordsworth and the New Testament.

The bedding of the children incorporates them in the cycle of nature, in the "peace for ever new" of the glade, and distinguishes them from the men whose urban existence permits only an unrenewable peace in the finality of the grave. But even within the city there is available—to men who know how to use it—the abiding renewal of the glade, a better sepulture because it guarantees resurrection. With the full extension of the glade's significance to include the life cycle of man, explicitly from cradle to grave, we are ready for the final petition and the final stage in the transformation of landscape into metaphor.

> Calm soul of all things! make it mine
> To feel, amid the city's jar,
> That there abides a peace of thine,
> Man did not make, and cannot mar.
>
> The will to neither strive nor cry,
> The power to feel with others give!
> Calm, calm me more; nor let me die
> Before I have begun to live.   (ll. 37–44)

Professor Allott is obviously correct to gloss the opening vocative with references to the *anima mundi* from Plato to Wordsworth.[7] But it blurs the poem's achievement not to point out, in addition, the ambiguity of the reference. In the manuscript there is immediately before the stanza, as Professor Allott notes, what looks like an "abortive beginning" to it: "Spirit who must be here." It is worth enquiring into the consequences of rejecting this alternative to "Calm soul of all things!" There is a small metrical difficulty in combining the first reading with "make it mine," and the simplest solution of eliding "it" would blur the syntax. Merely to substitute "spirit" for "calm soul" would achieve metrical and syntactical precision at the cost of losing an important attribute. But what is most striking is that where the first reading clearly distinguishes between

[7] Allott, pp. 257–58.

51

glade and spirit as *locus* and *genius loci,* the final reading ambiguously refers both to the glade and something more ubiquitous than
a *genius loci.* The speaker, the glade, and the calm soul are all
"amid the city's jar." The peace of the calm soul, unaffected by
man, has a counterpart in the pristine peace of "all things in this
glade" even when the observing speaker is gone.

The glade, literally and most simply, is a temporary refuge from
"the huge world, which roars hard by," and the speaker is, as the
authors of the *Commentary* put it, a "tired man grateful for a
present hour of rest and anxious lest the blessed mood depart."[8]
But the speaker's observing acceptance of the glade's life, the act of
making poetry out of visual and aural record, induces in him a calmness which the glade itself possesses by virtue of its total accord with
the "calm soul of all things." But "all things" include even the
speaker when "on men's impious uproar hurl'd" and his individual
soul shares in the universal soul. He petitions for a sense of peace
"amid the city's jar," because he wishes to translate the peace he
finds in a glade *surrounded* by the city's jar into a peace when he is
included in the city's jar. The life cycle he would substitute for the
city's restless progress to the grave is the constant renewal of child
and nature. The eye of the hurricane has three aspects: the lone
glade within the city but open to access, the one soul informing the
manifold of all things, and the calm center of a man externally engaged in the jarring distractions of adult life. By entering the lone
because rarely visited glade and becoming part of it, a man lives
out of his calm center and not his exterior troubles, and can address
the soul of all things because he is in harmony with it. The literal
glade becomes almost imperceptibly metaphorical. The careful
enumeration of detail which is a necessary prelude to the final
mood makes the glade too insistently and objectively out there for
it to be a *paysage intérieur,* although the appearance of the child
in the glade is so like the speaker's recollection of his own rural
childhood that the glade appears momentarily to represent the
speaker's consciousness. The metaphorical potential of the glade is
released by the poet's imaginative concentration upon it, even
though the glade remains throughout a literal glade. In this respect, *Kensington Gardens* is a process poem reminiscent of Keats's
Ode on a Grecian Urn. But where in Keats the imaginative process
is made explicit in the final stanza, and the gains of imaginative

8 *Commentary,* p. 199.

entrance into the life of the urn's frieze are spelled out, in Arnold
the imaginative process remains implicit and issues instead in moral
explicitness. The concluding imperatives of Arnold's poem are less
assured and leave more room for that anxiety "lest the blessed mood
depart" noted by the authors of the *Commentary* than the tri-
umphant indicatives of Keats's final lines. But Arnold's poem is as
much as Keats's a paradigm of its own meaning. The poem itself
is an example of how to achieve the calmness the speaker seeks at
the end.

That the achievement did not come easily is evident from a
comparison of the manuscript draft with the final poem.[9] The
manuscript contains versions of twelve stanzas and a prose note for
a thirteenth. The stanza omitted from the final poem is placed
second in the first edition and in the manuscript:

> The clouded sky is still & grey—
> Thro: silken rifts soft winks the sun:
> Light the clear foliaged chestnuts play:
> The massier elms stand grave & dun.

Apart from the pathetic fallacy of "winks" and "play," sufficient
perhaps to push the poem into the sentimentalism it elsewhere
barely avoids, the chief objection to this stanza is that it is unnecessary. Not only does the further enumeration of trees blur the effect
of the pines standing at the end of the first stanza, but additional
visual detail, part of which takes us above and therefore out of the
glade, is not needed for the full objective realization of the place.
If the stanza had been included, with or without minor alterations,
it would have constituted a not too distracting blemish. But if
Arnold had included a stanza based upon his prose note, he would
certainly have ended with a different poem, and most probably with
a poem in which his final meaning was blurred to the point of con-
tradiction. "Every day all these appear, live, go thro: their stages
whether I see them or no. I in an unnatural state of effort & personal wrappedupedness, do not see them." He had already written
out a version of the stanza recording the continuity of the glade's
life in his absence, and the first sentence of his note would therefore
have produced a repetition. The second sentence could possibly
refer to his mode of life in the town, but the phrasing of "do not

[9] The draft is given in *Commentary*, pp. 196–98.

see them" suggests that he is physically able to see them and is prevented only by psychological distraction. It suggests in fact that he has brought the city's jar into the glade instead of leaving it behind. If he had written out such a stanza it could only have been placed at the beginning of the poem as an initial record of lingering distraction before the glade begins to do its work. But it would have needed elaboration in other and perhaps fuller terms than those of the first sentence in order to serve as such a prelude. Arnold's wise decision to suppress this misbegotten embryo is an indication of his total sense of the poem and what it should do.

Another indication is the thorough rearrangement of the stanzas between manuscript and final form. The ordering of the first, third, and fourth stanzas is identical in both versions; the suppressed stanza is second in the manuscript, while the final second stanza, the aural record of the glade, comes eighth in the manuscript, immediately after the contrast between the "huge world" and the rural cradle. The angler is in the same fifth place but is separated from the "huge world" stanza by the affirmation of the glade's activity in the speaker's absence. With the aural record following the rural Pan, the manuscript places the stanza of "impious tumult" at the end, and thus closes the poem with the gloomy affirmation

That peace has left the upper world
And now dwells only in the grave.

The remainder of the manuscript follows the final order except that the pessimistic prose note immediately precedes the petition to the "calm soul of all things" and thus renders the exhortation a despairing cry de profundis which is appropriately silenced in the peace of the grave.

It would be a superficial response which found in the versions of Kensington Gardens simply one more example of the two voices that have been detected so often in Victorian culture: the melancholy despair of a private record dressed with qualified optimism for public consumption. Unquestionably, the manuscript order produces a picture of peace in nature which the speaker cannot really share because he is too involved in the roar of human life to do more than utter a despairing cry for help. But if the two-voices interpretation is insisted upon, then it must be affirmed that the version for public consumption is a far better poem than the private record.

It is so because the manuscript version in effect denies what it has already established. The description of the glade is an implicit record of the speaker's achieved calm. The final version, unlike the manuscript, recognizes the implication and proceeds in accordance with it. The best that can be said of the manuscript is that it flatly juxtaposes nature's peace and man's turbulence, and makes no further effort to integrate the details of description and reflection than Surrey's *The soote season,* with its thirteen lines joyfully celebrating nature's renewal and its final, curt note that the speaker alone is unhappy. But to say even this of the manuscript version of *Kensington Gardens* it is necessary to overlook both what is already implied by the opening description and the fact that the latter half of the poem is not a coherent expression of despair but rather an unsequacious veering from calm to turmoil and floating image to floating reflection. Of such a poem as the manuscript version Arnold could properly advise his sister not to waste time in attempting to find its integrity. The final version, however, makes clearer what Arnold must have meant by finding in Gray's poems "an evolution sure and satisfying." If the rearrangement of the stanzas results also (as it does) in a note of greater optimism and moral assurance, then it may be no more than support for Arnold's contention that aesthetic wholeness can only come out of moral wholeness and clarity of moral vision.

iii

The evolution which satisfied Arnold in Gray's poems need not be of precisely the same kind as the evolution observable in *Kensington Gardens.* Collins' *Ode to Evening* need not be "a river which loses itself in the sand" because it fails to achieve an evolution like Gray's or Arnold's. It fails, if it does, by not finding an evolution appropriate to its own way of apprehending landscape, or by apprehending landscape in a way which denies the possibility of evolution. In the Emerson lecture Arnold does not specify which are those best poems of Gray which possess an evolution lacking in the *Ode to Evening.* The essay on Gray contributed to Ward's *English Poets* mentions only two poems, the *Elegy* (not, we learn, Gray's best) and *The Progress of Poesy,* which does indeed exemplify that prized evolution.[10] But *The Progress of Poesy* comes by its evolu-

10 *Works,* IV, 72.

tion in part through the chronological sequence of the progress genre, and it would be fairer to Collins to compare his *Ode to Evening* with Gray's *Ode on the Spring*.

An initial reading of *Ode on the Spring* is likely to prompt feelings that here is a simple little poem which achieves such complexity as it possesses and redeems the triteness of its moralizing by a lightly ironic turn upon itself. An opening stanza enumerating some of the pleasurable sights and sounds of spring is succeeded by a stanza placing the speaker out of the prevailing sun in a shade conducive to moralizing reflection. The results of this reflection are contained in the next two stanzas, the first describing the activities of insects and the second applying that description as an analogy for the activities of man in polite society. The unsurprising conclusion of this comparison of man with insect is that the inevitable agents of transience: fortune, age, and death, make the gay life not worth having. The fifth and final stanza contains the ironic return: since all are subject to transience, it is as well to make the most of the moment by indulgence in principally sexual pleasure. In these terms, any evolution the poem possesses is likely to be satisfying only if we are prepared to rest in an obvious movement that alternates between description and reflection. The evolution will appear sure only if we are convinced that the descriptive details of the first two stanzas are a necessary prelude to what follows.

Arnold praised Gray's best poems, not only, although principally, for their evolution, but also for "a diction generally pure in an age of impure diction." It was also clear, however, that he found Gray's diction not altogether free from the "viciousness" of the age; he certainly thought it inferior to the diction of *Ode to Evening*. What Arnold meant by the impure diction of the eighteenth century scarcely needs detailed explanation. The judgment is familiar to us from the many critical elaborations, including Arnold's, upon the preface to the *Lyrical Ballads*. Very briefly, it meant for him a misapplied Miltonism: "as when the moon refulgent lamp of night," or a misapplication of human attributes and emotions to natural phenomena: "no cheerful murmurs fluctuate in the gale." Such formulas involved keeping the eye on a received poetic diction instead of on an object to be accurately delineated. Since Arnold's day we have been taught to find in much natural description in eighteenth-century poetry an attempt at accurate and precise delineation by means of current scientific categories and the terms of philosophical definition.[11] The origin of phrases like "the feathered kind" in systems of biological classification meant that their use in poetry could imply the system from which they were drawn. It remained for the poet to show himself responsive to the implication and to shape his poem in terms of the moral or physical order his diction suggested. Much of the diction, in fact, involved the latent assumption that it is valid to draw analogies between man and nature or nature and God, because the presumed existence of an order in nature necessarily implied the existence of an ordering principle.

Gray's ode avoids the dangers of the full argument from design[12] by contenting itself with a simple moral analogy between man and nature. But in working out this analogy, his use of a received diction makes an invaluable contribution to the integrity of his poem. The extent of this contribution has been well discussed by P. F. Vernon, who has pointed out the way in which the final three stanzas of moralizing draw upon the conventional descriptive details of the first two stanzas.[13] It is not too much to say that Gray's poem could not exist without the pre-existence of a diction that removes such phrases as "the insect youth" and "the sportive kind" from the realm of the unexpected. The kind of mildly ironic surprise the poem achieves is possible only within a context of predictability.

The first stanza evokes the amorousness of spring in color, sound, and smell:

> Lo! where the rosy-bosom'd Hours,
> Fair Venus' train appear,
> Disclose the long-expecting flowers,
> And wake the purple year!
> The Attic warbler pours her throat,
> Responsive to the cuckow's note,
> The untaught harmony of spring:
> While whisp'ring pleasure as they fly,
> Cool Zephyrs thro' the clear blue sky
> Their gather'd fragrance fling.   (ll. 1–10)

[11] John Arthos, *The Language of Natural Description in Eighteenth-Century Poetry* (Ann Arbor, 1949).
[12] Arnold's sense of the fallaciousness of the design argument is spelled out in *God and the Bible, Works,* VIII, 96–97.
[13] P. F. Vernon, "The Structure of Gray's Early Poems," *Essays in Criticism,* XV (1965), 382–87.

The genteel eroticism commences with the opening display of
rosy bosoms for our appreciative scrutiny; it is fully realized with
the entrance of great Venus herself; it is implicit in the song of the
sadly outraged Philomela, which aptly responds to the lugubrious
note of the cuckolds' bird; and it is suggestively diffused through
the whispered pleasures and gathered fragrance of the West Wind.
The presidential entrance of Venus at this season reminds us that
one of her aspects was the *magna mater* of Lucretius, in which form
she brought harmony to the world by arousing the procreative
instincts of all creatures.

From this evocation of the principle of spring the speaker deliberately dissociates himself, seeking instead the emblems of age and
gracelessness:

> Where'er the oak's thick branches stretch
> A broader browner shade;
> Where'er the rude and moss-grown beech
> O'er-canopies the glade,
> Beside some water's rushy brink
> With me the Muse shall sit, and think
> (At ease reclin'd in rustic state) .   (ll. 11–17)

This Virgilian posture is adopted for un-Virgilian reasons. The
speaker, it is clear, finds in the shade, not a cool respite from the
midday sun (the poem was originally called *Noontide, an Ode*),
but a suitably dun accompaniment to his pensive rejection of the
purple brilliance of spring. The closing parenthesis has about it a
note of self-satisfaction just sufficient to invest the sententious
moralizing which follows with an air of patronizing superiority. It
is this tone which is put properly in its place by the lightly ironic
return of the final stanza.

By withdrawing from amorous pleasure, the speaker finds it easy
in the third and fourth stanzas to reprove the soaring gaiety of the
rich for a failure to recall that they, like the earthbound, laboring
poor of "panting herds" and creeping insects, must inevitably end
in the dust. To the speaker's glum *respice finem,* the insects oppose
in the fifth stanza a cheerful *carpe diem*:

> Poor moralist! and what art thou?
> A solitary fly!
> Thy Joys no glittering female meets,
> No hive hast thou of hoarded sweets,

No painted plumage to display:
On hasty wings thy youth is flown;
Thy sun is set, thy spring is gone—
We frolick, while 'tis May.   (ll. 43–50)

The presence of the "glittering female" is the chief difference between the "poet's" view of the insect-socialite life and their own view of it. Where in the third stanza the display of a "gayly-gilded trim" denoted only frivolity, in the fifth the display of "painted plumage" is a necessary consequence of meeting a "glittering female"; it is the ritual of courtship. In much the same way, the insects of the third stanza merely "taste the honied spring" of field flowers, those of the fifth have laid up for themselves a hive of sweet domesticity. The poor moralist's partial view comes from his solitary detachment, the view of the insect-socialites comes from full absorption in nature, their harmony with the spirit of spring as it is set out in the opening stanza.

The reply of the sportive kind thus resolves both the tone and the argument of the moral discourse, and it does so by allusive recall of the values established in the opening stanza and too quickly forgotten by the speaker, who is an ironic persona of a kind familiar, if in many guises, in Augustan literature. The value of the persona here is that its use enables the poet to engage in conventional moralizing and yet dissociate himself from the tone of sententious complacency which inevitably accompanies such trite moralizing. This satisfying resolution of the poem is evidence of a satisfying evolution, although it is achieved by finding an appropriate diction in a set of terms that scarcely qualify as generally pure in the Arnoldian sense. The "impure" diction is appropriate because it employs the conventional morally classifying pairs of adjective and noun necessary for the establishment of the insect-socialite analogy, because it employs the conventional personifications of moral sententiousness as a necessary prelude to the final ironic return, because it employs the conventional allusions to literature and literary mythology necessary to recreate the tradition, the context of predictability, within which the poet can securely effect the modulations of tone that produce pleasurable surprise.

iv

There are no surprises in Collins' *Ode to Evening,* unless it be the felicitous rendering of the celebrated lines on the bat and beetle:

> Now Air is hush'd, save where the weak-ey'd Bat,
> With short shrill Shriek flits by on leathern Wing,
> Or where the Beetle winds
> His small but sullen Horn. (ll. 9–12)

Here, unquestionably, is the Arnoldian natural magic that "interprets by expressing with magical felicity the physiognomy and movement of the outward world." The lines recall, perhaps deliberately, the bat, the shard-borne beetle and alien crow of Macbeth's murderous reflections on the late-riding Banquo.[14] As in *Macbeth*, although to different ends, much of the effectiveness of these lines comes from the focus upon a single bat and beetle, for this is a landscape inhabited only by solitaries: the poet, the personified Evening, the pilgrim with whom the beetle collides. Bats, one feels, really have no business swooping around in bands; they disturb the decorum of twilight by doing so.

Ode to Evening is an evocation of a mood fully responsive and appropriate to the principle of evening; it is an attempt to capture an essence by the enumeration of attributes, an essence which inheres in the physical details of the attributes and the human response to them. Collins says as much, although less conceptually:

> Now teach me, *Maid* compos'd,
> To breathe some soften'd Strain
> Whose Numbers stealing thro' thy darkning Vale,
> May not unseemly with its Stillness suit. (ll. 15–18)

This essence is personified into the figure of Evening, which is then, by means of implicitly transferred epithets, credited with the moods induced in the speaker at this time of day: pensive, reserved, composed, religious. The moods are induced by the physiological consequences of evening: the diminished clarity of visual record and the compensating increase in the clarity of aural record: the sharp awareness of the "brawling Springs," which only in this sense can be said to belong to evening rather than the whole day.[15] Thus, to reverse the process, the sensations experienced in concentrating upon landscape detail induce a mood which is transferred to a personification of the natural phenomenon primarily responsible for the

[14] Alan D. McKillop finds additional "antecedents of the passage" in Spenser, Milton, and Gay: "Collins's *Ode to Evening*—Background and Structure," *Tennessee Studies in Literature*, V (1960), 79.
[15] See, e.g., Arnold's *Bacchanalia*, ll. 1–3.

quality of the sensations. "Process," however, is too evolutionary a word to describe the mode of the poem. *Ode to Evening* works through the accretion of detail and mood rather than their linear extension. Because all details contribute to a single mood (but not a single scene), the poem has an evident thematic unity. It is less clear that it possesses inevitable sequence; hence Arnold's stricture.

In a poem as image-laden as *Ode to Evening,* what is striking is its heavy dependence upon syntactical evolution. Technically, each of the three sections is an irmus, the schematic figure of the rhetoricians in which attention is held by delaying the main clause of a sentence with a long succession of subordinate clauses.[16] The figure is most successfully used in the first section, which opens with a conditional "if" that remains unresolved until line 15. The resolution is delayed by a series of principally temporal clauses, each contributing its landscape image. Even when the main clause has been completed in two short lines, an almost obsessive reluctance to let the sentence be leads to a relative and a temporal clause that account for four more lines. The tendency of the irmus toward syntactical flabbiness is most apparent in the second section, like the first, of twenty lines. The initial temporal subordinate accounts for eight lines, the remaining twelve contain three coordinate main clauses, the second with a dependent relative and the third with a parenthetic conditional and three relative clauses. If we take as a standard of excellence in the irmus—as a touchstone, indeed—the opening lines of *Absalom and Achitophel,* we can perhaps determine that its successful use depends upon an inverse ratio between subordinate and main clauses: the longer a main clause is delayed, the more pregnantly it should make its point. What Collins achieves is rather like a syntactical equivalent to the stock comic scene in which we witness the conclusion of a symphony: the musical pattern had seemed complete, the audience about to clap, but the final chords are repeated, and repeated, until, when it does end, the audience is unprepared. Collins' second section, especially, might as reasonably continue further—or stop earlier. Both the long sentence and the succession of images through which it winds are capable of considerable extension, and it is only the completion of

---

[16] The poem is divided into four-line stanzas, but I follow H. W. Garrod, *Collins* (Oxford, 1928), p. 75, in his division into three larger units, the breaks occurring after ll. 20 and 40. Garrod's division is endorsed by Henry Pettit, "Collins's 'Ode to Evening' and the Critics," *Studies in English Literature,* IV (1964), 361–69.

the metrical pattern, the five pairs of trimeters alternating with five paired pentameters, which determines that the section should end where it does. It is indeed a river which loses itself in the sands of prosody.

What gives the poem an air of losing its way, is the weak relationship between syntactical progress on the one hand and the unprogressive details of description and reflection on the other. It is not merely that the details are no more than tropical beads on a schematic thread, for the rhythmic exigencies of the syntax are such that they can lead to a quite unfruitful break in the sense:

> If chill blustring Winds, or driving Rain,
> Prevent my willing Feet, be mine the Hut,
>> That from the Mountain's Side,
>> Views Wilds, and swelling Floods,
> And Hamlets brown, and dim-discover'd Spires,
> And hears their simple Bell, and marks o'er all
>> Thy Dewy Fingers draw
>> The gradual dusky Veil.   (ll. 33–40)

The habit of describing one natural feature as overlooking another may excuse the hut's viewing the scene, but it is an unwarrantably wholesale attribution to the hut of its owner's capacities to say that it hears a bell and is cognizant of dew. One may well wonder, moreover, how either the hut or its owner can distinguish the dew in driving rain. This habit of pursuing a syntactical rhythm to the neglect of what has been descriptively or reflectively established perhaps accounts for the odd consort of virtues finally collected beneath the benign influence of Evening: *"Fancy, Friendship, Science, smiling Peace."* We may grant the poet his fancy as exemplified by the imaginative descriptions of landscape. We may obviously grant him the full establishment of peace. But the moods evoked in the first two stanzas have little to do with science in its normal eighteenth-century sense of knowledge, and almost the whole emphasis of the poem has been on a congenial solitude that has nothing to do with friendship. More than anything else, the conventional consort of virtues, the pat moral conclusion, is evidence of an uncertain grasp on the subject. Collins seems to know how his poem should move, but not for how long, and not how it should end. Arnold's image of the river is very precise: the syntax, the succession of images, flow on; there is no inherent reason why they should not flow longer. Moods are indefinite things, and since the mood cannot work itself out, the poem dives into the sands of moral personification, and disappears.

Ode to Evening exemplifies the disintegrating tendencies of the Arnoldian natural magic: the indulgence in technic at the expense of *architectonicé*. It does so because it lacks a firm concept of Evening personified to inform and control the enumeration of its attributes. The mood of evening is coherently evoked. There is sufficient consonance in the descriptive details. But the figure of Evening is imperfectly realized, a crucial weakness because it is this figure which the title indicates the poem will address, this personification out of which something is to be made. The first section succeeds best in this as in other respects. There the idea of evening is coherently personified as a shy and thoughtful maiden, turning away from a tacit invitation to couch with the splendidly virile sun:

> O *Nymp*h reserv'd, while now the bright-hair'd Sun
> Sits in yon western Tent, whose cloudy Skirts,
> > With Brede ethereal wove,
> > O'erhang his wavy Bed. (ll. 5–8)

Evening stands aside, quietly awaiting her time to return, and that this will be a leisurely pedestrian return is indicated by the fact that the poet's song, in harmony with her mood, proposes to steal through the valley, as he himself muses slowly. But this figurative clarity is obscured in the second section, where we learn that Evening has a "shadowy Car" prepared for her, and will presumably use it. We never see her charioted, for the next and final account of her activities is the observation of her "Dewy Fingers" drawing a "gradual dusky Veil" over everything. This presumably solitary labor is in fact a reversion to the shy maid of the first section, and it comes awkwardly after her metamorphosis into a quasi-regal figure with a chariot and attendant Pleasures, Hours, Elves, and "many a *Nymph*" busying herself with shedding "the fresh'ning Dew" and thus rendering superfluous, one would think, the later performance of this office by Evening herself. Without those fingers observed by the hut to scatter dew in the driving rain, the metamorphosis of the second section would have properly led into the near synthesis of the third, where the meek maid of the first section with the queenly train of the second maintains a "quiet Rule," her hair rinsed with spring showers, her lap filled with autumn leaves, her robes torn by winter blasts. But even here we find that Summer can think of nothing better to do than "sport, / Beneath thy ling'ring Light." It is true that the northern evening in summer is remarkable for its long twilight, but in what sense does the maiden Evening have a lingering light? What, moreover, is achieved by the rude assaults of Winter? It is impossible to fix a naturalistic referenc for the torn robes of Evening. Her clothes cannot be shadows or darkness, as they would be unaffected by the wind. The allegorical vehicle of Evening has quite parted from the naturalistic tenor of evening. The allegorical figure, whose relationship to the thing or quality personified was never securely established, marks its independence by elaboration in terms appropriate only to the thing as person and not at all to the thing as thing. "This is the worst of the allegorical," Arnold once assured Clough, "it instantly involves you in the unnecessary—and the unnecessary is necessarily unpoetical. Goly what a Shite's oracle! But profoundly true."[17]

v

The shite's oracle, however profound, is not infallible. The kind of interpretation available to natural magic, the felicitous expression of outward physiognomy and movement, can effectively coexist with allegory, at least in the simplest form of personification. Allegorical personification need not encroach upon moral profundity; it may be the appropriate expression of the essence of a natural phenomenon, that unifying concept or initial idea without which the poet is likely to be prevailed upon by the multitudinousness of the outward physiognomy and movement. Such is the case in Keats's *Ode to Autumn,* where the idea of plenitude exemplified in the details of harvest abundance involves or evolves into a sense of perfection: the fullness of all things is the coexistence of all things in a moment and for a moment; philosophically, the perception of being in becoming. The first two stanzas, setting out, as it were, the autumnal principle immanent in nature and ubiquitously personified in nature, culminate in an image of time infinitely extended and of time slowed down until it virtually stops. The third stanza finds the sounds of other seasons latent in the sounds of autumn. The songs of spring may be gone, but the bleating of full-grown lambs reminds of their bleating when new-born. The robin

---

[17] *Clough Letters,* p. 60; [Nov.-Dec., 1847?].

is identified by the red breast he reassumes in autumn and the song he utters most consistently in the same season. The twitter of gathering swallows presages their flight and thus reminds of winter, but their flight is not yet. The mournful wail of gnats rises or falls as the wind lives or dies: eternal becoming, constant renewal. The evidences of change and mortality in nature are apprehended in the season of plenitude at the point where they verge upon immortality and changelessness: movement implying stasis. The physical fullness rendered in the first stanza evolves by way of the spatial ubiquitousness of the second into the metaphysical fullness of the third, all times in one time. Keats's autumn is the moment when the seasonal cycle most closely approaches heaven's bourne, that point where, by the act of imagination, we stand at the edge of the mortal world of becoming and observe its perfect realization in the immortal world of being.[18] Arnold, it will be remembered, called *Ode to Autumn* "pure poetry of natural description." Whatever the "pure" means, it scarcely extends to an interpretation of nature which goes beyond the felicitous rendering of its outward physiognomy and movement. Such a rendering of the surface was likely to issue, as Arnold realized, in glorious bits and images. It was likely to issue in the products of an Arnoldian Keats, prevailed on by the world's multitudinousness. But the Keats of *Ode to Autumn* has an idea, certainly of his subject and perhaps of the world, and in rendering that idea, in interpreting the essence of autumn through a representation of its outward manifestations he achieves in his poem a sure and satisfying evolution. The problem of uniting reflection and description has almost disappeared in this total embodiment of thought in descriptive detail.

It was perhaps unfair to come down on Arnold's phrase about "pure poetry of natural description." Elsewhere, in the Guérin essay, Arnold finds a formula which exactly describes *Ode to Autumn* and the nature of its interpretation. When Keats and Guérin "speak of the world they speak like Adam naming by divine inspiration the creatures; their expression corresponds with the thing's essential reality."[19] Perhaps only of *Ode to Autumn* among Keats's poems can it be said that this formula fully accounts for the kind of interpretation in the poem which brings both significance

[18] I follow the account of Keats's thought given by Earl R. Wasserman in *The Finer Tone* (Baltimore, 1953), esp. pp. 15–16. Wasserman does not himself apply it to *Ode to Autumn*.
[19] *Complete Prose*, III, 34.

and coherence to its descriptive details. Each of Keats's other major odes bases itself upon the relationship between an observer and some object or quality. The poems constitute a process, a movement into or out of imaginative fulfillment. The "essential reality" of nightingale or urn, of Psyche or Melancholy is expressed in terms of a human response to them, in terms of the proper or improper way to apprehend them. The process of imaginative apprehension is an overt issue in these poems, and it is the process, accordingly, which constitutes their evolution and significance. But in *Ode to Autumn* the process is completed prior to the poem, and it thus has only latent significance within it; evolution and significance are here dependent upon the expression of the thing itself. The mind responsible for that expression is not an issue.

vi

The kind of success Keats achieves in *Ode to Autumn* differs from those that Earl R. Wasserman finds most characteristic of Romantic poetry.[20] Professor Wasserman locates the major problem of landscape poetry in the Baconian disjunction between the "shews of things" and the "desires of the mind," especially as that disjunction was elaborated upon or philosophically resolved by Hobbes, Locke, Berkeley and Hume. So stated, the problem was most acute—because imperfectly grasped and solved—for eighteenth-century poets, who, with more reason than Arnold, might have complained that they were left "hanging between two worlds." From early in the seventeenth century there was a gradual, if by no means constant, weakening of the old Renaissance world of natural and supernatural correspondence. This was a world in which an eagle was not merely like a king; it was a king, and to name an eagle was to imply a king. Analogies between the cosmic, political, and natural orders were ontological. To describe the rising of a river and the disastrous overflow of its banks demonstrated the dangers of tyranny or insurrection, because government with its controlling guarantees of liberty and order was an exact and full equivalent in the political realm of a river in the natural realm following a course marked out by restraining banks. With the development of phenomenology in the seventeenth century, the universe was increasingly explicated in terms of laws which

---

[20] Earl R. Wasserman, "The English Romantics: The Grounds of Knowledge," *Studies in Romanticism*, IV (1964–65), 17–34, and "Nature Moralized: The Divine Analogy in the Eighteenth Century," *ELH*, XX (1953), 39–76.

had no significance beyond their explanation of natural processes. The *mundus symbolicus* was succeeded by gas laws and Newton's *Optics*. But if the objects of perception no longer possessed human significance in themselves, man's ingenuity was equal to the task of associating them with the required significance. Rivers overflowing banks could still prompt an analogy with a tyrannous or rebellious overthrow of restraint, no longer, it is true, as demonstrations of a political truth, but as illustrations of it. Analogies that were once part of metaphysics became, equivocally, part of rhetoric, the art of argument.

The shift scarcely mattered aesthetically for poems which moved from moral discourse to illustrative analogy, for the requirements of the discourse effectively limited the vocabulary used in the analogy. If you want a governmental river overflowing the banks of checks and balances, then you omit the willows and the rushes along its edge. The problem occurred in landscape poetry proper, where the move was, nominally at least, from described object to moral implication. The description may have value, painterly or botanical, in itself; the moral analogue may have value in itself; but the two values were not fully coincident. The consequence was likely to be the existence in the poem of two syntaxes, one descriptive, one moral. If you are so ill-judging as to number the streaks of tulips or the blades of grass then you remove your natural object from the generalizing level at which it readily issues in moral reflections united with description because they share a syntax with it.[21] Thus it is that, when the typical eighteenth-century poet

is not merely organizing sense data into some picturesque, sublime, or beautiful distribution, he usually devotes himself to humanizing the external scene by associating it with some emotion, moral theme, historical episode, moving narrative, or autobiographical experience. The scene becomes significant only by stimulating the poet to link it with man by some loose association. . . . The eighteenth-century poet is forever interrupting his scene-painting to find its moral or emotional analogue.[22]

[21] Hazlitt, e.g., half recognizes this problem in the lecture on Thomson and Cowper, although he characteristically underrates its difficulty: we imperceptibly connect "the idea of the individual with man, and only the idea of the class with natural objects. In the one case, the external appearance or physical structure is the least thing to be attended to; in the other, it is every thing," William Hazlitt, *Collected Works,* ed. A. R. Waller and Arnold Glover (1902), V, 101.
[22] Wasserman, *Studies in Romanticism,* IV, 20.

The way out of this dilemma of poetic disintegration is, for Professor Wasserman, properly Romantic. Where the Renaissance poet found values pre-existent in the objects of perception, and the eighteenth-century poet associated the objects of perception with separately existing values, the Romantics located value in the act of perception itself. Variations in the modes of major Romantic poetry result, at least partly, from the different epistemological systems adopted by Wordsworth and Coleridge, Keats and Shelley. But, however variously, their best poems create rather than record the world they perceive, because it is only in the act of knowing, of experiencing, that the world comes properly into existence. And as the world comes into existence so, necessarily, does the poem which creates it, for the evolution of the poem is the process of knowing the world it creates. It used to be called organic unity, and no one could really quarrel with the term, because it was sufficiently protean to serve principally as a usefully imprecise value judgment. Professor Wasserman seeks the gains and risks the dangers of philosophical precision: "We may conceive of poetry as made up superficially *of* features, such as nature images, melancholy, or lyricism; but it is made *by* purposes, and epistemology is poetically constitutive."[23] Professor Wasserman would no doubt agree that there are poetically constitutive purposes other than the epistemological, even in Romantic poetry. But the pregnancy of his epigram invites a tacit rebuke from *Ode to Autumn,* which is not epistemologically constituted. If we wish to assign it to a philosophical category, we can say that *Ode to Autumn* is made of nature images and made by metaphysical purpose: the realization of an essence informing the sensory manifold without reference to the way in which that essence is experienced.

Epistemology may well bring significance and coherence to some landscape poems, but it is not therefore the only available mode. Epistemology is not the key problem, nor is it true that the eighteenth-century "resort to analogy only dodges the problem, since it both pretends to a relation between subject and object and yet keeps them categorically apart."[24] The "only" problem in landscape poetry is meaningfully to unite interpretation and description, and epistemology is but one, although perhaps the most satisfying, solution to that problem. The activities of Gray's glittering moral

[23] Wasserman, *Studies in Romanticism,* IV, 33–34.
[24] Wasserman, *Studies in Romanticism,* IV, 20–21.

insects, Collins' sullen and mood-suggesting beetle, Keats's metaphysically expressive gnats, and Arnold's suggestively moral-psycho-
logical thrush all imply attitudes to nature and to the expression of
naturalistic detail in meaningfully coherent poems. There is a
similarity between Collins' attempt to capture the essence of evening and Keats's rendering of the essence of autumn. The difference between them is not merely that between success and comparative failure, for, where Keats seeks a true metaphysical essence,
Collins finds an "essence" in the moods of human response. There
is a similarity between Gray's Virgilian posture in the shade and
Arnold's in Kensington Gardens, but the Arnoldian evolution of
literal scene into implicit metaphor for a kind of life differs funda-
mentally from Gray's evolution of morally implicit scene into explicit moral analogy. These few examples far from cover the available possibilities, and another insect and season will help fill out the
spectrum, without, of course, completing it.

vii

Thomson's *Seasons* has serious claim to be considered the most
inclusive poem in English since the Renaissance. By comparison,
The Prelude has a massively homogeneous simplicity, and perhaps
only *The Task* approaches *The Seasons* in omnivorousness. Its inclusiveness extends to varieties of genre: loco-descriptive, narrative,
lyrical, didactic; to varieties of style, tone, philosophy, theology,
scientific observation. Perhaps its very inclusiveness limits its
achievement. But it ought, one feels, to be a better poem than it is.
It constitutes such a rewarding critical study that it is disappointing
to find it irretrievably minor work. First or last, criticism that is not
a self-blinding lucubration must mark its failure. "Posterity," Arnold
once wrote, "alarmed at the way in which its literary baggage grows
upon it, always seeks to leave behind it as much as it can, as much
as it dares,—everything but masterpieces."[25] Who can doubt that on
such a march *The Seasons* would be an early, if daring, discard?

A brief discussion of *The Seasons* cannot do justice to it; but *The
Seasons* is perhaps accustomed to critical injustice by now,[26] and
this is scarcely the place to attempt a reassessment. But it may help

---

[25] *Works,* X, 326.
[26] For an account of the critical reaction to *The Seasons* see Ralph Cohen, *The
Art of Discrimination: Thomson's The Seasons and the Language of Criticism*
(Berkeley and Los Angeles, 1964).

a little to focus on the inadequacies of a relatively short section which originally had separate existence: the first version of *Winter,* published in 1726.

Winter 1726, like *The Seasons* as a whole, emerges as an exemplary type of the disjunctive use of analogy which Professor Wasserman finds throughout eighteenth-century landscape poetry. "The characteristic bipartite structure" of much eighteenth-century descriptive poetry manifests itself in a separation of sensory report and reflection, a separation syntactically evidenced by the use of simile (as in nature, so in man) instead of metaphor.[27] Thomson, in fact, shows himself cognizant of the uses of metaphor in working out his multiple variations on concord and discord in the social, natural, political, and cosmic orders. Thus, a husbandman's "lusty steers" are "cheered by the simple song and soaring lark," so that

> unrefusing, to the harnessed yoke
> They lend their shoulder, and begin their toil. (*Spring,* ll. 32–43)

The pathetic fallacy converts the ploughman's solitary task into a group task in which he is assisted by anthropomorphic cattle. Abundance is the keynote of *Autumn*: "Full, perfect all, and swell my glorious theme" (l. 8), and the dedication of the book to Arthur Onslow, Speaker of the Commons, is made appropriate by representing Onslow as the autumnal fullness and fruition of patriotism:

> The patriot-virtues that distend thy thought,
> Spread on thy front, and in thy bosom glow. (*Autumn,* ll. 13–14)

The ripeness with which Thomson fills all fruit to the core is social and political as well as vegetable: fruit swells, the song swells, and so does patriotic Onslow; he even possesses an embosomed glow to correspond to the bloom of apples and plums. What Ralph Cohen has identified as "the metaphoric descriptions in natural and human postures, creating a stylized 'family' of nature," have a large contribution to make to the "loose type of unity" with which he properly credits *The Seasons.*[28] Thomson's procedure in such descriptions is similar to Gray's in *Ode on the Spring,* and a loose unity results instead of Gray's tight integrity because in the much

---

[27] Wasserman, *ELH,* XX, 71.
[28] Cohen, *The Art of Discrimination,* pp. 129–30.

longer poem there are many passages in which man and nature cannot comfortably share a metaphor. Such passages are usually those given over to a careful enumeration of the details of sensory report. The more precise the detail, the more the eye is on the object, the less readily will it yield a unifying analogy. "Cautious generality," warns Professor Wasserman, "is the proper area for the artist working within the eighteenth-century framework of analogical thought: analogies may be based on light, but not the western sky's peculiar tint of yellow green; on the ebb and flow of the waters, not the rare chambered nautilus."[29]

The relative shortness (405 lines) of *Winter 1726* permits a sharper concentration on the strengths and weaknesses of Thomson's poetic mode. Even in the 1069-line final version of *Winter*, it emerges that the poem operates on a loosely chronological line with scenes illustrative of the season's progress from the last days of autumn through storm, snow, freezing and thaw to final desolation and the promise of spring. This chronological progress emerges much more clearly and is therefore a more effective ordering principle by virtue of the first version's stricter economy in illustrative scenes (it lacks, for example, the final version's two-hundred-line excursion through the frigid zone [ll. 794–987]) and in the reflections prompted by these scenes (the first version's forty-line roll-call of the illustrious dead [ll. 253–92] becomes 148 lines in the final version [ll. 424–571]). But what weakens its effectiveness as an ordering principle in 1726 (and *a fortiori* in 1746) is the circumstance that the chronological progress has no corresponding progress in the reflections upon the meaning and significance of the season. Wordsworth could meaningfully subtitle *The Prelude* the "Growth of a Poet's Mind," for what makes a poem even longer than the 1746 *Seasons* cohere is the continuing sense of the poet's onward pressing into the meaning of life, nature, imagination, and the poet's calling. The Thomsonian poet knows it all at the outset of his poem, which accordingly lacks an imaginative evolution of the kind Wordsworth adopted. Nor does it employ the rhetorical evolution of Pope's or Dryden's epistles or Gray's *Ode on the Spring*, in which an argument, an attitude, the personality implied by tone of voice, or the sense of a topic's significance are worked out and resolved with a firm and consistent awareness of an audience which may (as in some of Pope's epistles, but not Dryden's) be assigned

[29] Wasserman, *ELH*, XX, 45.

a vocal contribution to the discourse. (Part of the effectiveness of the ironic return in *Ode on the Spring* comes, we can say, from the surprise conversion of solitary meditatiod into dialogue: poetry to be overhead becomes poetry heard—with embarrassing consequences for the poetic persona). Thomson's poem is static, rather than dynamic; it proceeds by accretion, not discovery.

This static quality can be demonstrated through a consideration of the poem's thematic unity, for this it demonstrably possesses. The subject of the winter season is something to be apprehended and expressed on the one hand through the senses, principally the eye, and on the other through the thought, reason, and fancy. It is the two powers, the fancy and the eye, which Denham introduced into and manipulated throughout *Cooper's Hill*.[30] But where Denham unified his poem by making his eye serve his fancy, and by permitting his fancy to shape the ocular report of the landscape into an analogy for political life, Thomson adopts a stricter and more Lockeian distinction between perception and reflection. Crucially, the poet can associate with Contemplation, can reflect, only when he lays "the medling Senses all aside" (ll. 199–201). What is here explicit is implied, perhaps more interestingly, in a seemingly casual little scene near the beginning of the poem, most of which Thomson omitted from the later editions. Beginning his account of winter with the last, lazy, sunny days of autumn, the poet moves (rather abruptly) to a particular incident:

> Behold! the well-pois'd *Hornet,* hovering, hangs,
> With quivering Pinions, in the genial Blaze;
> Flys off, in airy Circles: then returns,
> And hums, and dances to the beating Ray.
> Nor shall the Man, that, musing, walks alone,
> And, heedless, strays within his radiant Lists,
> Go unchastis'd away.
>
> . . . .
>
>   Then is the Time,
> For those, whom *Wisdom,* and whom *Nature* charm,
> To steal themselves from the degenerate Croud,
> And soar above this *little* Scene of Things.   (ll. 23–36)

The hornet permits the particular observation, the closely marked detail, from which general reflection may proceed. But while the

[30] For a discussion of the role played by these two powers in *Cooper's Hill* see Earl R. Wasserman, *The Subtler Language* (Baltimore, 1959), pp. 45–88.

observing poet describes the hornet, the musing poet is chastised by it, and heedless of it. The hornet and its description belong to the sensory life of the poet, which is (painfully) inimical to his contemplative life.

It is this opposition, even antagonism, which is recalled throughout *Winter 1726*. Because nature in this season is harsh, afflictive, destructive, an appreciation of the providentially benevolent plan for the world can only be achieved in the face of the contrary evidence. The human villains of the poem are consequently those who do not go beyond nature, but reproduce its cruelty. The fools are those who take the superficial cruelty for the whole truth. While the musing man seeks to lay his "Passions in a gentle Calm" (l. 38), the villains are those

> giddy Youth, whom headlong Passions fire, [to]
> Rouse the wild Game, and stain the guiltless Grove
> With Violence and Death.   (ll. 104–6)

They are men who

> with the Gun
> And faithful Spaniel, range the ravag'd Fields,
> And adding to the Ruins of the Year,
> Distress the Feathery, or the Footed *Game*.   (ll. 321–24)

When the musing and contemplative poet has laid aside the meddling senses, he can scorn the "lying *Vanities* of Life," the troubles, hopes, and disappointments of "deluded Man" (ll. 202–9). In such a condition he is superior to the "devoted *Wretch*" who superstitiously finds in the groaning of the winds portents of "Woe, and Death" (ll. 186–89).

Superior to passion-bound villain and fool alike, the deistical reflector finds

> th' Eternal *Scheme*,
> That Dark Perplexity, that Mystic Maze,
> Which Sight cou'd never trace, nor Heart conceive,
> To *Reason's* Eye, refin'd, clears up apace.   (ll. 380–83)

The problem is superficially cleared up because an analogical application of the seasonal cycle to the life of man, closing in wintry death, prompts a reminder that both man and nature will be reborn into eternal life, into an unfading spring. But there is no discovery, no progression of thought. The reasoning man obviously knew this all along, since he was able to see that, however storm-tossed or wrecked on wintry seas, a miserable man will be led to safety by *"Providence, that ever-waking Eye"* through "all this dreary Labyrinth of Fate" (ll. 355–58). The reasoning man is aware that when the storm dies into calm it is because "the *Almighty* Speaks" (l. 192). He is aware that the "Father of Light, and Life" is available to teach him to know good and avoid vice and folly (ll. 210–15). The reasoning man is weak on logic, of course. His conclusion is deistical-stoical, reason being opposed to sense and feeling in its apprehension of logos. But how does reason solve a *mystic* maze? Reason, in fact, solves nothing at all. Thomson claims that a recollection of eternal life (somehow deduced by reason) explains why in temporal life the good often suffer and the evil prosper. Boethius contented himself with explaining that both good and bad fortune are, in their different ways, trials of virtue. But Thomson prefers the chilly asceticism of insisting that prosperity inevitably brings corruption: palace luxury prompts low thoughts (ll. 393–94). There is no allowance in *Winter 1726* for the prosperously virtuous, since virtue is apparently restricted to conditions of hardship and to the middle life of semi-retirement with a few choice friends. Moreover, the heart-reason opposition of the conclusion contradicts the sentimentalist burden of lines 66–73, where the bearing of "the swelling Thought aloft to Heaven" is accompanied by what the "forming *Fancy*" conceives and by sympathizing benevolence for others: "all the *Social Off-spring* of the Heart." If, then, the heart can reach heaven, why can it not grasp the divine plan?—because, when not on sentimental charitable duty, the heart is associated with passions, which in turn associate men with the tempestuous ravages of winter. The muddle is not insoluble, but Thomson clearly has not thought through his philosophy and theology, a failure the less excusable in a static, didactic poem where the poet starts from a position of understanding and "proceeds" to explain and illustrate that position.

The two main ordering principles—chronological progression and thematic recurrence of topics—exist in no significant aesthetic relationship. The consequence is a loosely untidy poem, with a revealing uncertainty in its reaching for an audience. The poem veers between the confessional tone of *The Prelude* and the expository tone of Pope's epistles. But where Pope frequently channels his exposition through an interlocutor, the developing relationship between whom and the poet can provide a rhetorical evolution, those whom Thomson addresses are outside his poem; the form is always apostrophe. In *Winter 1726,* and especially in its opening lines, what we get is ambiguously directed exhortation: "See! Winter comes" (l. 1), "Behold! the well-pois'd *Hornet*: (l. 23), "let me wander" (l. 41), "bear me then" (l. 74), "See! where *Winter* comes" (l. 112), "Lo! from the livid East" (l. 216), "See! sudden . . . / The Woods" (ll. 224–25), "But see who yonder comes!" (l. 285), "See, on the hallow'd Hour" (l. 297), "But hark!" (l. 325), "And hark!" (l. 334). To what is evidently a stylistic trick, or tic, of exclamation, must be added the frequent apostrophizing of abstractions and generic groups: youths, vain men, ye learned. This half-sermonizing, half-exclaiming to himself leaves the poem uncertainly directed; now giving comfort to the oppressed, now praising God, now chastising the luxurious, now recounting experiences, and addressing no one in particular.

The poem, then, lacks the kind of rhetorical evolution that comes from establishing a meaningful relationship between author and audience. It lacks the modified evolution which Denham achieved by allowing his wandering eye to "discover" fresh matter for his fixed thoughts, thus gradually shaping a total landscape into a total political analogy. It lacks the evolution which comes from subjectively realized landscape, where the coherence and dynamic derive from the poet's imaginative pressing into the meaning of his experiences, or his imaginative absorption of experience, as Wordsworth imaginatively absorbs the solitary reaper and the leechgatherer, or as Keats imaginatively enters the life of the urn's frieze. For Thomson's landscape, however much it may be made to yield human analogies or evidences of a divine plan, is objective: the hornet waiting out there to chastise the heedless, musing poet, who, seemingly undisturbed, passes on in meditation. In *Winter 1726* the world of second causes, of phenomena, is separated from the principle of meaning, the first cause. In the dead season, especially, the relationship between first and second causes is indirect. Spring bodies forth his harmony, summer his light and glory, autumn his plenitude: the observer is required to explicate the explicit. But in winter he must perceive implications that in fact depend upon a questionable theology. Thought and sensation pull in different directions, as T. S. Eliot long ago observed, and only a valiantly deistical declaration at the end leaves them in uneasy harmony. Thomson removed the hornet from later versions, but its shade hovers over *The Seasons* as a potentially painful reminder that in objective landscape the details of description are forever striving to escape the control of reasoned or imaginative significance.

viii

The very strength of this tendency constitutes much of the aesthetic challenge faced by the poet of landscape. It is also a considerable stimulation to the critic who seeks the integrating principles of poems made out of such material. The words of literature are potentially two-way signs, pointing both to the inner relationships which bring coherence to a work and to the external objects which moved the poet to attempt a work. All literary products have an equivocally exterior context consisting of ideas, events, autobiographical experiences, animate and inanimate objects, traditions of expression. From this context, the components of which exist in no significant aesthetic relationship to each other, a work is properly made when it effects or "discovers" due connections between its disparate and discrete raw materials. Co-existing with the inner coherence of these connections there is, in varying degrees of strength, a reference out and back to the raw materials. This reference, potentially so disintegrating because it focuses upon the discreteness of the raw materials, has value for a reader because it permits him to identify the common originating experiences out of which the poem has made a new experience. The great challenge of landscape poetry is that the criterion of the eye on the object so increases a poet's obligation to the faithful representation of part of his raw material that a reader (and often a poet also) can too readily rest in the recollection of common experiences without proceeding to an apprehension of the new experience that has been or could be made out of them. How much easier, for example, is the task of the satirist, who is permitted great license in fictional distortion. Shaftesbury and Hervey are just sufficiently recognizable through the characters of Dryden's Achitophel and Pope's Sporus to satisfy a mind principally occupied in responding to the general satiric truths embodied in these portraits and contributory to the fictional and discursive coherence of the whole poems in which they occur.

Nonetheless, a measure of distortion is usually inevitable for a poet who wishes to make a whole new experience out of topographical features, autobiographical experiences, ideas of God or of man and nature, and, perhaps too, such literary or quasi-literary traditions of the mythographical embodiment of natural phenomena as, say, the Philomela story. When this distortion, this sacrifice to the ensemble, occurs in the rendering of topographical features, it will often take the form of selective omission in the interests of shaping landscape in terms of an intellectual or emotional interpretation. But it may take the form of adding to or tacitly extending the geographical site referred to in order to complete the significance with which that site is invested. Thus, in Arnold's *Resignation* the description of a walk across the fells from Wythburn to Keswick terminates by "the wide-glimmering sea." Because Keswick is an inland town, there has been speculation that Arnold's phrase is a licentious reference to Derwent Water, the lake by which Keswick stands, or else Arnold is to be understood as omitting a description of the carriage ride from Keswick to the Irish Sea some miles away which originally concluded the outing commemorated in the poem. From the poem itself it seems that the day's outing did not terminate at Keswick. Most of the description is devoted to the hike across the fells, but at the end we are summarily told that the hikers gained "the town, the highway, and the plain," making reasonably clear that after reaching Keswick they proceeded along the main road to the flatter coastal strip of Cumberland, traveling "many a mile of dusty way." Strictly speaking, however, nothing is clear from the poem alone, for *Resignation* names no places. The walk is plotted and speculation arises almost entirely as a result of the itinerary note Arnold added to the poem twenty years after its first publication. When this note is further glossed with family records and the memorial stone at Wythburn marking the starting point of the walk, we quickly find ourselves lost in an attempted reconstruction of the biographical occasion. We are silently assuming that the poem principally commemorates an outing, instead of using some aspects of the outing in order to objectify the poem's interpretation of life. What the Wythburn stone really commemorates is the common habit of reading out and back from the poem to its originating contexts, whether they be a particular landscape at a particular time, the *Bhagavad Gita,* or *Wilhelm Meister.* Such reading out may take the form of annotating from what are understood to be sources, and when criticism rests in sources, its contribution is invariably a disintegration and redistribution of the poem into its originating contexts. But poetry is to be read, and not, it must be hoped, only by professional critics. The naming of a place (if only in a note) provides a source which it needs no learning to identify and understand and which can be compared with the poet's representation as a check on his mimetic accuracy. It licenses the poetic equivalent of accepting or rejecting a portrait because it is or is not very like. Both landscape poet and portrait painter may, if they choose, exploit, manipulate, and ultimately contend with what can be called the lay response. They may also, of course, reject the layman and represent a sitter in cubist perspective for the informed satisfaction of a few.

Such a rejection takes many forms in landscape poetry, from the symbolic landscape of a Blake to a *paysage intérieur*. Most of these forms have in common the composition of a landscape out of separate features, some at least with an identifiable mimetic origin, into a whole which has no identifiable mimetic equivalent. No matter how much Shelley makes out of Mont Blanc and the Ravine of Arve, the mountain and the ravine are verifiably there, both in and out of the poem. But Prufrock inhabits a terrain that coheres only in his mind, even though its components may be separately identified by a reader. Blake's Thel undertakes a journey from innocence to experience and encounters on the way such recognizable objects as a cloud, a lily, a lamb, or a worm. But their mimetic potential is checked by their possession of the gift of speech and by the fact that they manifestly occur as stages in a psychological progress. They objectify, they provide concrete equivalents for states of mind, but their mimesis is minimal: nearly all their reference is in to the total poetic interpretation, hardly any is out to their naturalistic equivalents. Symbolic landscape of this kind loses or shuns the lay reader because it provides him with no common experience to work from. By way of compensation, such readers as it does attract are allowed no license to rest in common experiences to the neglect of the aesthetic constitution of the work.

Much of the charm of poetry employing an identifiable landscape comes from the poet's association of emotions and ideas with natural features in a manner which can be identified and shared by a reader. As Hazlitt puts it:

If we have once enjoyed the cool shade of a tree, and been lulled into a deep repose by the sound of a brook running at its foot, we are sure that wherever we can find a shady stream, we can enjoy the same pleasure again; so that when we imagine these objects, we can easily form a mystic personification of the friendly power that inhabits them, Dryad or Naiad, offering its cool fountain or its tempting shade. Hence the origin of the Grecian mythology. . . . It is the same setting sun that we see and remember year after year, through summer and winter, seed-time and harvest. The moon that shines above our heads, or plays through the checquered shade, is the same moon that we used to read of in Mrs. Radcliffe's romances. . . . The cuckoo, "that wandering voice," that comes and goes with the spring, mocks our ears with one note from youth to age; and the lapwing, screaming round the traveller's path, repeats forever the same sad story of Tereus and Philomel![31]

Because, for Hazlitt, "the interest we feel in external nature is common, and transferable from one object to all others of the same class,"[32] the mimetic use of landscape may be said to minimize the tendency of the private mode of poetry to remain uncommunicatively within a circle of private associations. A poet's individual response to landscape is sufficiently conditioned by his sense of the general response to enable his particular interpretation to take place securely within a general experience. When a poet has nothing to bring beyond a more or less felicitous expression of the general experience, we get something like the easy nostalgia of *The Old Vicarage, Grantchester*. When a poet brings too idiosyncratic an interpretation and fails properly to embody it in the landscape, a reader's move from the initial common experience to the particular interpretation is blocked by the enigmatic private associations. The lapwing is heard to utter inexplicable cries of joy; witches gather in the glade in Kensington Gardens. The psychological symbolism of landscape is at odds with the mimetic identity. Something of this kind appears to have happened in the other Lake District poem of Arnold's 1849 volume, *The Hayswater Boat*.

ix

The general lines of what Arnold would be about in *The Hayswater Boat* are clear enough. The first two of five eight-line stanzas describe the upland tarn of Hayeswater. They recapitulate a likely

[31] *Collected Works*, ed. Waller and Glover, V, 102–4.
[32] *Collected Works*, V, 100.

common response to such a scene by using simile to associate it with man:

> A region desolate and wild.
> Black, chafing water: and afloat,
> And lonely as a truant child
> In a waste wood, a single boat:
> No mast, no sails are set thereon;
> It moves, but never moveth on:
> And welters like a human thing
> Amid the wild waves weltering.
>
> Behind, a buried vale doth sleep,
> Far down the torrent cleaves its way:
> In front the dumb rock rises steep,
> A fretted wall of blue and grey;
> Of shooting cliff and crumbled stone
> With many a wild weed overgrown:
> All else, black water: and afloat,
> One rood from shore, that single boat.   (ll. 1–16)

The increasing popularity of the Lake District has still not extended to Hayeswater, and even today the uphill walk from Patterdale and Brothers Water (Arnold's sleeping valley) beside the Hayeswater Gill (the cleaving torrent) involves that ascent from the habitations of man to the regions of solitude which is a recurrent motif in Arnold's poetry. The tarn itself has a bleak uncommunicativeness which is barely disturbed by the prim brick box declaring the utility of Hayeswater as a reservoir serving the needs of Penrith. It is not hard to stand by Hayeswater and recapitulate the common experience invoked by Arnold in the first two stanzas. Moreover, to anyone moderately instructed in the trope of the ship of life, the presence of an unoccupied rowing boat on a tarn so seemingly remote from humanity might easily suggest the aimless, isolated existence of man. Simile is just the syntax to express the low-level imaginativeness of this response. But the poet, building on this common experience, proposes to take us beyond it. What particularly attracts his attention is the precise distance of the boat from the tarn's edge, "one rood from shore," six or seven yards. It is a seemingly inexplicable distance, and to account for it the similes of common experiences must give place to the allegory of individual interpretation:

Last night the wind was up and strong;
The grey-streak'd waters labour still:
The strong blast brought a pigmy throng
From that mild hollow in the hill;
From those twin brooks, that beached strand
So featly strewn with drifted sand;
From those weird domes of mounded green
That spot the solitary scene.

This boat they found against the shore:
The glossy rushes nodded by.
One rood from land they push'd, no more;
Then rested, listening silently.
The loud rains lash'd the mountain's crown,
The grating shingle straggled down:
All night they sate; then stole away,
And left it rocking in the bay.   (ll. 17–32)

The inexplicable is explained by invoking the fanciful. The pigmy throng is presumably made up of little folk, those fairies who inhabit the lone places of England as well as the bottoms of gardens. These spirits of the place concentrate in the boat the qualities diffused throughout the scene in an unidentifiable hollow, in a small beach now, it seems, sacrificed to the water supply of Penrith, in the twin brooks of the upper Gill which feed the tarn from the high ground to the south, and in the weird domes of the strangely humped lateral moraines along the south-west edge of Hayeswater. We have an allegorical equivalent for an imaginative process. There is the scene, the object, and here the observer, the subject. The object becomes properly known by investing it with qualities of the subject, by locating in the object itself the emotional reflections of the subjective perceiver. But the allegorical vehicle retains the distinction between subject and object by making the anthropomorphic throng the agents of this imaginative transfer. Lest the reader should be tempted to take the pigmies literally, the final stanza emphasizes that the interpretation of the scene is wholly imagined by the speaker:

Last night?—I looked, the sky was clear.
The boat was old, a batter'd boat.
In sooth, it seems a hundred year
Since that strange crew did ride afloat.

81

The boat hath drifted in the bay—
The oars have moulder'd as they lay—
The rudder swings—yet none doth steer.
    What living hand hath brought it here? (ll. 33–40)

Thomson's hornet does not live at these heights, but its demise is accomplished at the cost of introducing the worst of the allegorical: its instant involvement of the poet in the unnecessary. Why four groups of pigmies? and why should they inhabit just those landscape features rather than, say, the weedy cliff of the second stanza or the black waters of the first? The very preciseness with which the pigmy homes are distinguished suggests that the poet associates a quite distinct emotion or reflection with each of the four places. But there is no way of making these distinctions from within the poem, and they could never be made more than plausibly from without: possible readings not inimical to the poem but not demanded by it. In fact, such outside aid (from Arnold's other poems) brings only confusion. If the hollow is one of the recurrent glades, with which should it be glossed: Mycerinus', Callicles', Iseult of Brittany's, Merlin's, the Scholar Gipsy's? If the weird domes make suggestive burial mounds of the moraines, with whose should they be glossed: the Duke and Duchess of Savoy's, the Scholar Gipsy's, Tristram and Iseult's, the criminal of Bokhara's? The sand pigmies share a location with the Gipsy Child and the Forsaken Merman. The relationship of the boat to the shore, close but isolated because out of reach, recalls Arnold's interest in the meeting point of land and water in *Dover Beach, To a Gipsy Child, The Forsaken Merman, The Neckan,* or *To Marguerite—Continued.* But in *The Hayswater Boat* the meeting point is exploited not for moral or emotional significance but as the excuse for allegorizing the imaginative process. Instead of prompting the poet to ask what does it mean, it prompts him to ask how do I convey my sense that it is meaningful? In making a concretely allegorical answer to the second question, he fails to answer the first, but at the same time suggests it could be answered. The whimsical objectification of imaginative process is not sufficiently significant in itself to carry a poem whose interpretation of the scene never advances definably beyond the associations of human isolation and helplessness effected by the similes of the opening stanza. Thus, the attempt to build upon the evoked common experience results only in fanciful enigmas. In terms of the 1853 Preface Arnold has produced an allegory of the state of his mind in a representative landscape, but in striving to imply an explanation and justification of his use of allegory he neglects to convey a clear sense of his state of mind. The shite's oracle that allegory involves a poet in what is unpoetical because unnecessary notes the fate of at least *The Hayswater Boat*: it was the only poem from the 1849 volume which Arnold never republished.

x

The Hayswater Boat offers an implicit answer to the question overtly considered in *Epilogue to Lessing's Laocoön*: how does a poet make poetry out of landscape? It is a question which recurs throughout Arnold's criticism and poetry, although it is particularly dominant in the volume of 1849. It is not too much to say that the matter of many of Arnold's poems lies separate in his letters. The reflections on poetics and on the political, social, and intellectual life of the time which we find in the letters to Clough can be placed beside those many letters to his mother and his unmarried sister which contain descriptions of landscapes around England and the Continent. Some of his unsatisfactory poems are so because the material of these two groups of letters is merely juxtaposed and not synthesized. "D—n description," he once exclaimed to Clough, and proceeded to describe the mountains, water and trees of Switzerland.[33] Both the exasperation and the compulsion are crucial for the kind of landscape poetry Arnold produced: the driving sense of the need to keep the eye on the object and the concurrent sense that the mere description which results from this activity is not enough.

Locke's distinction between sensation and reflection, his separation of perceiving subject and perceived object by locating some qualities definitively in the one, some in the other, rather codifies than causes the problem. To find, wittingly or not, an answer to Locke, to create an object by rendering the complex process of perceiving it, is one solution to the problem. Another is to find that objects in themselves, independently of a perceiving subject, exist in significant relationship to each other, and body forth a *concordia*

[33] *Clough Letters,* pp. 91–92; Sept. 29, 1848.

discors or such evidences of design as imply a designer. Such a solution is likely to involve a quasi-rhetorical process of proving that objects do in fact exhibit the significant relationship attributed to them, as Pope and Denham argue political conclusions from the evidence of harmonious disorder in Windsor Forest or the view from Cooper's Hill. Another solution is to find significance in the essence rather than the relationship of objects, to find that essence to be something more than, although manifested through, the attributes apprehended by the senses. Such an essence might be the implication of metaphysical fullness in the material plenitude of autumn, or the achievement of selfhood—quiddity or haecceity—which Hopkins located in the achievement of Christhood or Christlikeness. A fourth solution, quasi-rhetorical like the second because it typically involves argued proof, is to see in natural phenomena like Gray's insects separate analogies for human problems and situations. The fifth solution is to find in landscape an objective equivalent—or correlative—for a state of mind or way of life compounded of thought and emotion, as Arnold's lone glade and Collins' single beetle locate in objects the poet's subjective sense of solitude. This solution, indeed, brings us into the world of many of Arnold's poems, or many of Tennyson's for that matter, although it by no means fully accounts for all of them.

A classification of this kind involves, no doubt, categorization as arbitrary as the assignment of *Epilogue to Lessing's Laocoön* to the lyric genre. There is implicit in it a suppression of symbolic or interior landscape, or of landscape used solely as brief metaphor.[34] It implies a completeness it has no right to pretend to. It implies in the word "solution" that here are five ways of writing successful landscape poetry, whereas they are at best ways of writing landscape poetry which may be successful. It implies that the categories are always readily distinguishable and perhaps mutually exclusive, whereas little thought is needed to point out, for example, that objectification of mood may coexist with identification of essence and also involve the cognitive fusion of subject and object. Keats objectifies an initially indeterminate mood by coming to know the essence of an unseen nightingale whose only sensory attribute is its

---

[34] I am also omitting poetic landscapes of the seventeenth century and earlier which make use of allegory and emblem to invoke or recreate agreed values: e.g., the virtues of plants and stones. Arnold wrote long after the breakdown of the old symbolic world, and the aesthetic problems he faced align him with eighteenth-century and Romantic poets, not the Renaissance.

song and which must therefore be supplied with an accidental context from the poet's imagination.

If, despite these dangerous fallacies, the classification has value, it is because it indicates that poetry which makes extensive use of landscape, especially objectively existent landscape, confronts aesthetic problems which cut across the traditional genre distinctions. It should further indicate that there are various ways of confronting these problems, and that the varieties are conditioned as much by the poet's individual sensibility and imaginative capability as by the ideas of theology, epistemology, aesthetics, or cosmology available to him. If the classification is allowed to imply the explications on which it is based, it should finally indicate that the kind of generalization it engages in has value, if at all, in prompting some of the questions which will lead to a fuller apprehension of particular works. It may well be that, properly speaking, there are no varieties of landscape poetry, but only various landscape poems.

Landscape in 1849

ARNOLD'S POETRY, T. S. Eliot once remarked, "has little technical interest. It is academic poetry in the best sense; the best fruit which can issue from the promise shown by the prize-poem."[1] The remark is sufficiently enigmatic and suggestive to qualify as an oracular placing of Arnold which could only be spoiled by elaboration. If (and why not?) we are to understand by "academic" an experience of life largely conditioned by books and the intellectual processes associated with them, then the remark is by no means inapposite to Arnold. Few things could be more "academic" than his assurance to Madame du Quaire that *Merope* "is calculated rather to inaugurate my Professorship with dignity than to move deeply the present race of *humans.*"[2] There is unquestionably an air of verse exercise hanging over the early *Fragment of an 'Antigone'* (1849) or the *Fragment of Chorus of a 'Dejaneira'* (1867).[3] In between he published not only *Merope* (1858), but, quite within the historical spirit of the prescribed prize poem on Cromwell, he elected again and again to find his subjects in the historically and geographically remote. The 1849 volume alone has poems about an oriental potentate of the early nineteenth century,

---

[1] T. S. Eliot, *The Use of Poetry and the Use of Criticism* (1959), p. 105.
[2] *Works*, XIII, 80; Feb. 9, 1858.
[3] Allott (p. 64) and *Commentary* (pp. 162–63) feel that, despite its late publication, the *'Dejaneira'* is an early composition, probably written about the same time as the *'Antigone.'* Both pieces contain consolation for death, but the *'Dejaneira'* reads in its final stanza as if moved by the death of Thomas Arnold. Such an occasion might explain the possibly delayed publication.

a Pharaoh of the third millennium B.C., and a young monk of the fourth century A.D. It is scarcely to be supposed, however, that we would continue to read at least some of these poems on the decorous subjects of schoolboy or undergraduate if they did not transcend their element of an exercise. The letter to Madame du Quaire explaining his motives in writing *Merope* continues with a modest assertion and an even more modest hope: "I have such a real love for this form and this old Greek world that perhaps I infuse a little soul into my dealings with them which saves me from being entirely *ennuyeux*, professorial, and pedantic."

i

To call a poem or a piece of criticism academic is often a way of asserting its irrelevance without engaging in the difficult and tedious task of defending a view of life which finds books of small moment. Academic criticism, it is true, attracts the special odium of translating literary works into ingenious patterns with but small apparent reference to the works themselves: a passion for intellectual tidiness is inappropriate to the products of poets, which are rarely as tidy intellectually as the mental habits of an academic critic would have them. The case of academic poetry is slightly different; there the reality so damagingly neglected by the writer is not the poem he pretends to discuss but the life stuff he is supposed to share with his audience. He marks his divorce by a preoccupation with alien situations and tangential issues: not for him the smell of steaks in passageways.

The raising of tangential issues is by no means the inevitable consequence of busying oneself with alien situations. Such a preoccupation may well be directed to revealing in what way a superficially alien situation is relevant to the present. So runs the defense of *Empedocles on Etna* with which Arnold prefaced his rejection of it. He has not, he insisted in the 1853 preface, omitted the poem "because the subject of it was a Sicilian Greek born between two and three thousand years ago": quite the contrary. A man like Empedocles, born into an age of faith, of Orphic metaphysics, and surviving into an age of Sophist scepticism, is the very paradigm of Victorian man, born into an age of Christian faith and surviving into an age of scepticism.

Into the feelings of a man so situated there entered much that we are accustomed to consider as exclusively modern; how much, the fragments of Empedocles himself which remain to us are sufficient at least to indicate. What those who are familiar only with the great monuments of early Greek genius suppose to be its exclusive characteristics, have disappeared: the calm, the cheerfulness, the disinterested objectivity have disappeared; the dialogue of the mind with itself has commenced; modern problems have presented themselves; we hear already the doubts, we witness the discouragement, of Hamlet and of Faust.[4]

Hamlet is very much to the purpose. This Scandinavian folk hero, whose exploits were transmitted to Shakespeare through books, is a very Elizabethan man, a contemporary of Robert Burton. The assumed value and relevance of the past implied in Arnold's defense of *Empedocles,* is also implied by an Elizabethan Hamlet or a Restoration Achitophel.

The historical and the exotic are not academic in terms of Arnold's defense of *Empedocles;* but they begin to be so in terms of his rejection of it. After concurring with Aristotle that any accurate imitation or representation is agreeable and interesting, he invokes Schiller as witness that all art "is dedicated to Joy, and there is no higher and no more serious problem, than how to make men happy. The right art is that alone, which creates the highest enjoyment."[5] Schiller's dictum is innocuous enough, being in these words little more than an intensified form of stressing the pleasurable in the age-old debate over the *dulce* and *utile.* But Arnold proceeds to discriminate between situations which are or are not joyful in themselves. That is to say—in rhetorical terms—the artist does not create joyful objects by the distribution and expression of his material; he finds them in the material itself. Situations which no poetic skill can render joyful "are those in which the suffering finds no vent in action; in which a continuous state of mental distress is prolonged, unrelieved by incident, hope, or resistance; in which there is everything to be endured, nothing to be done."[6] The rejection of pathos unaccompanied by praxis becomes crucial for a poet like Arnold, so conscious of a damnable aridity and unpoetic spirit in his age. A poet believing himself so circumstanced and rejecting the unqualified expression of despair is forced either to

[4] *Complete Prose,* I, 1.
[5] *Complete Prose,* I, 2.
[6] *Complete Prose,* I, 2-3.

flirt with the academic in a choice of historical or exotic subjects which he makes little attempt to render contemporary or to engage in enspiriting prognostication from the heights of Pisgah. The first way produces *Balder Dead* and *Merope;* the second leads ultimately to some of the poems in the volume of 1867.

Arnold discounted spectacular suicide as meaningful praxis, and dismissed *Empedocles* from the 1853 volume. Curiously enough, he included in that volume *Mycerinus* from 1849, even though it is a poem which pre-eminently fixes upon a situation in which "there is everything to be endured, nothing to be done." In 1849 *Mycerinus* stood second, following the sonnet later called *Quiet Work.* In 1853 it stood third, separated from *Quiet Work* by *Sohrab and Rustum.* The effect of this displacement is to reveal the action of *Mycerinus* more sympathetically. In 1849 the burden of *Quiet Work* tacitly reproaches *Mycerinus* for exclaiming against a cruel destiny, for succumbing to a disappointed melancholy when his demands upon life are refused. In 1853 the patient, modest acceptance of things recommended by *Quiet Work* is transmitted to *Mycerinus* by way of the sad nobility of *Sohrab and Rustum,* with its finally calm acceptance of a harsh destiny. What *Sohrab and Rustum* does for *Mycerinus* in 1853 is create a situation to which the lesson of *Quiet Work,* while not inappropriate, is certainly harder to apply. When, in 1849, the sound of Mycerinus' revelry "mix'd with the murmur of the moving Nile," it was principally a reminder that he had neglected his "wondering people" and allowed himself to drift. But in 1853 it reminds also of the Oxus, that "foil'd circuitous wanderer," and the hum from the Persian and Tartar encampments. It reminds that some life streams are more difficult to navigate than others, more difficult than the calm assurance of *Quiet Work* allows.

ii

The quasi-epigraphic status of *Quiet Work* in a number of Arnold's early volumes is most apparent in that of 1853, where it is italicized, and is acknowledged by Arnold in a later description of it as "an introductory piece."[7] It is a function which the sonnet performs well by its summary of issues which recur throughout the 1849 volume and the later poetry:

> One lesson, Nature, let me learn of thee,
> One lesson which in every wind is blown,

[7] Allott, p. 106.

One lesson of two duties kept at one
Though the loud world proclaim their enmity—

Of toil unsever'd from tranquillity!
Of labour, that in lasting fruit outgrows
Far noisier schemes, accomplish'd in repose,
Too great for haste, too high for rivalry!

Yes, while on earth a thousand discords ring,
Man's fitful uproar mingling with his toil,
Still do thy sleepless ministers move on,

Their glorious tasks in silence perfecting;
Still working, blaming still our vain turmoil,
Labourers that shall not fail, when man is gone.

It is not, certainly, a striking handling of the sonnet form: the scrupulous maintenance of the Italian rhyme scheme has no appropriate accompaniment in the progress of the thought. Even if we concede that there is no necessity to turn the thought between octave and sestet, something more may reasonably be asked than a mere restatement with minor elaborations. In 1849, it is true, the tutorial relationship between man and nature in the octave turns into a spatial relationship of generalized landscape in the sestet by virtue of the fact that the sleepless ministers perfect a "glorious course." As Professor Allott suggests, this word makes stars of the ministers. Such a suggestion gives added point to the "sleepless" by implying a night scene, when man should sleep, but the stars do not. It further emphasizes the contrast between "man's fitful uproar" and nature's silence: the stars are sleepless because it is their nature to be unsleeping; man is simply unable to get to sleep. The night scene, then, with the stars above epitomizing the unhurried purposefulness of all nature and silently upbraiding the human discords below, makes in 1849 for a satisfactory pictorial application in the sestet of the octave's burden at the same time that it properly realizes the spatial potential of "on earth." But Arnold chose to alter "glorious course" into "glorious tasks," perhaps because he felt that the implied stars unduly limited the operations of nature instead of epitomizing them. For all that, the poem makes its points with becoming clarity, once Arnold had solved his little problem in numeration: he originally sought "two lessons" in nature, and fancied a distinction between the tranquil toil and uncompetitive labor of the second quatrain.

One way to learn the lesson (or lessons) of nature is revealed in *Kensington Gardens,* which records a rare if qualified success in the early poems in achieving the desired harmony, the patient quiescence, which is, by virtue of the contented angler, as much a matter of tranquil labor as of tranquil meditation: the contemplative life has here a proper and meaningful issue in activity. Most often, the early poems, up to *The Scholar-Gipsy* in 1853, present variations upon the "thousand discords" to which man is subject, and investigate possible, but generally illusory, escapes from it. Increasingly in the later poems, and especially in the volume of 1867, there is an assurance, a belief in the efficacy of means to quiet the discord. *Quiet Work*'s endorsement of patience, tranquillity, and work (which may tentatively be glossed as purpose) implies the typical danger signals in Arnold's poems: impatience, fretfulness, and aimlessness. This moral explicitness functions as a gloss on some of the implications of *Mycerinus.* That is to say, it confirms the propriety of a reading which finds in the poem a condemnation, however qualified, of the hapless Pharaoh's acts and decisions.

Some of the more interesting aspects of *Mycerinus* are those which result from Arnold's modification of his source in Herodotus.[8] What Arnold shares with Herodotus is given in the note first included in 1853 (in 1849 there is only a bare indication of source) :

After Cephren, Mycerinus, son of Cheops, reigned over Egypt. He abhorred his father's courses, and judged his subjects more justly than any of their kings had done.—To him there came an oracle from the city of Buto, to the effect that he was to live but six years longer, and to die in the seventh year from that time.

Arnold also took from Herodotus the King's consequent decision to pass his remaining years in day- and night-long revelry. The modifications introduced by Arnold are principally the suppression and the change of a motive and an apparently trivial restriction in the landscape setting of the second half of the poem.

The suppressed motive is that of the gods in cutting short the life of Mycerinus. In Herodotus the King, on learning his fate, sends a second time to the oracle to discover the reason for it. He is told that "his good deeds were the very cause of shortening his life; for he had done what was contrary to fate; Egypt should have

[8] Given in Allott, p. 26, and *Commentary,* pp. 35–37.

been afflicted for an hundred and fifty years, whereof the two kings before him had been aware, but not Mycerinus. Hearing this, he knew that his doom was fixed." In Arnold there is no second oracle and no 150-year affliction of Egypt to be flouted by the King's justice. The result is that what is arbitrary in Herodotus—the original doom upon Egypt—is shifted forward to fall wholly upon Mycerinus. Arnold handles this change with fine equivocation:

'I will unfold my sentence and my crime.
My crime—that, rapt in reverential awe,
I sate obedient, in the fiery prime
Of youth, self-govern'd, at the feet of Law;
Ennobling this dull pomp, the life of kings,
By contemplation of diviner things.

'My father loved injustice, and lived long;
Crown'd with gray hairs he died, and full of sway.
I loved the good he scorn'd, and hated wrong—
The Gods declare my recompence to-day.
I look'd for life more lasting, rule more high;
And when six years are measured, lo, I die!'   (ll. 7–18)

In Herodotus the King's just ways were indeed a crime against the divine disposition of things, but by suppressing explicit reference to that disposition, Arnold's Mycerinus seems to speak in angry sarcasm; as the poem has it at the end of the King's address to his people, "so spake he, half in anger, half in scorn" (l. 79). Where the Mycerinus of Herodotus devotes himself to feasting in resignation, Arnold's devotes himself out of bitter frustration.

The changed motive concerns the perpetual feasting of the King. After hearing his doom, the King in Herodotus "caused many lamps to be made, and would light these at nightfall and drink and make merry; by day or night he never ceased from revelling. . . . Thus he planned, that by turning night into day, he might make his six years into twelve and so prove the oracle false." The feasting is thus incidental to the turning of night into day in order to "cheat" the oracle. But for Arnold's Mycerinus to turn night into day serves the principal purpose of living what is left of his life as a hedonist dream of extended and uninterrupted pleasure. This purpose is also served by the change Arnold introduced into the setting for the King's revelry. In Herodotus, Mycerinus "never ceased from

revelling, roaming to the marsh country and the groves and wherever he heard of the likeliest places of pleasure." The groves, which
in Herodotus are but one stage on an aimless, pleasurable itinerary,
are the sole location of the feasting in Arnold: Arnold's Mycerinus
moves his court "to the cool region of the groves he loved" (l. 84).
The consequence of this change in motive and location is to intensify the moral significance of Mycerinus's decision and action.

Mycerinus makes extensive use of an image beloved of poets and
critics alike: light and dark. The nightly revelries of the source are
sufficient to prompt such an image, but do not themselves imply the
traditional equation of light as truth and dark as error. It is these
equations which Arnold employs to carry some of the moral implication of his poem. Light first enters the poem as a Platonic
effulgence:

> 'Yet surely, O my people, did I deem
> Man's justice from the all-just Gods was given;
> A light that from some upper fount did beam,
> Some better archetype, whose seat was heaven;
> A light that, shining from the blest abodes,
> Did shadow somewhat of the life of Gods.'   (ll. 19–24)

Such Platonic idealism is no longer acceptable because the divine
curtailment of the King's life is manifestly "unjust" by mortal
standards, which cannot, therefore, be an image, however imperfect,
of divine justice. The fallacy of this argument, focused by the uncompromising *therefore,* is to assume that the imperfection of mortal justice does not result from a difference in motive which leaves
mortal justice less pure than heavenly. Mycerinus, in effect, rejects
the possibility that a failure to achieve the perfectly disinterested
love of right marks the point where man falls short of the archetype. He is led to the position because, as he makes clear, his practice of justice before the oracle was not an end in itself: "I look'd
for life more lasting, rule more high" (l. 17). Disappointed in his
expectation of reward, Mycerinus engages in theological speculations that pass in review possible definitions of the nature of gods
and supernatural law. He concludes with the Lucretian hypothesis
of cheerfully negligent deities unmindful of the world below:

> 'Or in deaf ease, on thrones of dazzling sheen,
> Drinking deep draughts of joy, ye dwell serene?

'Oh, wherefore cheat our youth, if thus it be,
Of one short joy, one lust, one pleasant dream?
Stringing vain words of powers we cannot see,
Blind divinations of a will supreme;
Lost labour! when the circumambient gloom
But hides, if Gods, Gods careless of our doom?'   (ll. 47–54)

Where his pre-oracular theology saw the gods shedding archetypal light, his final embittered Epicureanism shrouds the gods in gloom. Where his initial Platonic metaphysics issued in an appropriate ethics—his urge to political justice by divine inspiration was accompanied by the self-government of temperance—his final, hypothetical theology moves him to an intemperate hedonism. The change from divine archetype to divine negligence, from refulgence to gloom, from temperance to intemperance is appropriately marked in his announcement of his decision:

'The rest I give to joy. Even while I speak,
My sand runs short; and—as yon star-shot ray,
Hemm'd by two banks of cloud, peers pale and weak,
Now, as the barrier closes, dies away—
Even so do past and future intertwine,
Blotting this six years' space, which yet is mine.'   (ll. 55–60)

A simile invoked to illustrate the brevity of the time remaining to Mycerinus thus implies the quality of life he has decided upon: a wilful closing out of the light in order to sport in gloom, like his hypothetical Lucretian deities.

The simile becomes landscape fact by the restriction of his feasting to the groves with their "tranquil gloom." Just as his disappointment had led him to characterize whatever is shadowed forth on earth by the archetypal light as "mere phantoms" and "vain dreams" (ll. 25–27), so his abandonment to hedonism constitutes a choosing to live the dreams of "the feverish time of youth" (l. 89), for dreams are properly accompanied by shadows and gloom. But the upward glance of the King's theological speculation in the first part of the poem is not forgotten in the final revelry:

There by the river-banks he wander'd on,
From palm-grove on to palm-grove, happy trees,
Their smooth tops shining sunward, and beneath
Burying their unsunn'd stems in grass and flowers;

> Where in one dream the feverish time of youth
> Might fade in slumber, and the feet of joy
> Might wander all day long and never tire.   (ll. 85–91)

While the trees know both the regions of light and the regions of shadowy dreams, the King's choice to enter the glade, marked as it is by the clouding over of a star, permits him only a broken glimpse of the light above (ll. 98–99).

Without ever endorsing the King's initial Platonism, the poem yet makes clear that his substitute hedonism (it is too intemperate to be properly Epicurean) is misguided. The speculative hypotheses of lines 100–111 present the reaction of Arnoldian man to the King's situation, interleaving hedonism, as it were, with an unelaborate Stoicism. The earlier association of the King's new life with dreams, both in the words of his address and in those of the noncommittal narrative in lines 79–99, is appropriately and strikingly reapplied in what might be called the section of narrative with commentary that runs from line 100 to the end:

> It may be that sometimes his wondering soul
> From the loud joyful laughter of his lips
> Might shrink half startled, like a guilty man
> Who wrestles with his dream; as some pale shape
> Gliding half hidden through the dusky stems,
> Would thrust a hand before the lifted bowl,
> Whispering: *A little space, and thou art mine!*   (ll. 100–106)

A Roman might have checked his laughter at the sight of a decorative skeleton on his cup, the nagging *memento mori* in the midst of revelry, and have been further sobered by the cup's lugubrious motto of *gnothi seauton*—know thyself. Arnold's Mycerinus, wrestling guiltily with a dream, perhaps finds the skeleton revivified and walking free of the cup, but still ready to interpose itself between cup and lip and utter the old cry of *memento mori*. And at such a check to revelry Mycerinus perhaps turns, with the Roman, to know himself:

> It may be on that joyless feast his eye
> Dwelt with mere outward seeming; he, within,
> Took measure of his soul, and knew its strength,
> And by that silent knowledge, day by day,
> Was calm'd, ennobled, comforted, sustain'd.   (ll. 107–11)

Such a self-knowledge, Stoic or Socratic, would be a return to the virtuous self-government of the days before the oracle, but the entrance into the groves and endless feasting has effectively denied this possibility. And so the hypotheses end, and with them the indirect moral commentary, the implication of what Mycerinus should have done:

> It may be; but not less his brow was smooth,
> And his clear laugh fled ringing through the gloom,
> And his mirth quail'd not at the mild reproof
> Sigh'd out by winter's sad tranquillity;
> Nor, pall'd with its own fulness, ebb'd and died
> In the rich languor of long summer-days.   (ll. 112–17)

Evidently, his mirth should have quailed, and should have palled: we have moved from indirect reproof to the most explicit condemnation of Mycerinus the poem will engage in.

The failure to adopt winter's sad tranquillity in his unhappiness involves him in "all the tumult of the feast" (l. 96), a riotous disorder which contrasts with his self-government and his wise rule before the oracle. His unquenchable mirth in summer's "rich languor" recalls the description of himself as once he was: "the strenuous just man" (l. 29). Mycerinus, we can say, substitutes hectic lack of purpose for quiet work. The work of a king is his government, his duty to his people. But like the work of anyone else, it should follow the patient, unambitious processes of nature itself. Mycerinus, strikingly, quite fails to learn lessons from nature in the cycle of the seasons (ll. 112–21). His looking for a life longer and a rule more celebrated than his father's leaves him, when these are denied, with no resource to check his plunge into the "fitful uproar" of pointless feasting, where he is silently upbraided by the procession of the seasons and the star which shines in its course even though it is obscured for Mycerinus.

Mycerinus, in effect, makes most of the mistakes Arnold later reproved in his social and religious essays. In particular he mistakes the existence of natural laws, however enigmatic, for proof of the existence of natural rights,[9] and he makes the even more egregious error of basing his conduct on metaphysics, of basing himself

---

[9] Arnold wrote in an essay on *Copyright* for the *Fortnightly Review* (1880): "for me the matter is simplified by my believing that men, if they go down into their own minds and deal quite freely with their own consciousness, will find that they have not any natural rights at all," *Works*, XI, 241.

upon a belief in objectively existent, supernatural sanctions and on a hope for supernaturally donated rewards.[10] He quite fails to see with the eyes of the later Arnold that God and his attributes are but a poetic way of describing the tendency within man which makes for righteousness.[11] But to point out such consonances between early poem and late prose—real as they are—unquestionably vulgarizes the poem by destroying its mood of qualified sympathy for the hapless King, a man who, like Arnold and at least some of his contemporaries, finds himself depending upon a religion whose support has suddenly become illusory. In such a situation there remains duty, a life plan which is none the worse for being a shade reminiscent of Rugby.

iii

In 1849 *Mycerinus* was followed by the well-known sonnet *To a Friend* with its notorious first line and its famous praise of Sophocles. Each of the three writers who give the speaker intellectual support—Homer, Epictetus, and Sophocles—is provided with a briefly realized landscape setting. Homer sees, "though blind," "the Wide Prospect" of Europe; Epictetus continues to expound his Stoic philosophy in Nicopolis after his expulsion from Rome by Domitian, "Vespasian's brutal son"; Sophocles, undulled by business and untempted by passion, sings of Colonus and sees life steadily and whole. The qualities of vision associated with the poets and the philosopher's perseverance in the face of cruel injustice read, in the 1849 ordering, as a tacit reproach to Mycerinus. Blind Homer's wide view of landscape contrasts with Mycerinus' removal to the grove: the self-blinding of a clouded star. Unlike Mycerinus, who in Arnold's poem lost his self-control in youth, Sophocles retained his "even-balanced soul, / From first youth tested up to extreme old age." The kinds of support which Arnold finds in "the bad days" of the mid-nineteenth century: clarity of purpose and vision, acceptance of such physical infirmity as blindness or lameness, perseverance in adversity, these are, evidently, the supports which Mycerinus should have sought in the bad days after the oracle. *To a Friend* shares with both of the poems which preceded

---

[10] Both *Literature and Dogma* and *God and the Bible* address themselves at large to dispersing this error.
[11] E.g., in *Literature and Dogma*, *Works*, VII, 43 ff.

it in 1849 a concern with work: Sophocles undulled by business recalls the unemulous toil of *Quiet Work* and "the strenuous just
man" that Mycerinus ceased to be. The false ruler in *To a Friend,*
"Vespasian's brutal son," is reminiscent of Mycerinus' unjust, impious, and destructive father. The mundane discords of *Quiet Work*
are fully exemplified in the hectic feasting of Mycerinus and glanced
at in the picture of Sophocles not made wild with passion. But to
the figures of laborer, ruler, and reveler, *To a Friend* adds the
poet, and thus prepares for the next poem in 1849, its title poem,
The Strayed Reveller.

What makes *The Strayed Reveller* difficult is that, unusually for
Arnold, it lacks the features which permit a value judgment upon
the action and professions it contains. It is Arnold's fullest poetic
statement about the nature of the poet and his creation *(Resignation,* with which *The Strayed Reveller* may naturally be compared,
attempts, by contrast, to define the poet's calling in terms of a much
wider consideration of other possible lives) . But the statement is
made without the sort of comment, however indirect, which could
tell us whether or not it constitutes a full and adequate aesthetic.
The place of the poem within the wider context of Arnold's views
on poetics in these early years is not an issue within the poem. But
some readers have understandably wished to make it so, and have
found in the poem an implicit rejection of Keatsian Romanticism in
accordance with its explicit rejection in the contemporary Clough
letters.

Even without the Clough letters rejection must have been a
tempting reading in 1849. There is nothing in *The Strayed Reveller* like the interleaving of a Stoic hypothesis in *Mycerinus.* But to
pass from *Mycerinus,* with its sympathetic condemnation of the life
of intense feeling, to *The Strayed Reveller's* appropriation of exactly that life to the conditions of poetic creativity makes almost
irresistible a condemnation of creativity on these terms. The guilty
dreams of moral reproach which may have haunted Mycerinus in
the grove seem latent in those half-waking dreams of the Strayed
Reveller which issue in poetic creation. Mycerinus, with his "throng
of revellers" (l. 83) , would seek forgetfulness in "the lifted bowl"
(l. 105) , but is (hypothetically) checked by an apparition of
memento mori. There is no skeleton on the "deep cup" of Circe in
which the Reveller finds forgetfulness of his religious purpose (ll.
12, 64–69) , but it is difficult to avoid feeling that the intoxicating

loss of self-control it brings constitutes a tacit reproach. *The Strayed Reveller* was, in any case, immediately preceded in 1849 by *To a Friend,* not *Mycerinus.* There are few more striking disjunctions in Arnold than that between the sestet of the sonnet and the opening lines of *The Strayed Reveller:*

But be his

My special thanks, whose even-balanced soul,
From first youth tested up to extreme old age,
Business could not make dull, nor passion wild;

Who saw life steadily, and saw it whole;
The mellow glory of the Attic stage,
Singer of sweet Colonus, and its child.

Faster, faster,
O Circe, Goddess,
Let the wild, thronging train,
The bright procession
Of eddying forms,
Sweep through my soul!

It is customary to gloss the opening lines of *The Strayed Reveller* with the condemnation of Keats and Browning for "passionately desiring movement and fulness"; and such a gloss is clearly pertinent, although—unlike the Arnoldian Keats and Browning—the Strayed Reveller is far indeed from achieving "but a confused multitudinousness." It ought to be recalled that in the same letter to Clough Arnold goes on to confess that "I have had that desire of fulness without respect of the means, which may become almost maniacal: but nature had placed a bar thereto not only in the conscience (as with all men) but in a great numbness in that direction."[12]

Inexplicably, Arnold later classified *The Strayed Reveller* as a lyric poem, although its form, a dialogue containing narrative matter and exemplary lyric descriptions, is similar both to *Empedocles,* classified as dramatic, and *The Sick King in Bokhara,* classified as narrative. The form, in fact, is distractingly objective. It seems to promise the creation of a certain kind of poet, not noticeably Arnoldian, for the purpose of dispassionate consideration and judg-

---

[12] *Clough Letters,* p. 97; [after Sept., 1848].

ment, however implicit, along the lines of the Clough letters and the commentary in *Mycerinus* and *Quiet Work*. The objectivity, the separation of the Reveller from Arnold, prompts us to read the poem as T. S. Eliot properly read *Heine's Grave*: as "criticism, and very fine criticism too; and a kind of criticism which is justified because it could not be made in prose."[13] But the kind of evaluative placing that we find in *Heine's Grave* is absent from *The Strayed Reveller*. One of the best descriptive formulas for the poem is M. G. Sundell's: "Arnold does not use the Reveller to discuss what sorts of poets are proper or improper; he uses him to portray the sacrifice that anyone must undergo if he is to become a poet at all."[14] More pertinent to *The Strayed Reveller* is T. S. Eliot's further comment on *Heine's Grave*, it "is good poetry for the same reason that it is good criticism: because Heine is one of the *personae*, the masks behind which Arnold is able to go through his performance."[15] But the Reveller is a Romantic, not a neoclassical persona: there is enough of Arnold in him to justify the later lyric classification, while the quasi-dramatic form keeps him sufficiently separate to make him a persona and not *poeta loquitur*. Before considering how much of Arnold there is in the Reveller, it will be proper to determine what sort of person the Reveller is in the poem.

It is the pre-existence of the Reveller which enables him to stray and which causes him to respond as he does to the new experience which comes from straying. The topography of the action is given clearly: a valley slopes up to high ground on which the Reveller lives alone in a hut; part way down the valley and apparently on opposite sides of it there are two buildings: the temple of Iacchus (ll. 37–39) and the palace of Circe (ll. 42–45); presumably farther down and on the valley floor there is a town (ll. 36–37). The solitary youth loves the music of Pan (ll. 65–67), but is also eager to join the religious festivities of Iacchus. The other revelers assemble in the town, and the youth makes his own way to meet them at the temple (ll. 35–39). It is because his solitary existence leads him to take a different path to the religious festival that he passes near and sees the beech-surrounded palace of Circe, empty and without the smoke of ritual observance (l. 45). Ulysses asks Circe whether the youth is "Iacchus' darling" or whether he is "beloved of Pan" (ll.

---

[13] T. S. Eliot, *The Use of Poetry and the Use of Criticism*, p. 111.
[14] M. G. Sundell, "Story and Context in 'The Strayed Reveller,'" *Victorian Poetry*, III (1965), 161–70; quotation from pp. 164–65.
[15] *The Use of Poetry and the Use of Criticism*, p. 112.

79–80), and the answer should be that, whatever their feelings for him, he loves both. Love of Pan accounts for his solitary hut; love of Iacchus accounts for his leaving it and coming upon the palace of Circe. At the palace he gains three things: the drowsy intoxication of the cup, knowledge of the stories told him by Silenus at noon (ll. 261–69), and an awareness that in order to retell the stories he must vicariously suffer the pain of other men's experience:

> such a price
> The Gods exact for song:
> To become what we sing.   (ll. 232–34)

This creative, if temporary, metamorphosis is the poetic equivalent of the bestial metamorphosis normally associated with the Circean cup and glanced at in the lions which the youth finds sleeping when he first approaches the palace (l. 48). It is, of course, the interpretation of creative empathy as a kind of metamorphosis which accounts for, and justifies, the location of the action at Circe's palace—even if it involves some minor geographical adjustment to do so. Circe, then, is the appropriately enigmatic muse of (at least this kind of) poetry, the "strangely smiling Goddess" (l. 286) of a palace of art. It is a palace visited by few, for most join the rout in the town and proceed to the temple of divine worship.

Those who do frequent the palace separately exemplify the constituents of poetry and the poetic act: Silenus with his fund of stories, Circe with the cup of inspirational metamorphosis, Ulysses, the wise, much-traveled man (ll. 105–13), who has lived the life the poet sings about and is prepared to honor him for his song. The Ulysses who hunts with Circe (ll. 70–74) is the wisdom of experience which comes vicariously to the poet when he not only knows the stories of old Silenus but, inspired by the cup, relives them in order to recreate them.[16] Ulysses is wise, but so are the bards (l. 207). Ulysses is the "proved, much enduring, / Wave-toss'd Wanderer!" (ll. 287–88), but so are the bards, for

> They see the Heroes
> Near harbour;—but they share
> Their lives, and former violent toil in Thebes,

[16] That the youth becomes a poet in Circe's palace rather than, as Sundell argues, a potential poet, is evident from the youth's numbering himself with poets: the price exacted from poets by the gods is "to become what *we* sing" (l. 234).

Seven-gated Thebes, or Troy;
Or where the echoing oars
Of Argo first
Startled the unknown sea.   (ll. 254–60)

Ulysses, it is true, has experienced these things for himself; the
poet's experience is second-hand. But to describe it as second-hand,
rather than vicarious, forces a moral distinction which the poem
does not appear to require. Such a distinction underlies Mr. Sundell's account of the two functions served by Ulysses: "he is a trust-
worthy reporter of how poets appear externally, and as the best of
active men he embodies the sort of life now closed to the Reveller."
Mr. Sundell accurately describes the poem as presenting "the drama
of initiation into the imaginative existence necessary for poetry,"
but he proceeds with a more questionable observation: "it portrays
the sacrifice of life for the possibility of creating art."[17] This interpretation assumes, what the poem nowhere suggests, that the
youth is a potential Ulysses, and that *The Strayed Reveller* adopts
a scale of values similar to that of Tennyson's *Palace of Art*. In
effect, it is true, the youth does make a choice, but not between the
life of Ulysses and the life of Circe's palace. His "choice" is between
the palace of art and the temple of divine worship. The distinctions made by the poem do not include that between actual and
vicarious experience; they are between the gods' unimpassioned objectivity and the poet's painful subjectivity, and between the revels
of art and the revels of divine worship. The revels of art, the consequences of the Circean cup, are solitary, creative, and painful. The
revels of worship, from which the youth has strayed, are communal
and painless. Both revels involve a going out of self. For the poet
there is both labor and pain in singing the lives of men (ll. 210–
11), but across the valley the youth sees "all day long"

Without pain, without labour,
Sometimes a wild-hair'd Mænad—
Sometimes a Faun with torches—
And sometimes, for a moment,
Passing through the dark stems
Flowing-robed, the beloved,
The desired, the divine,
Beloved Iacchus.   (ll. 274–81)

[17] *Victorian Poetry*, III, 167–68.

Religious festivity, the wished-for witness of the epiphany, would have united the youth with the rout that assembled in the town, with the maenads and fauns in the woods. The poetic revel takes place within: the rout in the woods is replaced by "the wild, thronging train, / The bright procession / Of eddying forms" that sweeps through the soul. The poet experiences vicariously the manhood that is truly lost only in the religious revel. He lives separately the identities of the thronging train within instead of losing his identity in the rout without. *The Strayed Reveller,* in fact, might almost be an answer to the wry dismissal of poets in Plato's *Ion:* "as the Corybantian revellers when they dance are not in their right mind, so the lyric poets are not in their right mind when they are composing their beautiful strains."[18] For Arnold, revels at the religious temple differ markedly from those at the palace of art, even though the first may help define the second.

Despite his perception that *The Strayed Reveller* is not a rejection of the Keatsian poet, Mr. Sundell errs, I feel, in making it too much the product of Matthew Arnold of Rugby: the duties of active life sternly reprove the man who strays from them in search of the pleasure in poetic pains. It was, in fact, for *Resignation* that Arnold reserved his consideration of the rival claims of life and art. The strongest support for Mr. Sundell's reading is that the intoxicated youth is as lacking in dignity as he is certainly lacking in self-control. But Ulysses sees him as decidedly beautiful and is ready to honor him, while the products of intoxication, the vignettes of men and heroes, have all of them a control and clarity matched elsewhere in Arnold perhaps only by the songs of Callicles, who also left a feast in order to sing. To employ the Arnoldian distinction, the quality of these vignettes is not the haunting suggestiveness of Celtic natural magic, but rather, and appropriately, the brilliant clarity of Greek radiance. If it is Keatsian, it is Arnold's Keats of

> What little town, by river or seashore,
> Or mountain-built with quiet citadel,
> Is emptied of its folk, this pious morn?

It is not the Keats of "magic-casements" and "fast-fading violets."[19] Of course the vignettes are appropriate to the Greek youth, taught by Silenus, inspired by Circe, and aspiring to the wisdom of

---

[18] *Dialogues of Plato,* trans. B. Jowett (New York, 1937), I, 289.
[19] *Complete Prose,* III, 377–78.

Ulysses. But they are not less appropriate to Arnold, loving nature and as temperamentally aloof as the young man at the valley's head, engaging in the lone observances of poetry and seeing them, as the Clough letters of these years testify, as somehow distinct from the communal observance of religion.[20] Above all, the vignettes are far from inappropriate to an Arnold who later confessed his "real love" for "this old Greek world" and hoped that he had infused sufficient soul into his representation of it to save it from academicism. If *The Strayed Reveller* is academic, it is because it constitutes a young poet's mythic representation of the nature of his calling in terms of the tradition he saw himself part of and in terms of literary materials he was to use again in order to define, and objectify, his own experience of life. It is small wonder that it was the title poem of his first volume, although it must be admitted that the only other natural candidate for the honor, *Resignation,* would have made but a glum alternative.

The Strayed Reveller, it must be remembered, is about poets and poetry in themselves. The poets of *Quiet Work* prop the mind of Arnold the man rather than Arnold the poet (so much may be presumed from the fact that Homer and Sophocles share this office with the philosopher Epictetus) . The cup and the seclusion that may be appropriate to a young poet are not necessarily appropriate to a ruler like Mycerinus. For all that, it must be admitted that there are many features of the poem which puzzle, both when it is read in itself and when it is placed in the context of the 1849 volume. The abandonment of restraint, the revelry in glades, are activities which seem to require the kind of moral condemnation they receive elsewhere in Arnold, but are not accorded here. It is no doubt to solve this puzzle that readings have been offered in terms of rejected

---

[20] See especially, "a growing sense of the deficiency of the *beautiful* in your poems, and of this alone being properly *poetical* as distinguished from rhetorical, devotional or metaphysical, made me speak as I did," *Clough Letters,* p. 66; [Feb. 24, 1848]. For similar statements see *Clough Letters,* pp. 84, 99, and the assertion, p. 59, that the social conscience of "a strong minded writer" will cause him to "lose his self-knowledge, and talk of his usefulness and imagine himself a Reformer, instead of an Exhibition." By September, 1849, Arnold confessed he was "more snuffing after a moral atmosphere to respire in than ever before in my life," *Clough Letters,* p. 109. Something of the old aestheticism recurs in a letter of September, 1853: "if one loved what was beautiful and interesting in itself *passionately* enough, one would produce what was excellent without troubling oneself with religious dogmas at all," *Clough Letters,* p. 143. But in between he wrote the "magister vitae" letter of October, 1852, insisting that poetry must include religion, "instead of existing as poetry only, and leaving religious wants to be supplied by the Christian religion, as a power existing independent of the poetical power," *Clough Letters,* p. 124.

Keatsianism or Mr. Sundell's interesting version of an opposition between active life and poetic loss of manhood. The point is that the poem seems to require a reading back to the known character and views of the author, to require the personal heresy, in fact; but then it proves not quite to square with those views: desire of movement and fulness does not produce confused multitudinousness. There are several possible explanations for this circumstance, all of them more or less speculative. Least satisfactory is to assume that the reworked myth contained some intransigent material—notably the effects of intoxication—which Arnold nonetheless went along with for the sake of the suggestiveness of metamorphosis. A second, and more winning, is that the poem should be referred not to Arnold's total aesthetic, but to one aspect of it considered without the qualifications he elsewhere gives. Arnold, it will be remembered, confessed to just that Keatsian tendency whose effects he had already reproved, but had found in himself not only a conscientious disinclination but an aesthetic inadequacy for its full expression. *The Strayed Reveller* could be, as Professor Allott partly suggests,[21] an attempt to suspend conscience in the interests of finding out how far inadequate he actually was in the poetry of natural magic. *The Strayed Reveller* is certainly the only poem in which the Arnoldian natural magic is indulged without its usual, and desired, accompaniment by moral profundity. The third possible explanation, which could combine with and modify either of the first two, is that the poem is as deliberately experimental in mode as it obviously is in prosody. Not only is it a young poet's poem about a young poet and poetics, but the long central passage of paired vignettes (ll. 130–260) has constantly the air of indulged virtuosity, of trying the effect of descriptive lists, numerous names, or that variation of meter to intensify the action of the meaning which is these days usually canonized as "muscularity":

> They see the Centaurs
> On Pelion;—then they feel,
> They too, the maddening wine
> Swell their large veins to bursting; in wild pain
> They feel the biting spears
> Of the grim Lapithæ, and Theseus, drive
> Drive crashing through their bones.   (ll. 223–29)

[21] Allott, p. 65.

It is, certainly, a brilliant piece of total mimesis, but, like much poetry which is unequivocally "muscular," the effects are a shade too obviously contrived, the craft is obtruded too insistently for the highest excellence to obtain.

iv

The import of *The Strayed Reveller*'s paired vignettes recurs in the choric amplifications of the next of the 1849 poems, *Fragment of an 'Antigone.'* But where *The Strayed Reveller* uses the vignettes to illustrate that poets must suffer the pain as well as witness the happiness of the lives they record in song, the *'Antigone'* uses the resources of mythology to illustrate the sad fate of the subjects of song themselves. The *'Antigone'* is Arnold's fullest explicit concentration upon the issues of law, natural and civil, and necessity which appear in various forms in many of his poems. Much, if not all, of the poem's interest derives, indeed, from its relevance to other and better pieces. The poem itself is too much an exercise in finding English equivalents for Greek poetic syntax to be satisfying; frequently, it hovers close to that solemn banality of Greek tragedy in English so delightfully parodied by Housman. But its relevance extends both back and forward in the 1849 volume.

The opening chorus focuses upon the fundamental dichotomy of classical tragedy. On the one hand, there is the true hero, who, scorning to be fortune's fool, "makes his own welfare his unswerved-from law," although not to the extent of infringing justice (ll. 7–8). On the other hand, there is the general human condition, to which even heroes are subject: the necessity of death and the obligations imposed upon a man by being born into one family, one city, one country. Tragedy results when individual self-fulfillment irreconcilably conflicts with the obligations imposed by the natural laws of kinship or inevitable mortality or the divinely ordained order expressed through government (ll. 21–22, 41, 48–49). Tragic irreconcilability comes especially, as in *'Antigone,'* when individual need coincides with one law in defiance of another. Antigone herself prefers the primal law of blood to Creon's law, while Haemon, unlike his Sophoclean counterpart, accepts Creon's harsh law, in part because its observance by Antigone would have permitted indulgence of his own "self-selected good" of love for Antigone (l. 29). He upbraids Antigone for preferring the dead to the living, for preferring death by Creon's law to love for Haemon. The chorus then offers a series of illustrative consolations, pointing out that the love which transgresses an "eternal law" is wrong (l. 75), and that all must die, even the favored of the gods.

The plight of lovers in conflict with higher obligations was to concern Arnold more fully in the volume of 1852. But the initial concern with individual good and public duty has obvious relevance to Mycerinus, who protested the law of his own mortality and neglected his obligations to his people in order to seize happiness for himself. This concern also looks forward to the next poem in 1849, *The Sick King in Bokhara*.[22]

Most of the weaknesses of *The Sick King* can be attributed to its prosodic form and its general mode of presentation. The poem's variations upon ballad measure combined with an appropriately simple, often prosaic, diction produce, too often, the kind of sing-song banality to which the ballads themselves often succumb and which Johnson so ruthlessly exposed. It is a quality which the ballads often manage to render acceptable by virtue of their charming naivety. But *The Sick King* constitutes a very sophisticated attempt to project the spiritual and social problems of Arnold's England in terms of a story with an oriental setting. Because its central purpose is sophisticated, the painful simplicities of meter and mode make an inappropriate manner for the expression of its matter. The mode is the quasi-dramatic form of *The Strayed Reveller,* but where the lack of an external narrator was principally of moment in *The Strayed Reveller* in its eschewal of a clear evaluation of the action and ideas, it matters in *The Sick King* because it leads to the artificial forcing of narrative exposition into the form of dialogue. Most obviously is this the case in the well-worn device of bringing on a character who is obligingly uninformed of recent events and must have the situation explained to him. We accept the device in Elizabethan drama because one scene of exposition is succeeded by five acts which build upon it. In *The Sick King* exposition accounts for just over half the poem. Moreover, the Vizier, he who is so usefully ignorant of events, is so because he has been seriously ill (ll. 22–25). Since the poem presents a sick king placed in judgment over a sick criminal in a sick city, the Vizier's sickness ought, one feels, to be of thematic moment. But where the other

[22] Allott, p. 60, following Lionel Trilling, *Matthew Arnold* (New York, 1949), pp. 104–5.

sickness is evidently a metaphor for the human condition, the Vizier's is principally a useful device. It is, in any case, not the only near-redundancy in the poem. The situation is explained to the Vizier by Hussein, a poet. A poet ought to be a significant addition to the counterpoint of views effected by the idealistic monarch and his pragmatic chief officer, but Hussein is not. The Vizier addresses him as "thou teller of sweet tales" (l. 11), but nothing is made of the fact that the tale he actually tells is far from sweet. There seems to be a potential significance in this difference between the traditional matter of poets and their current matter. As the poem stands, the potential is quite unrealized, and there is no obvious reason why Hussein's expository office could not have been discharged in the usual way by some anonymous palace inmate. Hussein, moreover, is assigned stage directions as well as exposition. He tells the unobservant Vizier that they have reached the royal apartments in order to prepare a reader for the sudden entrance of the King into their conversation (ll. 20–21), and he concludes his exposition by hearing outside the men bearing in the criminal's corpse (ll. 129–32). The weak and inappropriately naive manner does not, as it happens, diminish the interest of the sophisticated matter, although it obviously lessens the poem's total value.

There are two chief aspects of the poem's matter, and both have received the attention of annotators. The descriptive details of the setting and much of the central incident are drawn from Alexander Burnes's *Travels into Bokhara,* while the incident itself presents a situation capable of sustaining variants upon Arnold's preoccupation with law of all kinds and the necessities and obligations it involves. To annotate the poem thus, and withhold further comment, impoverishes the poem by tacitly representing it as but one more contribution to the long-lasting oriental fad in English literature— from the *Persian Eclogues* to *Hassan*—which bids for serious attention by virtue of its philosophizing. The connection between oriental setting and philosophical speculation thus becomes so tenuous as easily to snap under a reading which attends separately to guidebook accuracy and the place of the thought in Arnold's total views.

Such tacit disintegration of the poem is principally encouraged by the scrupulousness with which the local details are drawn from the source. It is a sound critical axiom that the greater a work's fidelity to its source the more completely is it inhibited from establishing significances not present in the source. Because Arnold's

Bokhara is so close to Burnes's Bokhara it is unlikely to be anything but a literal Bokhara. But the axiom overlooks the fact that
a poet who perceives symbolic potential in a literal source may release that potential with the slightest of modifications which do not
destroy the literal accuracy of his representation. The description
of the Oxus which closes *Sohrab and Rustum* makes use only of the
geographical details of the source—once again, Burnes's *Bokhara*—
but by discriminating between those details and humanizing the
river with unelaborate metaphor and unobtrusive pathetic fallacy
Arnold produces one of the most splendidly symbolic rivers in English literature. This coexistence of the literal and the symbolic, less
memorable and to different ends though it be, is also present in
Arnold's picture of Bokhara.

The key word for the poem is "sick." And the nature of its importance becomes obvious when we recall that physical disorder has
long been an acceptable metaphor for spiritual malaise. Such a
recollection draws together the two aspects of the poem which
normally lie separate. The physical details of the poem explain
how the self-accusing criminal succumbed to the literal fever which
caused him to curse his mother and brothers. The King's frustrated
philosophizing, his vain reaching for a moral principle lacking in
his civilization, causes him to be "ill at ease" (l. 4) and his head to
burn (l. 183). The importance of these conditions in the poem is
indicated by their being Arnoldian additions to the source material.
Professor Allott agrees with the authors of the *Commentary* that
"the sickness of the King and people was probably suggested by the
account of the Balkh fever, contracted on the banks of the Oxus,
which prostrated Captain Burnes and many members of his party
upon their arrival in Bokhara."[23] Perhaps it was, but it is the use
to which that suggestion is put which begins the transmutation of
travel book into poem. The central incident, the King's reluctant
punishment of the self-accusing criminal, is a conflation of two
stories which Burnes relates one after the other as instances of "the
rigour of the Mohammedan law."[24] From the first story Arnold
took the criminal's threefold appearance before the King. This
story also contains the King's reluctance to punish, the sentence of
death by stoning decreed by the ecclesiastical court, the King's

[23] Allott, p. 77; *Commentary*, p. 87. But see also, Burnes, *Travels into Bokhara*
(1834), I, 302, "the water [of Bokhara] is bad, and said to be the cause of
guinea worm, a disease frightfully prevalent in Bokhara."
[24] See *Commentary*, pp. 88–89.

throwing the first stone and his instruction to let the man escape if he wished, his sorrow when the man accepted death gladly, and his attendance at the burial. The second story adds only a hint for the nature of the crime with which the man accused himself: cursing his mother. Arnold's additions include a narrative of events that bring about the cursing (including the man's fever). His most important modifications are to make the King's unhappiness a spiritual sickness and to make the King bury the criminal in the grave that had been set aside for himself.

Both the spiritual sickness of the King and the physical sickness of the criminal are a consequence of the condition of life forced upon them by their civilization and environment. They are conditions involving an arbitrary division of society into haves and have-nots, a division widened by the harshness of climate and terrain. The prevailing drought, plague, and poverty make of the haves those who successfully exploit the labor of others to create for themselves cool sanctuaries: "in the desert, spacious inns," "houses, arcades, enamell'd mosques," "cherries serv'd in drifts of snow," "meat and drink at will" (ll. 197–213). The inevitable aspiration of the have-nots to the condition of the haves is checked by inflexible laws whose coercive effect is as much upon the conscience as it is upon the bodies of those who would upset the established order; theological damnation waits upon transgressors (ll. 99–104). They are conditions encouraging a Hobbist anarchy of individualism which is countered only by religious sanctions. Arnold's addition of the events which led to the criminal's curse makes it clear that the man endeavored, in a way appropriate to his lowly sphere, to approximate the hedonistic selfishness of the King's own existence. In time of drought, with the river serving the city from the heights of Samarkand nearly dried up and the rainfall tanks "to a putrid puddle turn'd" (l. 61), the sinner finds a small pool of water "under some mulberry-trees" (ll. 67–68). This water he takes to cool his fever, and tries to keep to himself. When it is found and drunk by his mother and brothers, he curses them. It is clear from the King's apostrophe to the sinner's corpse that he sees the parallel with his own situation:

Thou wast athirst; and didst not see,
That, though we take what we desire,
We must not snatch it eagerly.

> And I have meat and drink at will,
> And rooms of treasures, not a few.
> But I am sick, nor heed I these;
> And what I would, I cannot do. (ll. 210–16)

But in drawing the parallel, the King also reveals the limitation of his own perception. He fails to see that what is wrong with the civilization is that it consists of people taking what they desire. The King accepts—and tacitly endorses—the fundamental selfishness, and reproves only its greedy excess of snatching eagerly at desired objects. He himself, after all, has no need to snatch: all that he can desire materially is provided for him by a system exemplified in the opening lines of the poem when Hussein interrupts the Vizier's customary collection of tribute from transient merchants to swell the royal wealth. It is the King's sense that he has only half-grasped the significance of the parallel, that he does not see clearly in these moral issues (l. 182), which accounts for his sickness. Nor does the sinner see clearly: he located his crime, as the law taught him, in the cursing of his mother, not in the selfishness of wishing to keep the water for himself. And yet the King is sorry for the sinner and wishes to help him escape the consequences of his crime. The King's sympathy, his pity for suffering and sin, is an altruistic impulse in a civilization of selfishness whose laws are devised only to keep that selfishness in manageable order.

The King is unable properly to identify and justify his altruism because, as the Vizier makes clear, it is contrary to the principles by which all, including the King, govern their lives. The Vizier's speech is the largest single addition to the source material, and its importance is to clarify and to generalize the rule of life in Bokhara. The Vizier reproves the King for tendencies which are, historically considered, sentimentalist, but which take on here the usual Victorian form of humanitarianism. Such tendencies are wrong because, if indulged, they make life intolerable:

> who, through all this length of time,
> Could bear the burden of his years,
> If he for strangers pain'd his heart
> Not less than those who merit tears?
>
> Fathers we *must* have, wife and child,
> And grievous is the grief of these;
> This pain alone, which *must* be borne,
> Makes the head white, and bows the knees. (ll. 145–52)

The value of law is that it assumes the burden of individual conscience. Once endeavor to reassume that burden and there can be
no end to the claimants for humanitarian consideration:

> Look, this is but one single place,
> Though it be great; all the earth round,
> If a man bear to have it so,
> Things which might vex him shall be found.   (ll. 157–60)

Although the examples surveyed by the Vizier are all located in the
middle east, it is evident that Bokhara exemplifies European as
much as oriental civilization. The Vizier's first example is of two
armies on "the northern frontier" preying upon each other. When
the poem was next reprinted in 1855, after, that is, the outbreak of
the Crimean War, the "northern frontier" was changed to "the
Russian frontier" (l. 161). Even in 1849 "all the earth round" is
sufficiently comprehensive. It is the Vizier's generalizing, then,
which realizes the always latent reference of Bokhara to Victorian
England. Bokhara with its commercial preoccupation, with its material and spiritual aridity, is fully consonant with the familiar picture
of the Victorian desert, the spiritual life stifled by economic individualism. It remains for the Vizier to make the consonance implicit in the poem and not a mere external gloss.

But the relevance would at least partly emerge without the
Vizier's generalizing. For all its oriental setting and its Mohammedan code, *The Sick King* is a Christian poem. The language is
often painfully stilted, but it also strives, frequently, to achieve a
biblical cadence, or at least to echo recognizably biblical phrases.[25]
Some of these echoes are no doubt attributable to literary convention and the social similarities of Semitic peoples. Mohammedan
and Jew alike are traditionally given to speak of sinners and cursing, of burdens and fruits, of dead dogs and stones. But when, in
the execution of the criminal, Arnold changes Burnes's description

[25] It seems that Arnold was striving to achieve a kind of Homeric simplicity in
his poem both by meter and diction. One month after the publication of *The
Strayed Reveller* volume, Arnold was offering advice on Clough's projected
translation of the *Iliad*. He urged Clough to be plainer in diction, to stop trying to imitate Greek syntax, and to "read the Bible: Isaiah, Job, &c." On the
question of meter, Arnold was equally specific: "Drat Hexameters. Try a bit
in the metre I took for the sick king," *Clough Letters*, pp. 103–4; [March, 1849].
When Arnold came to lecture at Oxford *On Translating Homer* in the winter
of 1860–61, he rejected the short ballad measure in favor of English hexameters,
but still accounted the Bible a true model for the diction of an English Homer,
Complete Prose, I, 126–39, 148–53, 156.

of how the King "threw the first stone" into "the King took a stone, / And cast it softly" (ll. 117–18), he uses a word which is more poetic because it is biblical. "He that is without sin among you, let him first cast a stone."[26] The King casts the first stone in accordance with the law, but he casts it softly out of an uneasy sense that he is himself not without sin. The Vizier uses a metaphor which associates the physical conditions of Bokhara with its political and economic system:

> these all, labouring for a lord,
> Eat not the fruit of their own hands;
> Which is the heaviest of all plagues,
> To that man's mind, who understands. (ll. 169–72)

The Vizier means that it may plague the mind of the understanding laborer, but it is an uncertain sense of this inequity which plagues the mind of his lord, the King, and makes him sick. As Paul wrote to Timothy, "the husbandman that laboureth must be first partaker of the fruits."[27] Perhaps most striking of all is the resonance set up by the Vizier's denial of the practicality of paining one's heart for strangers. When the Son comes to judge the world, the nations shall be divided into sheep and goats. The sinful goats will be damned:

> For I was an hungred, and ye gave me no meat: I was thirsty, and ye gave me no drink. I was a stranger, and ye took me not in: naked and ye clothed me not. . . . Inasmuch as ye did it not to one of the least of these [my brethren], ye did it not to me.[28]

The King knows that the criminal "wast a sinner. . . . / wast athirst." He knows too that he himself has "meat and drink at will." But he fails to make the necessary connection. The King is a man born into goathood and struggling to express his sense of sheephood. He cannot see his way clearly, but what he desires is to substitute for a rule of law the rule of love. Against him all the facts of his civilization are ranged. If the first major benefit of the source material is to provide a setting of physical aridity that can correspond to spiritual aridity, the second is the similarity between Mohammedan and Old Testament emphasis on the law, with the reluctance of the King suggesting the struggle of the New Testament

[26] John 8: 7.
[27] II Timothy 2: 6.
[28] Matthew 25: 42–45.

to come into being. For this reason the poem sounds with half-echoes of the good Samaritan and the publican in the temple.

Years later, Arnold wrote in a chapter of *Literature and Dogma* devoted to "The True Greatness of Christianity,"

We have only to look at our own community to see the almost precise parallel, so far as religion is concerned, to the state of things presented in Judæa when Jesus Christ came. The multitudes are the same everywhere. The chief priests and elders of the people, and the scribes, are our bishops and dogmatists, with their pseudo-science of learned theology blinding their eyes, and always,—whenever simple souls are disposed to think that the method and secret of Jesus is true religion, and that the Great Personal First Cause and the God-head of the Eternal Son have nothing to do with it,—eager to cry out: *This people that knoweth not the law are cursed!* The Pharisees, with their genuine concern for religion, but total want of perception of what religion really is . . . are the Protestant Dissenters. The Sadducees are our friends the philosophical Liberals, who believe neither in angel nor spirit but in Mr. Herbert Spencer. Even the Roman governor has his close parallel in our celebrated aristocracy, with . . . its profound helplessness in presence of all great spiritual ideas. And the result is, that the splendid promises to righteousness made by the Hebrew prophets, claimed by the Jews as the property of Judaism, claimed by us as the property of Christianity, are almost as ludicrously inapplicable to our religious state now, as to theirs then.[29]

Thus Arnold in 1873. Twenty-five years earlier he might have made a poem out of such a parallel. But he found it instead in the obscure impulse of a Mohammedan potentate early in his own century. *The Sick King in Bokhara* is Arnold's *Waste Land.* He found a myth in the oriental fad of his time, while T. S. Eliot went to the Arthurian fad of his. To those who will may be left the task of deciding which is the more academic poem.

v

The King of Bokhara planned to bury the sinner in

> a fretted brick-work tomb
> Upon a hill on the right hand,
> Hard by a close of apricots,
> Upon the road of Samarcand.   (ll. 221-24)

[29] *Works*, VII, 372-73.

Both the location of the grave and the fact that it was in the King's own mausoleum were Arnoldian additions to the source. What these additions accomplish is to make a particularly appropriate grave for two men who sought a merely physical escape from conditions whose physical harshness expressed also a moral and spiritual inadequacy. The transience of the refreshment found at night beneath mulberry trees is brought hard home to the sinner, and the vulnerability of the King's conscience to onslaughts from the hot city renders ineffectual his isolation in a cool palace of social inequity. The inadequacy of attempts to escape the bad times by selfish withdrawal prompts a desire to perpetuate that escape in death: the sinner seeks death and the King prepares for his. The hedonistic withdrawal of Mycerinus to the groves of the Nile and of the King of Bokhara to his palace is ineffectual because it leaves the one king vulnerable to the promptings of social conscience and the other to the promptings of moral conscience. Arnold also found such withdrawal ineffectual. In the sonnet *To George Cruikshank* the artist's etchings of "the rank life of towns" prove sufficient to destroy Arnold's country contentments, which are prompted as much by social as by geographical isolation from the horrors of life among the London poor. The pleasures of life in the country among "men to middle fortune born" are fittingly expressed by the mythological artificiality of "breathless glades, cheer'd by shy Dian's horn," with its glance at the sports of country gentlemen, and this fragile if "heavenly solitude" is easily broken by the rough intruders of the etchings with their reminder of the depravity to which man is incident.

To George Cruikshank is one of nine sonnets which succeeded *The Sick King* in the volume of 1849. The sonnets are all concerned with the nature of man as it expresses itself in a social or moral sense and in a capacity for nobility, heroism, evil, success and defeat. Many insist upon a common humanity whose essential nobility can be obscured but not eradicated by the theologian who uses a faculty psychology to disintegrate the moral and spiritual conscience which constitutes that nobility (*Written in Butler's Sermons*), or by a mistaken attempt to find in natural phenomena evidence of the conscience informing man (*In Harmony with Nature* and *Religious Isolation*). In *To George Cruikshank* the fact of crime and vice demonstrates that "the nobleness of man / May be by man effaced," but this surface obliteration is of the potential nobility of individual man, not the fundamental nobility of mankind. Nonetheless, such individual effacement is so overwhelmingly common as to cover all men with a "network" of "selfish occupation—plot and plan, / Lust, avarice, envy." This net is so strongly repressive as to be like "high / Uno'erleap'd Mountains of Necessity," whose existence marks the idealistic impracticality of republican attempts to bring about a millennium of universal social justice, even though republican sympathy for "the armies of the homeless and unfed" is nothing but laudable, particularly when set beside the moral myopia of what appears to be the aristocratic sentimentalism of a Shaftesbury, ethics, perhaps, easily practiced by country gentlemen of middle fortune but inevitably choked in "the rank life of towns" (*To a Republican Friend,* the same *Continued,* and *To George Cruikshank*). The distinction running throughout these sonnets between the nobility of man's essential nature and the viciousness of tendencies which overlie it is not a very winning alternative to faculty psychology. But it is conventional nineteenth-century humanitarianism, and Arnold may have been encouraged in it by the sort of speculation informing three sonnets that consider the full heroic realization of man's potential nobility. *Written in Emerson's Essays,* indeed, might as well have been written in Carlyle's lectures on heroes. The assertion that "the seeds of god-like power are in us still; / Gods are we, bards, saints, heroes, if we will," is exemplified in the sonnet *To the Duke of Wellington,* which presents the hero as warrior-statesman, possessed, as it were, of a Machiavellian *virtù* but scorning the attendant *fortuna* in his splendid contribution to history. The celebrated sonnet on Shakespeare, easily the best of this group of nine, presents the hero as poet, as Professor Allott recognizes in his annotation of the poem with quotations from Carlyle.[30]

Shakespeare is the best of these sonnets partly because it is the only one which sustains syntactical clarity and felicity of diction and partly because it finds a fully appropriate, consistent, and suggestive landscape metaphor to express its idea of heroic achievement. The mountain is an appropriate metaphor for the man because it expresses both the extraordinary clarity of vision at its summit and the painful half-knowledge of ordinary men at its base. The only other sonnet which successfully handles its landscape metaphor is *To George Cruikshank,* but the metaphor is much simpler and less

[30] Allott, p. 50.

suggestive than that of *Shakespeare,* and the sestet in any case exhibits that syntax cramped to near obscurity which is common in many of these sonnets. The remainder generally fail both syntactically and metaphorically. In the latter respect they fail by seeking, as it were, metaphors for metaphors, or by juxtaposing separate landscape metaphors which are topographically inconsistent. *To the Duke of Wellington* has wheels of life which are first wagon wheels moved by the ordinary laborers in the field and then, apparently, mill wheels turned by the stream of heroic purpose, a stream, moreover, which is somehow increased by hedonists "spinning sand." The water of streams in turn suggests the wide ocean of history in crossing which the hero follows "one clue," like Theseus in the labyrinth. *Written in Butler's Sermons* is a dizzying sequence of metaphors and similes for the nobility of common humanity which is enthroned somewhere down there but expresses itself as an archipelago linked by submerged reefs or the summits of a mountain range linked by "aërial arches." This sort of confusion is avoided by *In Harmony with Nature,* which banishes all but the most insignificant metaphor. The result is a set of declarative verses quite without moment as a poem.

Arnold's imagination accommodated itself best to a literal landscape he had seen or read about, whose metaphoric relevance to thoughts or actions occurring in it he could release in the course of its detailed description. Metaphor or simile proper is usually most successful in his poems when it coincides with literal landscape and, by alluding to it, helps release the landscape's own potential, as the Vizier's comment that it is a heavy plague to be denied the fruit of one's own labor intensifies the suggestion of spiritual and social malaise in the physical plague of Bokhara. Arnold's general failure in the sonnet is perhaps a consequence of trying to force into a constricted form an expansive talent which needed room to develop symbolic suggestion out of literal description. It must be admitted, however, that he was also capable in his expansive poems of neglecting the principle of Thomson's hornet and of so elaborating description as to repress instead of release symbolic potential.

vi

It is just this over-elaboration of descriptive detail which helps make a "mumble" of *The New Sirens,* one of four poems in the

1849 volume which present the saddening inadequacy or vulnerability of the emotional life. In his struggle to find a situation and
landscape to convey his attitude to sexual passion and pleasure and
the reasons for rejecting it, Arnold makes his poem too long. As a
consequence, the significance of the setting—the tree-surrounded
palace of the New Sirens in a valley—and the significance of the
diurnal round—the transition from night to dawn to afternoon—
become blurred by undue repetition. Explication, by piecing
together and making coherent the diffused significances, unduly
tidies the poem in the high academic way. But *The New Sirens* is
sufficiently interesting to excuse the consequent blurring of value
judgment, and Arnold has already led the way with a commentary
which clarifies some obscurities by omitting part of the poem's
import.[31]

The form of the poem is a monologue in which a poet (the singer
of line 6, the laureled one of line 31) apostrophizes the New
Sirens in a catechism on the validity of the life of the heart and the
senses which they lead in opposition to the life of the mind and the
soul. Like the Strayed Reveller, the poet has come down from the
clear mountain tops, lured down by sounds of the New Sirens'
pleasure. Just as the youth in *The Strayed Reveller* strayed from
his purposed worshiping of Iacchus, so, much more fully and explicitly, this member of a band of poets has wandered from the
springs of knowledge in high places and his sight of the morning
star (ll. 33–37). He is an exile from knowledge, from wisdom (l.
75), from opinion, judgment, conviction (ll. 81–82). The palace of
the New Sirens is set, like Circe's, in a valley, cut off from the inspiration of the heavens which may be scanned from summits (ll.
139–46) and hard by a grove of cedars where silence falls stifling
"the climbing soul" (l. 72).

The sirens of antiquity were fierce, beautiful, and uncomplicated,
luring men from their path in life to a swift, exquisite death (ll.
9–24, 49–56). These romantic New Sirens also distract from the true
path, the life of mind and soul, but, instead of killing, leave a sad
ennui after the rapture, an emotional hangover after a night of joy.
The sirens of old inhabited the shore line and beckoned men to
emotional shipwreck. The New Sirens substitute for such finality

[31] For Arnold's commentary see Allott, pp. 34–35; *Commentary,* pp. 47–49; or
Clough Letters, pp. 105–7.

the slow setting of the tide (l. 220), a "flux of guesses— / Mad delight, and frozen calms" (ll. 195–96). Their reliance on the wisdom of heart rather than head (ll. 77–83) is inadequate because man cannot live all the time in his emotions, and in the unavoidable intervals between joy he cannot escape dissatisfied ennui because he is sustained by no continuous purpose in life (ll. 115–30). In antiquity these embodiments of sexual love were only an occasional if killing distraction from the active life of "those Kings with treasure steering / From the jewell'd lands of dawn" (ll. 21–22). Their revels were lonely (l. 20), for there were few passers-by, and it was always possible for a Ulysses to withstand their charms (l. 44). With the passing of antique sensuality, the prompters of love moved inland to join the poets on mountain tops in a watch for "purer fire" (l. 140). Whether or not the fire was that of a Platonic idealism (the most likely historical gloss), love wearied in the quest for exalted expression, the solitary "life of the spirit" in which the poet persevered, and descended into the valley to practice "the vehement emotional life of passion."[32] In this romantically enervating middle ground,[33] their attractions are felt equally by the lone poetic seekers they have left in high places and the "troops, with gold and gifts" (l. 23) from "the seats of men" (l. 150).

It is in their inevitable intervals of lassitude between the moments of "mad delight" that their way of life is most vulnerable to reproach. For the bright morning star visible to the poets (l. 36) and the watch for "purer fire" (l. 140) they have substituted "some transient earthly sun" which brings only a "turbid inspiration" (ll. 151–52) instead of the true inspiration of heavenly light. To illuminate their nightly revel, they set "broad lamps" to "flash the brightness / Which the sorrow-stricken day denies (ll. 177–78). But these lamps cast upon the circumambient gloom only "a broken gleaming" (ll. 179–86), and palely reveal their artificiality in the cold, and to the Sirens, "unlovely dawning" (ll. 263–65). Romantic, emotional love is thus as ineffectual as the hedonism Mycerinus sought by the Nile. Mycerinus denied the heavenly light of a refulgent Platonic ideal; his life was a blotting out of the star, and his poor substitute, lamps in the shadowy groves. Just as Mycerinus in his hedonism was per-

---

[32] *Commentary*, p. 48.
[33] I borrow the phrase "middle ground" from John M. Wallace, "Landscape and 'The General Law': The Poetry of Matthew Arnold," *Boston University Studies in English*, V (1961), 91–106. For Wallace the "middle ground" of the glade is Arnold's "ideal landscape," principally because it permits a valuable detachment.

haps upbraided by thoughts of sustaining self-knowledge, a recollection of his past life, so in the intervals of joy it may be that the New Sirens recall their past spiritual life, still perhaps not completely lost in the life of the senses (ll. 135–40). It is at least unlikely that they successfully devote the intervals of lassitude to reliving in the memory the pleasures of the night; the poet's catechism evidently requires a negative answer here:

Is the pleasure that is tasted
Patient of a long review?
Will the fire joy hath wasted,
Mused on, warm the heart anew?   (ll. 131–34)

The poet's succeeding speculation on the possibility of recalling a past spiritual life is to be answered, it seems, like the analogous speculation on the thoughts of Mycerinus in the grove, with a "probably not, but it ought to be so."

The New Sirens was originally subtitled "A Palinode," but it is not clear which previous poetic statement it is supposed to retract. The authors of the *Commentary*, noting that in 1849 the poem was preceded by *A Modern Sappho,* imply that this is the work containing the rejected thesis.[34] It is true that the poems make a superficially neat emotional antithesis. The woman's view is succeeded by a man's; assertions of inevitable transience are preceded by assertions of constancy in the face of infidelity. There is the parallelism of titles: the Sirens are new because they replace fierce, final sensuality with lingering emotionalism; the Sappho is modern, presumably because she substitutes for the ecstasies of fulfilled love the not less deranging pains of rejected love. *A Modern Sappho* reads, in fact, rather like the vain endeavors of a Marianne Dashwood to convince herself when spurned by Willoughby that she is her sister Elinor and he is Colonel Brandon. But that it is a vain endeavor

---

[34] *Commentary*, p. 46. I agree with Warren D. Anderson, *Matthew Arnold and the Classical Tradition* (Ann Arbor, 1965), pp. 27, 29, in finding *The Strayed Reveller* to be a "companion piece" of *The New Sirens,* at least in the context of the 1849 volume. The poem was not reprinted until December, 1876, when it appeared separately in *Macmillan's Magazine* with the original title and subtitle and a prefatory note by Arnold which ran, in part, "to a work of his youth, a work produced in long-past days of ardour and emotion, an author can never be very hard-hearted" (*Works,* XV, 355 *n.*). When the poem appeared in Arnold's collected works from 1877 on, the subtitle was dropped. Allott, p. 33, says that the subtitle "implies that the poem is a recantation of what A. once believed in common with the new sirens." Allott's explanation would seem to be true of the 1876 reprint, where "A Palinode" could only refer to the prefatory note.

is evidenced by the insistent, throbbing anapaests, the feminine rhymes, the quivering heart and burning head, and the final awareness that her asseverations of constancy are unlikely to command her for long. Far from retracting, *The New Sirens* merely reiterates more diffusely and with a wider speculative range the distracting torments of the emotional life exemplified in *A Modern Sappho.*

If we look instead to the association of landscape features with ways of life and states of mind, a more likely referent of "palinode" is the title poem in 1849. The poetic revel of *The Strayed Reveller* is presented, I have argued, without the qualification of evaluative commentary. The poem presents the conditions of creativity. It does not glory in them, nor, in itself, does it condemn their apparent involvement in Keatsian emotionalism or their contingent suspension of the good active life. The reproving gloss supplied by the ineffectually escapist revels of Mycerinus or the King of Bokhara loses its relevance by the noncommittal presentation of *The Strayed Reveller* itself and by their own lack of concern with the ingredients of poetic life and creativity. But *The New Sirens* is concerned with this life. The topography of the two poems is almost identical, but *The New Sirens* annotates the landscape with a moral explicitness lacking in *The Strayed Reveller.* The visionary intensity imbibed from Circe's cup makes a poet of the youth; the speaker of *The New Sirens* was already a poet by virtue of the elevated solitude which the Strayed Reveller left behind. Like the New Sirens themselves, the lured poet is in danger of losing contact with the springs of knowledge and visions of heavenly truth, which are presumably the conditions of true creativity, by imbibing a transient emotional intensity from the "love-potions" offered by the Sirens (l. 87). The Strayed Reveller finds a muse in his middle ground; the poet finds love goddesses whose activities are frowned upon by the muse of "upland valleys" (ll. 25–26). The relationship of *The New Sirens* to *The Strayed Reveller* is exactly that of palinode, but, unlike, say, that of *Troilus and Criseyde,* the palinode is wholly external. The fact of rejection or retraction lies between the two poems; we are not justified in moving it into *The Strayed Reveller,* nor, despite the sub-title's invitation, are we justified in moving it into *The New Sirens.* The only way a poet can properly retract an achieved poem is to destroy it before publication or extensively rewrite it, and the latter recourse still leaves the original beyond his jurisdiction.

vii

At one point in his reproving catechism of the New Sirens the poet finds himself uneasy about the neatness of his moral categories and their sharply distinguished landscape correlatives. He begs the Sirens to prove him wrong, for their attractions are such that he would believe them if he could:

> Would you freeze my too loud boldness,
> Dumbly smiling as you go,
> One faint frown of distant coldness
> Flitting fast across each marble brow?
>
> Do I brighten at your sorrow,
> O sweet Pleaders?—doth my lot
> Find assurance in to-morrow
> Of one joy, which you have not?
> O, speak once, and shame my sadness!
> Let this sobbing, Phrygian strain,
> Mock'd and baffled by your gladness,
> Mar the music of your feasts in vain! (ll. 159–70)

The poet of *The New Sirens* puts the temptation behind him, stiffening himself by recalling the permanence of truth on the mountain top and the transience of joy and beauty. It remains for the Forsaken Merman to put part of the case for the Sirens, although he too chooses a "sobbing Phrygian strain" for the purpose.

Of all his later classifications by genre, the most baffling is Arnold's inclusion of *The Forsaken Merman* in the group of narrative poems. The classification is so indefensible that the authors of the *Commentary* may well be right to speculate that Arnold's motive was a desire to eke out an otherwise sparse group. There is certainly narrative content in the poem, but its mode is plainly that of monologue, a Victorian version of the old complaint. What matters is the consequence of the mode for critical interpretation. The counterpoint of views in *The Sick King* allows for moral implication in the opposition of views: disagreement must be argued down. The third-person narrative which succeeds monologue in *Mycerinus* permits the interleaving of moral hypothesis as comment upon the life and decisions of the king. But *The Forsaken Merman* is noncommittal in a way reminiscent of *The Strayed Reveller,* where the youth's account of things passes unchallenged by the other speakers. Everything is from the Merman's point of view; even the description of Margaret's wistful nostalgia for the life she has left in the sea caves is his speculation (ll. 96–107). Since the Merman is neither manifestly perverse nor indubitably the sole repository of truth, the poem is peculiarly susceptible to misreading in terms of a critic's moral preferences. W. Stacy Johnson, for example, may be wrong to see Margaret's recall to the land by the Easter bell as a symbolic resurrection from natural to moral life.[35] He may, as Howard W. Fulweiler argues,[36] be presenting "Easter from the point of view of Margaret" and a Christianity assumed to be valid, instead of, as the poem gives it, "from the point of view of the depths" and an alien, unchristian creature to whom religious observance is only one of the major causes of his wife's desertion. But Professor Johnson's reading, if wrong, constitutes a minor misplacement of emphasis beside Mr. Fulweiler's uncompromising imposition of value categories upon the poem. For Mr. Fulweiler the land life is monotonous, repressive, and death regarding; the sea life is the abode of love and imagination, it is life enhancing and revelatory of "the fundamental mysteries of the universe." For Margaret, we learn, "Easter is not a symbolic resurrection from death to life; it is, as she implies to the merman, only a legal observance to save herself. . . . She is reborn not into life, but into spiritual death." What Margaret actually says is

> 'I must go, for my kinsfolk pray
> In the little grey church on the shore to-day.
> 'Twill be Easter-time in the world—ah me!
> And I lose my poor soul, Merman! here with thee.'   (ll. 56–59)

It is the Merman, and not Margaret, who assumes that what is involved is a mere legal observance, a prudent laying-up of credit for an after-life by occasional donations of time:

> 'Go up, dear heart, through the waves;
> Say thy prayer, and come back to the kind sea-caves!' (ll. 60–61)

Whether or not Margaret is wrong in her hopes from devotion, and the poem does not say, the Merman, as befits an alien creature, evi-

[35] W. Stacy Johnson, *The Voices of Matthew Arnold* (New Haven, 1961), pp. 84–89.
[36] Howard W. Fulweiler, "Matthew Arnold: The Metamorphosis of a Merman," *Victorian Poetry*, I (1963), 208–22; especially pp. 211–12.

dently fails to understand what it involves. As for Margaret's "spiritual death," even the Merman credits her with a simple contented joy as well as intermittent sad nostalgia (ll. 87–95).

Mr. Fulweiler praises "Arnold's skillful employment of present participles" to increase "the effect of incessant and mechanical activity." There is "constant movement" in the town, "a monotonous and colorless whirring, whizzing, humming, murmuring, and praying behind walls." We must not assume that this participial sequence actually occurs in the poem. Margaret has a whizzing spinning wheel and there is humming, surely cheerful, throughout the town. Nothing whirs, and the "murmur of folk at their prayers" is not participial (l. 72). Mr. Fulweiler also suppresses some inconvenient participles which do occur: most notably, the Merman's description of Margaret "singing most joyfully" as she spins. The "constant movement," the "incessant and mechanical activity" of the town comes to a stop when Margaret drops the spindle and the "wheel stands still" while she gazes nostalgically out to sea. It will also be stopped during the Merman's midnight trip to gaze at "the white, sleeping town" (l. 137) —yet another participle. There are good grounds, in fact, for locating the incessant activity in the depths, with their beasts that feed, snakes that "coil and twine" and their "great whales" who come "sailing [participially] by,"

Sail and sail, with unshut eye
Round the world for ever and aye.   (ll. 40–45)

The town may sleep, but among the creatures of the depths, the whales at least do not. If Arnold had really intended to use participles to suggest monotony and mechanical activity, one can only say that he sadly botched his business.

Mr. Fulweiler properly points out that a part of the underwater scene is conveyed in terms of color, named or implied: "a red gold throne" (l. 51), "a ceiling of amber, / A pavement of pearl" (ll. 118–19), while the town is limited to gray and white. Another difference is that the town is illuminated by "the blessed light of the sun" (l. 93) and the "clear . . . moonlight" (l. 126) while the sea cave is a place "where the spent lights quiver and gleam" (l. 37). The light above and the half-light below correspond, of course, to the reiterated vertical movement of the poem, the constant down and up. This correspondence recalls those other poems in 1849 which employ vertical movement, especially downward, in combination with light and half light. The Strayed Reveller goes from the "white dawn" of the high ground "down the dark valley" (ll. 24, 42). Mycerinus, it is true, accompanies his exchange of heavenly for artificial light with horizontal movement into the groves, but the placing of the King beneath palms whose tops know the sun brings before us the dropping of his eyes from high refulgence to the gloom of the "grove's centre" (l. 124). Most obvious is the poet's descent into the artificially lit palace of the New Sirens. The poet, moreover, salutes the Sirens as "lodgers in the forest and the cave" (l. 234), and it does seem that the Merman's underwater cave is another version of the New Sirens' palace, although quite without the explicit moral values of the palace.

The consonance of the two poems is further strengthened by the alien nature of their titular characters, and the amphibious Merman finds a counterpart in the antique sirens, before they moved inland:

> Who are they, O pensive Graces,
> —For I dream'd they wore your forms—
> Who on shores and sea-wash'd places
> Scoop the shelves and fret the storms?
> Who, when ships are that way tending,
> Troop across the flushing sands,
> To all reefs and narrows wending,
> With blown tresses, and with beckoning hands?
>
> Yet I see, the howling levels
> Of the deep are not your lair;
> And your tragic-vaunted revels
> Are less lonely than they were.   (ll. 9–20)

The Merman, in fact, joins the sad lassitude of the New Sirens to the haunts and the loneliness of the old. Like the New Sirens, he comes to the sad, regretful nostalgia that waits upon the inevitable end of the intense and dreamlike beauty of love in deep caverns "where the winds are all asleep" (l. 36). The diurnal round of the Sirens was evidently symbolic of the longer period required for the waning of beauty and love (ll. 207–26), a period literally represented by the time required for Margaret to bear the Merman's children beneath the waves. The poet asks the Sirens whether,

> when change itself is over,
> When the slow tide sets one way,
> Shall you find the radiant lover,
> Even by moments, of to-day?
> The eye wanders, faith is failing—
> O, loose hands, and let it be!
> Proudly, like a king bewailing,
> O, let fall one tear, and set us free!   (ll. 219–226)

Margaret also sighed, her eye wandered upward, and she asked for her freedom. When the Merman finds it permanent, he can but lament that "alone dwell for ever / The kings of the sea" (ll. 122–23). The Sirens bring down a lone watcher from the mountains, but they also turn their eyes to "the seats of men," whence are presumably drawn many of the "troops" that throng their "enchanted lawn" (ll. 23–24). The Merman's attention is all upon the town; there is no truth-seeking, but only the unresolvable antinomy of private love and a public life of work and communal worship.[37] Neither private love nor public life is bad, except in a failure to be permanent or permanently absorbing which leaves intervals for regretting what has been lost or surrendered, or perhaps never achieved. *The Forsaken Merman* records neither spiritual death nor moral resurrection, but only the sad inevitability of things.

viii

What is inevitable is the transience of joy. Intense feelings, whether of love or hedonist indulgence, must pass because they are feelings. They seem to offer the only relief from pain, but in fact intensify it by their nagging reminder of what was but cannot always be. There is no sustaining memory of joy in the midst of pain, for Arnoldian memory is the sad nostalgia of the Merman or Margaret, the sobering interruption of pleasure by a recollection of duty, mortality, or the burdens of man, or merely the decaying sense of Hobbes. The pleasure tasted by the Sirens at night is impatient of memorial review by day (ll. 131–34). In a poem eventually called *A Memory-Picture*, the speaker's endeavor to fix a "clear impression" of his mistress in his mind leaves him only the doubtful

[37] For Johnson, neither the "natural world" of the sea and love, nor the human and moral world of the town with its "work and worship" is an alternative "complete in itself," *The Voices of Matthew Arnold*, pp. 84, 88–89.

"prize" of a "dim remembrance" (ll. 57–62). Remembrance of things past is as transient, as lacking in fixity, as the things themselves. Both *The Voice* and *A Question* (called in 1849 only by its later subtitle, *To Fausta*) pile up images and statements of transience, many of them, especially in *The Voice,* similes from landscapes which in the narrative and quasi-dramatic poems form an objective correlative for emotions, states of mind, points of view, or ways of life. These tropes for transience include, in the opening stanza of *The Voice,* moonlight glancing on

> the sleepless waters
> Of a lonely mere,
> On the wild whirling waves, mournfully, mournfully.   (ll. 5–7)

It may be that the obscurity of *The Hayswater Boat* shrouds an idea of the pigmy throng as fairies bringing their traditional gift of delusive because only temporarily sustaining dreams. The humanized boat is left rocking aimlessly in the emotional waters of life because it had allowed itself to be manned—or mastered—by the vain hopes of whatever it was Arnold associated with the four landscape features.

Descent into the half-light of transience has, in *The New Sirens,* a counterpart in the suggested ascent to the full light of truth. But just as the poet half hopes his moral dismissal of the Sirens will be satisfactorily rebutted, so, later in the 1849 volume, we find it by no means certain that the springs of knowledge are near summits. Mycerinus may have been right to reject his own idealism: the poem is noncommittal; and *In Utrumque Paratus* poises the universe instinct with divine purpose, which Mycerinus rejected, against the Lucretian world of chance, which he half accepted. The impossibility of choosing definitively between the alternatives is conveyed in *In Utrumque Paratus* by their expression in terms of the same metaphorical landscape and the same physical relationship of man to that landscape. Man cannot know whether there is a divine first cause operating through the second causes of phenomena, or whether there is nothing beyond the phenomena themselves. But both hypotheses result in his isolation. Consciousness of divine purpose, to be meaningful, involves the individual decoction of its purity from the colorful distraction of manifold human life. It involves an ascetic ascent in "lonely pureness" to the springs of purity on mountain tops, gradually leaving behind "the pleasant human noises." The success of such an ascent is at best equivocal, for the summits are known only to the enigmatic stars and moon. If the materialist hypothesis is correct—and man cannot know—isolation still results. Contemplation of its probablity must lead man to sharp consciousness of his separateness from inanimate nature, which is unable to contemplate; and man is once again enthroned on lonely high places. But if the materialist hypothesis really is correct, then everything, including man, comes, by chance, from the same enigmatic matter: animate and inanimate are brothers, born of the obscure earth. We should rest poised between the alternatives because neither suggests a way of life that is indubitably meaningful, and because neither can be shown indubitably correct. The only certain consequence of such metaphysical speculation is to enforce an awareness of isolation, a leaving behind the pleasant human noises, a suppression of yearning for kinship with nature. The coexistence of the alternatives effectively cancels whatever there may be of value in either, and as effectively leaves the unpleasurable isolation of both. Well may the later Arnold have looked with assured scorn upon the metaphysics that led his youth astray:

At the mention of that name *metaphysics*, lo, essence, existence, substance, finite and infinite, cause and succession, something and nothing, begin to weave their eternal dance before us! with the confused murmur of their combinations filling all the region governed by *her*.[38]

But in 1849 he was still young and still hopeful that some fixity of purpose, some assurance might be found in metaphysics or in the existence of a God whose undoubted transcendence need not also imply a Lucretian negligence. Such at least is the hope of the litany Arnold finally called *Stagirius*, an unremarkable piece whose chief interest lies in it summary enumeration of almost every pessimistic topic in the 1849 volume, from uncertain faith and love to the transience of joy and the impotence of tears. The sole optimistic entry in this dispiriting ledger is hope that God will reveal his erstwhile strength and save man from the consequence of his own inadequacy. But, once again, the attempted ascent out of the false dreams of life brings no certainty of amelioration, for "the soul, mounting higher, / To God comes no nigher" because it is accompanied by

[38] *God and the Bible,* in *Works,* VIII, 55.

a humanist pride. This cry from the depths succeeds principally in charting the depths.

If appeals to God are of uncertain efficacy, no more is work a sure anodyne: the spindle drops from Margaret's hand and the strenuous justice of Mycerinus falters before the blank indifference of things. Most of the world rushes busily about, and the task of the Arnoldian poet is to lament its frenetic inattention to the sadness of transience and isolation. One attempt to define this poetic role is *The World and the Quietist,* an unsatisfactory piece because its solemnity of tone sorts ill with the essential frivolity of its argument: the poet's "mournful rhymes" have a useful social function because, by reproving the general hurry, they permit a view of the hurry from without and thus a fuller appreciation of what it achieves. The poem was addressed *To Critias,* probably Clough,[39] for it has the same combination of flippancy and seriousness as can be seen in the early letters to Clough.

A much better, but not entirely successful poem is *To a Gipsy Child by the Sea-Shore.* The poem is Wordsworthian in its attribution of ideas and emotions to someone encountered by chance who is not allowed or not able to speak for himself. In Wordsworth the consequence of imaginative reading into another person is that the person becomes drawn transfigured into the poet's own life and consciousness. The initial separateness of poet and stranger disappears in the course of the imaginative act: the reaper that we are exhorted to behold "single in the field" becomes by the end of the poem only her music carried off in the poet's heart. In Arnold, the Child begins and ends separate from the speaker, always an addressed second person, another example and thus an objectification of the speaker's own sadness. The Child's "gloom" and "meditative guise" (ll. 2–3) lead the poet, in attempting to explain them, to adduce instances of grief that have known motives. Despite the moving felicity of much of the poem's diction (the last two lines are among the finest that Arnold wrote) the poem fails in two ways. The fact of the Gipsy Child and its probable life is kept before us and thus renders half-incongruous the Child's association with "stoic souls" or disillusioned kings. In addition, little or nothing comes of the titular promise of a specific landscape, and we get instead a succession of brief, disparate landscapes and situations whose order is far from inevitable. The Child is too evidently the

[39] Allott, p. 100; *Commentary,* p. 56.

vehicle of a meditation, and a vehicle which does not comfortably carry all the thought it is asked to carry. The poem does stand, however, with *The World and the Quietist,* as an attempt to find something of value in the ability to perceive the sadness and pain recorded in many of the 1849 poems. As such they are preludes to the last and finest poem in 1849, *Resignation.*

ix

"It is more important," say the authors of the *Commentary,* "to remember the beauty" of *Resignation* "than its 'philosophy.' " That beauty they locate in "the description of natural scenery," and find in the poet's tearful view of the shepherd at dawn (ll. 170–90) a clear presage of *The Scholar-Gipsy.*[40] The poem's "philosophy" of detachment, of withdrawal from quotidian bustle in order to see, what those who continue to bustle cannot see, that men are but born, endure and struggle awhile, and then die, is identified by annotating the poem with references to Lucretius, Marcus Aurelius, Goethe, Senancour, or the *Bhagavad Gita.* But an appreciation of the poem's true beauty does not permit a choice between scenic description and philosophy; it insists instead that we attend to their mutual dependence and thus win through to a sense of the poem's integrity, within which both descriptive beauty and the memorable phrasing of philosophy can securely contribute their local felicities.

More clearly than any other piece in 1849, more perhaps than any other long poem by Arnold, *Resignation* confronts the aesthetic problem which countless didactic-descriptive poems of the eighteenth century failed to solve. This consonance results not only from the provision of landscape setting for meditations with little or no narrative content, for *Resignation* belongs, ultimately, to the revisitation species of the loco-descriptive genre. Among its antecedents are Gray's *Eton College,* Goldsmith's *Deserted Village,* Warton's Lodon sonnet, and Wordsworth's *Tintern Abbey*; one of its successors was to be Arnold's own *Thyrsis.* Revisitation, in its account of change in the scene, the observer, or both, makes for a kind of narrative content which loco-descriptive poems otherwise sought in the historical associations of places. But unlike its antecedents, *Resignation* is concerned with continuity, not change: both scene and observer are the same (ll. 106–7).

[40] *Commentary,* pp. 67–68.

On that sameness the whole poem is based. *Resignation* is not, like *Tintern Abbey*, a poem of development; it reads in some respects like the static exposition of a predetermined position in the manner of Thomson's *Seasons*. But this static quality, which in itself raises questions about why things occur in the order they do, is combined with and modified by the strong forward movement of the poem whose most obvious manifestation is the large space given to accounts of journeys and goals. This physical motion has a counterpart in the appearance of discovery which overlies the static exposition. The second hike of the speaker and Fausta must proceed far enough for it to be clear that it exactly repeats the first hike before the exposition proper can begin, before, that is, the lesson of the hikes is fully evident. The exposition, moreover, like the second hike, takes place in the present, and the resultant sense of an immediate experience taking place as we read through the poem further mitigates the feeling that the philosophy is predetermined. With the hikers seated in an "upland glen" (l. 99) and with the introduction of images and descriptions of a motionless observer, the poem's evolution is maintained, partly by incidentally recalling the physical progress of the early sections, but principally by making the final exposition an attempt to persuade the sceptical Fausta.

Resignation may be satisfactorily sectionalized in various ways, but the clearest indication of its structure comes from a simple tripartite division. The first section, ending at line 107, is given up to the description of journeys: the two hikes and the opening account of four groups of representative travelers; it ends with the walkers seated on high ground affording an extensive view, but principally of the town below. The second section (ll. 108–98) is the speaker's first application of the lessons of travel to the lives of gipsies and poets; it is descriptively dominated by the tableaux of the gipsy encampment and the poet's observation of the shepherd at dawn. The third section begins with Fausta's objection that the approved life of poets is both irrelevant to most men because beyond them and in any case involves a kind of escapism from actuality which leaves the poet stored with surface images and scenes but lacking in full appreciation of their significance. The speaker replies by first defending the reality of poetic insight and then insisting that, with modifications, it is relevant to those who are not poets, because they can learn from it the common humanity too often obscured by "individual strife" (l. 251). They can learn, in fact, just the lesson that was sought from nature in the opening sonnet of the 1849 volume. The speaker has already learned it and Fausta may too, even "though fate grudge to thee and me / The poet's rapt security" (ll. 245–46), even though, that is, they are not themselves poets. *Resignation* is too often taken as a poet's manifesto, whereas it is more properly seen as the manifesto of Arnold the man.

This division of the poem draws attention to the enclosure of the largely static middle section by an opening section of physical movement and a closing section of rhetorical movement, of arguing a case in a manner reminiscent of a neoclassical epistle. The poem's total evolution is assured by the occurrence in all three sections of the same descriptive motifs and discursive topics. What in one place is described literally and expansively appears elsewhere as brief metaphor or example: the hikers' pause just below the crest near the rise of a stream leading the way down is a suitable place to meditate upon the way in which

> each moment in its race,
> Crowd as we will its neutral space,
> Is but a quiet watershed
> Whence, equally, the seas of life and death are fed.   (ll. 257–60)

The tripartite division also focuses the one weakness of moment in the poem. *Resignation* is evidently a made thing, shaped—composed, Arnold would say—but a major ingredient in that composition is the note of unpremeditated discovery contributed by the present tenses, the suggestion of physical and intellectual activity taking place as we read. The suggestion is crucial for the poem's philosophy, its rejection of living for the future because it involves neglect of both past and present. Living properly and fully in the present means seeing life as "a placid and continuous whole" (l. 190); it means enriching present experience with the known past instead of impoverishing it by concentrating on the unknown future. Therefore, the description of the first hike is temporally placed by past tenses at the beginning and end, but is conveyed in between by what is technically a historical present which emphasizes the second hike's quality of *déjà vu* and dissolves the temporal distinction between the two occasions. The poem, we can say, must convey the sense of immediate experience because it is about the value of fully appreciating immediate experience. But the poem's aspiration to become the paradigm of its own meaning is checked by the evident disposition of the experience for the maximum philosophical effect. The check is principally administered by the opening description of other travelers and the discussion of their inadequate view of life (ll. 1–39). More than anything else, this prelude works against the naturalness of the succeeding account of walks and the reflections they prompt: as if Arnold stayed Fausta at Wythburn to discourse of Mohammedan pilgrims, crusaders, Goths and Huns before allowing her to proceed with the walk. Clearly the poem needs this prelude, and there is no other place in which it would fit. Most importantly, it alerts us to the values implicit in the account of the walks. Without it, *Resignation* would appear as double-gaited as the eighteenth-century poems discussed by Professor Wasserman, with their section of "description" followed by a section of "significance." On the one hand, then, there is the natural-seeming "improvisation" of the bulk of the poem, reminiscent among other things of Coleridge's conversation pieces, and on the other there is the studied effect of the prelude, necessary for a full understanding of the significance of the walk. It is as if Arnold failed properly to harmonize the two aesthetic principles he urged upon Clough in the same letter: the absolute propriety of form which makes for naturalness and the grouping of objects which he later expressed as "composition, in the painter's sense."

The chief value of the prelude is that it uses travel in its ancient association with the *via vitae* to represent a manner of living. We thus come prepared to see otherwise unperceivable implications in the description of the two hikes. All four groups bound upon religious and martial exploits are "too imperious" travelers and, like Fausta, are "time's chafing prisoner" because the passage of time is of significance only as it brings them closer to some future goal. They ignore the sweetness and misuse the light offered by "every laughing Hour" (ll. 30–36) because their restless onward drive makes them impatient of retracing any of their steps. The true pleasure of the hours inheres in just this retracing, for the eschewal of distant goals brings the patience needed to attend minutely to the occurrences of the present and thus enrich them. Thus it is that the topography of the walks is given in detail: it must be, for the walks exemplify, in contrast to the restless travelers, the kind of life which has leisure to enjoy detail. The eye on the object is a way of life and hence morally significant. It is true that so generalized a significance contains no criterion for selecting one detail rather than another: the ghost of Thomson's hornet still flies, skimming, perhaps, like Arnold's red grouse, "the shining ground" (ll. 70–71), but it is no longer hostile. The details of sensory life are fully appropriate to reflective life, because reflection consists in attending to the simple lesson that things endure. The philosophical conclusion of the poem follows exactly from the quality of life implied by the description of the walks:

Yet, Fausta, the mute turf we tread,
The solemn hills around us spread,
This stream which falls incessantly,
The strange-scrawl'd rocks, the lonely sky,
If I might lend their life a voice,
Seem to bear rather than rejoice.   (ll. 265–70)

To learn this from nature, unremarkable though it may be, we must first observe in patience. Not only do the walks exemplify a way of life sufficiently patient to respond fully to things of the moment and to accept without fret the repetition of experience, they also contrast with the restless journeyers in not seeking goals which blind to everything but their attainment. Like any planned walk, of course, they aim to reach a certain point, but to do so is not the main purpose of the walk. The purpose is to enjoy the walk in itself, and, by way of aiding that enjoyment, to set intermediate markers: "the valley's western boundary" (l. 47), the disappearance and reappearance of habitation, the town below—the process is too familiar to anyone who has walked in the country to require elaboration.

Such a life as is exemplified by the hikes would be too uninterruptedly idyllic to be practiced consistently by any but the wholly leisured. Accordingly, if summarily, the walkers go on to the town and experience some of the dusty discomforts of travel which were all that the restless voyagers of the prelude knew. But if some parts of the road through life are unavoidably unpleasant, we have available to us the patient renewal of experience which enriches life. The joyful refreshment of washing one's hands in the sea at night recapitulates the refreshment found by upland springs, the satisfaction of a life well if modestly spent: the bathing is a sacramental seal upon such a life.

The hikes exemplify or objectify a way of life which is devoted to more than just walking. The questers of the prelude similarly exemplify a way of life which expresses itself in more ways than the blinding proposal of martial or religious goals. Anyone, like Fausta, impatient of achievement, will experience the pain of "labours, self-ordain'd" (l. 14). The consummation to which they can look forward is not the joy of the sea at night, but the end presaged to the Hun when

> the sun
> Went lurid down o'er flooded plains
> Through which the groaning Danube strains
> To the drear Euxine.   (ll. 10–13)

The painful course of the Danube to the uninviting Black Sea marks for the Hun, if he can see it, the drab death which will close his arduous life. The termination for both the Hun and the hikers by the sea at night has, evidently, the conventional association with death. The fierce pressing on to goals only brings us to death without appreciating life; each moment is a watershed and we may choose to follow either of the streams which lead to life or death. But some there are, many indeed, who lack this choice. "The armies of the homeless and unfed" of *To a Republican Friend* are exemplified in *Resignation* by the gipsies, who are so occupied by the struggle to survive that neither the pursuit of goals nor intervals for patient reflection are available to them. They can do nothing but "rub through" life

> Till death arrive to supersede,
> For them, vicissitude and need.   (ll. 140–43)

It is a Cowperian rejection of hard primitivism as too close to the bread line to allow men an appreciation of living in nature.[41] For such people Arnold does not write, because he cannot. But he is equally unable to forget them. The rank life of towns obtrudes upon glades cheered by Diana's horn, and the pleasurable hike crosses the aimlessly nomadic path of the gipsies.

Resignation is a richly rewarding poem, yielding new felicities on every reading. One of the best ways to appreciate its richness is to follow through a motif, observing its manifestations as particular and generalized landscape feature, as developed and unelaborate metaphor. In this way one focuses upon the metamorphoses of the

---

[41] See, e.g., *The Task*, I, 557–91, where the gipsy life is also treated as harshly unattractive.

Danube into the brook which, a "bright comrade," leads the hikers to the town (ll. 76–77), into the upstreaming tide of the first hiking party (ll. 48, 62), into the implied rivers which feed the seas of life and death, into the fiery flood of thought that a strong ruler rolls through his people (ll. 155–57), into the course of all mankind, the general life (ll. 147, 191). One may focus too upon the motif of habitation: Rome or Mecca, the wayside inn, the upland farm, the town, the gipsy camp, the general life again (l. 252), or the bells of foam whose detachment from "this bank, their home," suggests to Fausta that poets achieve their vision by leaving *the common life of men*," by leaping over the pen (ll. 201–11). One may follow the motif of solitude and companionship, of action and inaction. What such a reading achieves—when it is more than the mere enumeration of occurrences offered above—is a full sense of integrity in the poem, a realization that landscape and occasion are a totally adequate embodiment of meaning. Much of that meaning may be referred to sources in Arnold's reading, but to do only that delivers the poem as a don's reverie in the country. We end not with reminiscences of the *Bhagavad Gita* or Senancour but an enigmatic "something that infects the world." That something, forgotten though it is by the busy activity of Fausta and the travelers of the prelude, is the harshness of the general lot: the "heaving multitude" moved by a strong ruler (l. 157), the transience of love, the unreality of power (l. 236), the pains of gipsy life as the population of the country grows and the law stiffens (ll. 133–35), the toil of the town and the dustiness of the road. *Resignation,* like the 1849 volume as a whole, bids us ask roundly, "what then, is an academic poem?"

Landscape in 1852

IT IS THE GLADE, the beech-surrounded palace of the title poem, which is the dominant landscape feature of *The Strayed Reveller* volume in 1849. The glade recurs in *Mycerinus,* the sonnet to Cruikshank, and *The New Sirens.* It is the upland glen of Resignation; it provides shelter from the battle below in *To a Gipsy Child* (ll. 21–24), and has counterparts in the submarine caverns of *The Forsaken Merman* and the cool palace, desert inns, the mulberry grove and shaded mausoleum of *The Sick King in Bokhara.* In 1852 the glade is the place where Callicles sings his songs to the world-weary philosopher above, where Tristram fails to find solace for his unhappy love and Merlin is imprisoned as a consequence of his ill-advised love, and where, in Kensington Gardens, a peaceful if temporary harmony is obtainable. But merely to point to this recurrence obscures the greater comprehensiveness of landscape in 1852 than 1849: in 1852 not only the glade figures largely, but the sea and shore, plain, town, river and lake, mountains and the empyrean. Features which in 1849 appeared only in one or two poems, often in order to define more clearly the qualities of the glade, occur in 1852 more frequently and as the main place of action or meditation. Then too, the largely unlocalized or exotic landscapes of 1849 are replaced in 1852 by many at least potentially identifiable sites in England and on the Continent: 1852 is more evidently a European volume than 1849. Finally, the almost exclusive use of landscape in 1849 to provide a setting for individual circumstances is extended in 1852 to include landscapes of historical process.

Time in 1849 meant the transience of individual emotion and impression, the diurnal round of *The New Sirens,* Mycerinus' last six years, or Margaret's few if fruitful years beneath the waves. In 1852 poems scan generations: the life of Empedocles from joyful youth with Parmenides to the coming of the Sophists; from the boyhood of Goethe to the death of Senancour; the rise and fall of empires in *Revolutions.* The volume of 1849 ended with *Resignation,* in which the quality of individual life is defined only partly in terms of its final end and only briefly, if importantly, in terms of temporal circumstance: rising population and changing law. 1852 takes us fully into the elegiac mode which is the most appropriate expression of Arnoldian melancholy. Apart from the legends of *The Strayed Reveller* and the *'Antigone'* fragment, only the lawbreaker of Bokhara dies within the poems of 1849; in 1852 the subjects of elegy include Empedocles, Goethe, Senancour, Byron, Wordsworth, Tristram, Iseult of Ireland, and the unnamed woman of *Lines Written by a Death-Bed.* The luckless affair with Marguerite is projected in *A Farewell* into a vision of chaste love hereafter. *Empedocles on Etna* ends not with the philosopher in the crater but the ascent of Apollo Musagetes to an "endless abode." There is frequent communication with the heavens, often as a way of suggesting an existence beyond the one life allotted to individuals, of suggesting a view of man's lot *sub specie aeternitatis.* This reaching for a wider temporal context than that of the 1849 poems is also exemplified by the sense of historical process: the change in individual circumstances effected by changing times. The volume of 1852 accordingly ends with *The Future,* Arnold's fullest landscape representation of the course of history.

i

Empedocles on Etna and Other Poems used sometimes to be discussed as the volume of Marguerite.[1] It contains five of the poems grouped in later editions under the heading of *Switzerland,* although Arnold altered the order and constituents of the group five times between the first arrangement in 1853 and the final in 1877. All but one of the *Switzerland* group identify the woman addressed as Marguerite either in the title or within the poem. Four of the five poems included in the 1852 volume occur in a cluster, although

[1] For a useful summary of earlier views, see Culler, pp. 117-21.

without a group heading and with the insertion between the third and fourth of two quatrains called *Destiny,* never reprinted by Arnold but probably, as Professor Allott notes,[2] a Marguerite poem by virtue of its philosophical generalizations about the torments of love. The displaced fifth poem in 1852, *A Farewell,* is the only one which does not identify the woman, although there are a few details of Swiss scenery in the first two stanzas. The cluster of five poems, including the unreprinted *Destiny,* was followed in 1852 by four poems which have been associated with the Marguerite group, although the case for the second and fourth is not strong: *Human Life, Despondency,* the sonnet later called *Youth's Agitations,* and *Self-Deception.* The cluster of five was preceded in 1852 by six poems, four of which were later included in a group titled *Faded Leaves,* while the other two, *Excuse* and *Indifference* (later called *Urania* and *Euphrosyne*) have been sometimes associated with the Switzerland group, but recently and more convincingly by Professor Allott with *Faded Leaves.* The woman is not identified in the *Faded Leaves* poems, and some commentators have associated her with Marguerite, thus giving in 1852 a group of fifteen poems immediately following *Empedocles on Etna,* which stands first, that have been assigned with varying degrees of probability to the same biographical occasion: Arnold's presumed affair or liaison with a girl he called Marguerite, apparently French, whom he met at the Hotel Bellevue in Thun in September 1848 and September 1849.

These fifteen poems were followed by *Lines Written by a Death-Bed,* commemorating the death of a young woman and prompting the perhaps impertinent recollection that Marguerite in other poems is given a complexion of languid pallor. The piece was never reprinted in its 1852 form: the last twenty-five lines became from 1867 a separate poem, *Youth and Calm,* while the first sixteen were inserted from 1869 into *Tristram and Iseult* as a description of Iseult of Brittany kneeling by the death bed of Tristram. Professors Allott and Bonnerot feel that *Lines Written by a Death-Bed* was part of the first draft for *Tristram and Iseult,*[3] and it is true that only minor alterations were needed when sixteen of its lines were added or restored to *Tristram and Iseult. Tristram and Iseult* followed *Lines Written by a Death-Bed* in 1852, and is associated with the Marguerite episode, partly by the nature of its story, and

[2] Allott, p. 144.
[3] Allott, p. 224.

partly because Arnold in 1852 said he had been first moved to write it by an account of the legend in the *Revue de Paris* which he read a few years before (probably in 1849) while at Thun. Thus, the poem in 1852 which is second only to *Empedocles on Etna* in its length and ambitious scope can be assigned fairly confidently to the occasion which led to the Marguerite poems. After *Tristram and Iseult* in 1852 came the *Memorial Verses* on Wordsworth, *Courage*, and *Self-Dependence*, in which the glances at passionate love are only brief and allusive, although their major preoccupation with means to be calm in time of trouble is certainly appropriate to the distressed lover of Marguerite. Moreover, their preoccupations recur in the next two poems, *A Summer Night* and *The Buried Life*, with an extension in the first into a consideration of the passionate life and in the second, explicitly, into a description of the love between man and woman which Professor Allott has paralleled with the Marguerite poems.[4] In 1852 it was the displaced Marguerite poem, *A Farewell*, which followed *The Buried Life* and appropriately terminated the run of poems dealing, directly or indirectly, with romantic love. The remaining eleven poems concern themselves, like *Empedocles on Etna*, with meditations on the world and human life which are not, except in *Consolation*, associated with the woes of lovers. There were thirty-five poems in the 1852 volume, of which seventeen deal, usually directly, with unfortunate love, and perhaps six more can be associated with it by virtue of shared landscape motifs or moral exhortations. It is because all or most of these poems have been or could be connected in some way with events at Thun in 1848 and 1849 that the volume has been called the volume of Marguerite.

But a more convincing elucidation of the biographical occasions behind the 1852 volume results from following with Professor Allott and the authors of the *Commentary* the Arnold family tradition that the poems later grouped as *Faded Leaves* should be associated, not with Marguerite and Thun in 1848 and 1849, but Arnold's courtship of Frances Lucy Wightman in 1850.[5] To the external evidence of family tradition may be added the internal evidence of physical difference between the women of the two groups: Marguerite is blue-eyed with ash-colored hair; the woman of *Faded Leaves* has brown hair and gray eyes (although not, it is true, in the poems of

[4] Allott, p. 271.
[5] Allott, pp. 229–30; *Commentary*, p. 168.

this group included in 1852). There is, too, a difference between the temperament of the two women accounting, in part, for a difference in the course of the loves. The woman of *Faded Leaves* is credited with a self-sufficiency which at times promises peace to her lover but at others manifests itself in a conventional cruelty. Marguerite is a light enchantress, perhaps inconstant and certainly dependent, without promise of sustaining calm for her lover.

The internal evidence is more important for an explicator than the external. It is interesting, but finally irrelevant, that in *Faded Leaves* Arnold addressed the woman he married in June 1851. It is disappointing, but of no critical moment, that it has proved impossible so far to identify the original of Marguerite. When the inevitable and, if controlled, unexceptionable biographical curiosity has been set aside, what matters is the presence of poems recording different loves for different women. It matters because it points to ways in which the volume achieves a unity in its central core of poems by virtue of similar but varied situations, the recurrence of topics and landscape motifs. Put most crudely, many of the 1852 poems are stages on the itinerary of two loves, one in England, one on the Continent. Crossings of the Channel properly figure in this itinerary and as properly express the depressing situation of absence from the loved one: the circumstance of being, most famously, "in the sea of life enisled." *Tristram and Iseult,* with its movement from Cornwall to Brittany, has thus a strong geographical, as well as emotional and conceptual, connection with the lyrics which precede it. The volume of 1852 is Arnold's first public expression of his life-long interest in the relationship between England and the Continent, although the relationship is emotional rather than cultural: it was not only Byron who bore through Europe "the pageant of his bleeding heart."[6]

As the last sentence should indicate, any artistic coherence between poems in the 1852 volume is at least partly a result of similarities in their biographical occasions and in the aesthetic response to similar situations: the sense of geographical location as a setting for and sometimes a definition of the mood. But there are three reasons for keeping biographical occasion in the background. The first is the critical commonplace that individual poems constitute an artistic transmutation of experiences about which very little is in

[6] *Stanzas from the Grande Chartreuse,* ll. 133–36.

this case certainly known. Even if each poem does relate to a specific incident, the probability is strong that in making a poem out of it Arnold omitted some details and added thoughts and feelings which did not occur to him at the time of the original experience. The second reason is that the poems in 1852 represent a selection: poems almost certainly written at the same time as those included in 1852 were not published until, in some cases, fifteen years later. The omission from 1852 of such poems as *Separation* from the *Faded Leaves* group, or what was finally called *To Marguerite* from *Switzerland,* together with the apparently long-delayed publication of *Calais Sands* and *Dover Beach,* makes for a difference in the total story implied by the lyrics. The story of the actual events is transmuted into—or, perhaps, obscured by—the story implied by the poems selected for publication in 1852. Change between the stories is effected not only by the adaptation of incident in individual poems and the selection of some poems rather than others for publication, but also by the ordering of the poems in 1852. The ordering is of greatest moment in the chronological displacement of *Faded Leaves* poems to a position before the *Switzerland* poems. In biographical and (probably) compositional terms, poems of 1850 precede poems of, principally, 1849: the courtship of Miss Wightman precedes the liaison with Marguerite. But it would be misleading to imply that the love lyrics of 1852 make a fully coherent story: they do not constitute Arnold's equivalent of *Modern Love.* Their coherence resides in their suggestion of amorous itinerary, and in the investigation and gradually evolving significance of landscape features.

Although the biographical evidence is scanty, there is enough of it to indicate why poems relating to two separate loves could be reorganized to suggest a single continuous emotional experience. To convert probability into biographical certainty, Arnold met Marguerite at Thun in September, 1848. This first encounter produced the poem finally called *A Memory-Picture* but published in 1849 as *To My Friends, Who Ridiculed a Tender Leave-Taking.* To 1848 also belongs, it seems, *A Dream,* first published in 1853 as part of *Switzerland,* but finally assigned with *A Memory-Picture,* which it immediately followed, to the group Arnold called "Early Poems." Both pieces differ from the other Marguerite poems in the presence of friends. In September, 1849, Arnold was again in Thun and apparently renewed his acquaintance with Marguerite, although this time, as far as the poems are concerned, unchaperoned. I say "apparently" because for the 1849 meeting the external evidence of the Clough letters is far from clear. In 1848 (on his return to England from Italy) he told Clough that he would remain a day at the Hotel Bellevue "for the sake of the blue eyes of one of its inmates," making it reasonably clear that the first meeting with Marguerite took place on the outward trip.[7] In 1849 he wrote Clough from Thun that he was "in a curious and not altogether comfortable state" and proposed the next day to cool his "aching head" in the mountains, a proposal illustrated by quotation from the Marguerite poem called *Parting*.[8] But there is no sure indication that Arnold met or expected to meet Marguerite in 1849, and it is possible that all the poems finally called *Switzerland* were, if not as wholly imaginary as Arnold later described them, at least the product of recollected and transfigured emotion, an imaginary extension into intimacy of the flirtation which emerges from *A Memory-Picture* and *A Dream*. This hypothesis would give all the Switzerland poems a relationship to the two "early poems" like that given explicitly to *The Terrace at Berne,* a product of a visit to Switzerland in 1859, in which Arnold speculates whether he will find Marguerite still at Thun. In either case, imaginary or actual, the second meeting with Marguerite produced all the poems finally called *Switzerland* with the exception of *The Terrace at Berne.* One at least, *Parting,* had some kind of existence at Thun in September, 1849, and probably all were written then or in the months immediately following. *Absence,* with its gray eyes of a "fair stranger" in which Arnold sees Marguerite's eyes, quite likely records the beginning of his acquaintance with Miss Wightman during the winter of 1849–50. *Faded Leaves* records moments in the courtship, culminating in a "counterblast" to Arnold's hopes "which drove him out of England and towards the [Swiss] Alps."[9] The effect in 1852 of placing *Faded Leaves* poems before *Switzerland* poems is, in biographical terms, to associate the Marguerite sequence with the 1850 trip, and to make it the renewal of an earlier, ill-starred love after

[7] *Clough Letters,* p. 91; Sept. 29, 1848.
[8] *Clough Letters,* p. 110; Sept. 23 [1849]. It is of note that the lines quoted from *Parting* contain no reference to Marguerite or love. Out of context, the lines simply gloss Arnold's need to recover in the mountains from an "aching head," the cause of which is not given. That Arnold was, apparently, writing a Marguerite poem at Thun in 1849 is not proof that he was then in contact with her.
[9] *Commentary,* p. 172.

the failure of an emotionally more desirable but equally ill-starred love in England.

It is necessary to emphasize the malign influence of the stars as the poet's, not the critic's, writing up of emotional experience: Arnold's attempt to find a view of the world (both physical and philosophical) that could adequately express his sense of the human situation. If we hold closely to the presumed biographical occasions of the lyrics, we are likely to feel that the philosophy—or, rather, the myth—is too portentous for the fact. If, that is, we follow the Arnold family tradition that the counterblast to Arnold's hopes in the courtship of Miss Wightman blew from her father, who doubted that Arnold could support a wife,[10] then we may be uneasy about the appropriateness of *Euphrosyne's*

> Two bleeding hearts,
> Wounded by men, by fortune tried,
> Outwearied with their lonely parts,
> Vow to beat henceforth side by side.   (ll. 5–8)

If *Euphrosyne* was addressed to Miss Wightman, then it is surely remote from the picture which emerges from scanty records of an obedient girl heeding her father's far from unreasonable decision. And that is the point. The lover of the 1852 volume is much given to reverie, especially nocturnal; his poems are the product of dream-weaving about the slightest of occasions. It is pertinent to recall Tom Arnold's account of the genesis of *To a Gipsy-Child by the Sea-Shore.* One afternoon Arnold and his brother were part of a crowd on the pier at Douglas. Standing in front of them was a "poor woman," perhaps a gipsy, carrying a child who looked back over her shoulder at Arnold with "sad dark eyes" and an unchanging expression. Arnold became "completely abstracted" looking at the child,[11] and, we are to understand, entered upon an imaginative process which ended in the association of the child with Stoics, warriors, kings, and angels. Just such an imaginative extension of the biographical occasion is apparent in the opening discourse of travelers in *Resignation,* and an attempt to render the process of extension seems to underlie *The Hayswater Boat.* A large gap between occasion and poem is, then, not unprecedented in Arnold, and should make us cautious of resting in biographical explanation.

---

[10] *Commentary,* p. 167; Allott, p. 230.
[11] Allott, p. 22.

The possibility of such a gap is one reason for speculating that Arnold may not have renewed his acquaintance with Marguerite in 1849—except in imagination. If the Scholar Gipsy can walk from the pages of Glanvill to make a poem about Arnold, Marguerite could walk from the memorial tablets of 1848 to make poems about Arnold's love in 1849.

ii

The lyrics of 1852 are in the first place poems about being in love and only secondly about particular affairs and particular women. The emotional and metaphorical homogeneousness of the volume of 1852 is a consequence of its investigating the human lot principally by placing the figures of sage and lover in representative landscapes. There is a reworking of the dichotomies of *The New Sirens*: head and heart, reason and passion, landscape heights and depths, light and gloom. But the sharp moral distinctions are dulled by a sense of greater complication and inevitability. The poet's regret that the New Sirens cannot offer a fully satisfying life is replaced by a sense, not only that return to the wisdom of mountain tops is difficult to achieve in the face of contrary impulses, but that even if the summit is reached, wisdom will no longer be certainly found there. The lover of Marguerite longs to escape from their idyll by the lake to the clarity and calmness of the heights, but when he turned to the Alps as he sailed down the Rhine from his other love, Urania and Euphrosyne, the quiet they offered was the cold finality of death. Isolation in both life and death is what Empedocles and Obermann found at the summit.

Like the poems on Empedocles and Obermann, the love lyrics of 1852 record, principally, a failure to come to terms with the conditions of life. Characteristically, no doubt, Arnold's Victorian unease at the confusion and complication of modern life is identified at times vaguely and at others fragmentarily. No one poem (and for that matter no one of Arnold's essays) defines the total ills of the mid-nineteenth century. The intellectuals' loss of religious certitude, the vanished sense of nature as a spiritual force, the decline of the aristocracy as a provider of great leaders, the impoverishment of reading matter, the aesthetic casualties of industrialization in town and country, the growing insistence of the underprivileged poor that they be acknowledged, the riots and revolutions of 1848, the vulgar competitiveness of commercial life: all these elements and more make up the familiar schedule of Victorian woes which can be traced in the works of Arnold, or Carlyle, or Ruskin, or Butler, or Tennyson. For Arnold, especially in 1852, the social malaise was complicated by the endemic ills of young manhood: the emotional upsets of love and the strong consciousness of universal mortality. Much of the social malaise, for Arnold, resulted from or in (cause and effect being interchangeable) a lack of individual purpose definable in terms of a confident sense of community.

There are few moments more characteristic of the 1852 volume than a brief description and simile in the third part of *Tristram and Iseult*. With Tristram and Iseult of Ireland buried in the chapel of Tyntagel, the second Iseult is left to live through the sad remainder of her days by devoting herself to her children. She walks with them along the coast of Brittany, tells a story,

And now she will go home, and softly lay
Her laughing children in their beds, and play
Awhile with them before they sleep; and then
She'll light her silver lamp, which fishermen
Dragging their nets through the rough waves, afar,
Along this iron coast, know like a star,
And take her broidery-frame, and there she'll sit
Hour after hour, her gold curls sweeping it

. . . .

Then to her soft sleep—and to-morrow'll be
To-day's exact repeated effigy.   (III, 76–83, 94–95)

What is projected by the succession of *ands* and *thens* is a complete lack of purpose. Action follows action in time but without other connection. The enervate life is exactly mimicked by the slackness of the verse, containing as it does a high proportion of unemphatic words: "and now she will go home," "or else she will fall musing" (III, 90), "until she have told" (III, 92). The weak line-fillers match the purposeless filling up of a life with inconsequential detail. There are, in fact, too many weak words: the repeated *ands* would have been sufficient. The passage as a whole is far from memorable, and its general limitations are sharply marked by the striking description of the fishermen, "dragging their nets through the rough waves, afar." Like Marvell before him, Arnold is evidently alert to the suggestions of physical strain in the combination of "through" and "rough." There is no boat to ease the labor of trawling, but only the fishermen dragging their burden through the resisting sea, and threatened by the "iron coast." Quite obviously, the fishermen's hard lot is a counterpart to Iseult's: both drag their way through life. In glossing Iseult's life the fishermen are equally glossed by her. Because they provide a descriptive counterpart to a way of life, their single activity itself suggests their whole way of life. The waters they fish are the sea of life. The concentration upon the suggestiveness of the image is marked by the assurance of the rhyme: "afar" / "star," in contrast with the weak rhyme that precedes it: "and then" / "fishermen." Equally of note is the typically Arnoldian move to the outside: the pointlessness of life conveyed by the separation from other men, not merely isolation, but an apartness mocked and intensified by the glimpse of a blank window or an enigmatic beacon. We know, what the fishermen do not, that the "star" which marks their way shines from a life as wearisome and as purposeless as their own. Within the castle Iseult has

> The children, and the grey-hair'd seneschal,
> Her women, and Sir Tristram's aged hound. (III, 97–98)

If it is "lonely for her in her hall" (III, 96), it is nonetheless true that "these she loves" (III, 100), and the companionship and community they bring ease to some extent the pain of unfulfillment. But for the fishermen without, there is no such domestic anodyne, and their lot consequently reveals more clearly the dull pain of Iseult's life, at the same time as the conditions of that life are generalized into the nature of human existence.

To pass alone through the land and sea outside the window is to know more certainly the actual loneliness of the life within the house. Inside there are distractions and delusions, misleading promises of companionship. It is necessary to go outside because only in the landscape can the conditions of life be properly identified. The landscape, moreover, can suggest without involving the poet in explanations of his loneliness that risk the vulgar, the sentimental, and the bathetic. A major value of the landscape is its lack of conceptual precision. The extent of that value can be determined by considering the second Marguerite poem, *Parting*.

Parting distinguishes more explicitly than any other of Arnold's poems the life within from the life without. The distinction works finally to pose human love and love of nature as alternatives, but,

before that, the imagined progress of the storm wind outside operates as a gloss upon the relationship between the speaker and Marguerite inside. It seems at first that the primary function of the
autumnal winds is to objectify the turbulence within the speaker:
his emotional disturbance drives him to escape from the cause of the
disturbance into the calm and clarity of isolation, just as the winds
rush from human habitation to the "cold, distant barrier" of the
Alpine summits (l. 11). But if this is one implication of the first
sixty-six lines, it is also true that the speaker's imagined ascent with
the wind up the mountain side counterpoints the descent of Marguerite down the stairs (l. 17), through the door and across the
room to the speaker (ll. 35–42).[12] Such a counterpoint works to
clarify the nature of the human relationship. To follow in the mind
the progress of the wind makes it clear that the physical closeness of
Marguerite's approach is a misleading distraction from the actual
distance between the lovers. By the time Marguerite reaches the
speaker and bends towards him, the counterpoint of his imagined
ascent enables him to express the distance between them—emotional,
psychological or social—in physical or spatial terms. In the room
Marguerite and the speaker almost embrace, but his imagined
itinerary outside the room has reached a point where he can say:

> In the void air, towards thee
>   My stretch'd arms are cast;
> But a sea rolls between us—
>   Our different past! (ll. 63–66)

The "void air" is that of the mountain heights; the sea rolling
between them is as divisive as "the vast seas of snow" (l. 28) he had
already passed by in his imagined ascent. Marguerite and the
speaker now confront each other, in effect, across an upland chasm,
and the physical separation makes clear, as their proximity in the
room could not, the futility of their relationship. The progress of
his meditation has convinced the tantalized lover that he can never
reach the fruit or the water, and must accept the conditions of
separation. These conditions are a lonely watch until death.

[12] In speaking of Marguerite's "descent" I am in fact pressing the poem a little,
for the speaker simply hears her voice "on the stairs." Whether we invoke the
presumed biographical occasion in the Hotel Bellevue or general Victorian
propriety, descent to the reception rooms seems more appropriate than ascent
to the bedrooms (unless Marguerite was a chambermaid). It really makes little
difference whether the imagined ascent of the mountain is counterpointed by
Marguerite's ascent or descent of the stairs.

The autumnal winds which rattle the window (ll. 2–3), and thus
capture the speaker's attention, pass quickly, in his mind, from the
evidence of habitation: the lake, "gleam-lighted" from the surrounding houses, and the scattered farms just above, to the unin-
habited uplands. To do so they must traverse the deciduous belt,
"where the high woods strip sadly / Their yellowing arms" (ll. 7–8)
and offer but a sere introduction to the later motif of embrace. Below and within, the clear voice on the stairs suggests the music of a
"bird-haunted English lawn" and a "sun-fleck'd mountain-brook"
(ll. 19–21). The glancing of the sun on moving water and the
ghostly ambiguity of "haunted" make of this descant a light and
fleeting counterpoint to the burden of the torrents' "rock-strangled
hum" and the thunder of the avalanche (ll. 29–32). The speaker is
too choked to sing well, and there is no promise of harmony in their
duet. As Marguerite comes closer and the speaker ascends farther
the musical discord is replaced by physical difference. Marguerite
in her "unconquer'd joy" (l. 40) is decidedly young, the speaker
has aged thoughts, as might have been predicted from his remarking the "yellowing arms" of the "high woods." As he reaches "the
clear, waning hill-side" (l. 45), Marguerite's "sweet blue eyes" and
"soft, ash-colour'd hair" (l. 37) are replaced by the aconite's "dusky
blue" flowers and pine trees with clouds "hung soft in their heads"
(ll. 51–54): the vision of *bella donna* becomes the vision of wolfs-
bane. There is no life here save for "the mountain-bee's hum" (l.
56). The bee is not Thomson's hornet, but Edgar's samphire-
gatherer hanging perilously on the cliffs of Dover and emphasizing
their height by his presence.

The landscape has conclusively demonstrated the incompatibility
of the lovers. It can record the fact, but it cannot explain it fully;
and Arnold wishes to explain it fully:

> a sea rolls between us—
>   Our different past!
>
> To the lips, ah! of others
>   Those lips have been prest,
> And others, ere I was,
>   Were strain'd to that breast;
>
> Far, far from each other
>   Our spirits have grown;

And what heart knows another?
    Ah! who knows his own?

Blow, ye winds! lift me with you!
    I come to the wild.
Fold closely, O Nature!
    Thine arms round thy child.   (ll. 65–78)

The explanation is plainly a disaster, even when the fullest allowance has been made for changing attitudes to the ritual of mating
and even if we read euphemism into the distress that Marguerite
has been kissed before (and there is nothing in the poem to support
a euphemism). To fly from this lightsome woman to the motherly
embrace of Nature is an adolescent action which sorts ill with the
manly hoarseness of the earlier emotion and the sad stoicism of upland contemplation. The poem has changed direction sharply and
has run out of control in doing so. Where earlier the landscape
had conveyed and objectified the speaker's emotions while superficially offering escape from a difficult situation, it is now wholly
limited to the surface meaning. In using natural phenomena as
metaphors for human qualities, because the human situation is difficult to explain in terms of itself, Arnold ends by anthropomorphiz-
ing nature:

To thee only God granted
    A heart ever new—
To all always open,
    To all always true.

Ah! calm me, restore me;
    And dry up my tears
On thy high mountain-platforms,
    Where morn first appears;

Where the white mists, for ever,
    Are spread and upfurl'd—
In the stir of the forces
    Whence issued the world.   (ll. 79–90)

The poem begins with a reminiscence of Shelley's *Ode to the West
Wind* and ends with a reminiscence of Shelley's *Mont Blanc*. Unlike *Mont Blanc*, however, Arnold's poem has not worked to understand through the landscape the principles of creation: the last

stanza is an affirmation unsupported by what has preceded it. The landscape had earlier provided objective equivalents to a melancholy mood: as the mind ascended it found more and more evidences of mortality, destruction and death. Suddenly, at the top, it confronts the not very compelling evidence of primeval life forces in a landscape that is wholly objective. The summit mists may inspire a mood, but they do not provide an equivalent for it. The poem is a non sequitur.

It is so, apparently, because the change from glossing the emotions in terms of the landscape to an attempted analysis of the emotions in themselves throws the poem mawkishly out of control. In striving to bring the poem under control again Arnold suceeds only in banishing the mawkishness, not at all in recovering the earlier poetic value of the landscape.

iii

One subordinate value of the landscape of *Parting* is that it associates the poem with other pieces in the 1852 volume by virtue of its rendering emotions felt within the house in terms of the landscape outside. In this way *Parting* recalls such a Marguerite poem as *A Farewell,* in which the first two stanzas describing the lover's ride along the peaceful, moonlit lake to the house where Marguerite's candle in the window summons him to bliss are an evident attempt to provide a landscape equivalent for the succeeding discourse on the pains of the emotional life:

> My horse's feet beside the lake,
> Where sweet the unbroken moonbeams lay,
> Sent echoes through the night to wake
> Each glistening strand, each heath-fringed bay.
>
> The poplar avenue was pass'd,
> And the roof'd bridge that spans the stream;
> Up the steep street I hurried fast,
> Led by thy taper's starlike beam.   (ll. 1–8)

The calmness of the lake's unruffled surface and the harmonious communion of the hoofbeats with all parts of the scene prove to be but a delusive happiness. The happiness is delusive because such moments are brief and infrequent in this life, while still suggesting for their duration that they could be, if one only knew how to make them so, the general condition of life on earth. We draw closer to the prevailing conditions of earthly life in the second stanza, for here the happiness is edged with impatience and changed from a calm acceptance of beauty into hurry towards a promising beacon. When the promise fails, when man's harmony with others proves more difficult to achieve and sustain than the harmony of sound beside the lake, the impatient goal-seeker of the second stanza understands what it is truly like to be outside and striving to hurry home:

> we wear out life, alas!
> Distracted as a homeless wind,
> In beating where we must not pass,
> In seeking what we shall not find.   (ll. 49–52)

The opening scene beside the lake then proves (or is asserted to be) delusive only if we assume it to represent the general earthly condition. It is more properly seen as an exact image of the peace and harmony which will prevail hereafter:

> How sweet, unreach'd by earthly jars,
> My sister! to maintain with thee
> The hush among the shining stars,
> The calm upon the moonlit sea!   (ll. 77–80)

In order to discover their "true affinities of soul" (l. 56) beneath "the eternal Father's smile" (l. 61), the lovers must banish Eros and substitute the chaste affection of brother for sister. Apart from the mawkishness of the concluding assurances, reminiscent as they are of the in memoriam columns of newspapers, the poem fails because it establishes its landscape inadequately. The details of the first two stanzas are too few, and permit only brief, allusive metaphors later in the poem, most of which is conveyed in a different syntax.

But the syntax of its landscape recalls *Parting* and points further to *Absence,* with its lover, as storm-tossed on the sea as the representative "mortal" of *Human Life,* struggling "towards the light" of "wiser thoughts and feelings" than he can find with Marguerite "upon time's barren, stormy flow." The delusive peace of moonlit waters and harmonious communion recur in the second stanza of *To Marguerite—Continued,* and once again it is opposed by the divisive actualities of the human condition, "in the sea of life enisled." Arnold is evidently seeking in these poems a landscape through which to convey the obvious, if melancholy, retort to Donne: every man *is* an island.

The success of *To Marguerite—Continued* depends in part on Arnold's finding an adequately detailed landscape to convey his Victorian sense of alienation. But to phrase it thus, blurs, perhaps obliterates, the special excellence of *To Marguerite—Continued,* for, in contrast with the other *Switzerland* poems, it is not a poem in which the unification of discourse and description is at all problematic. Certainly, the first stanza offers in its "sea of life" a trope which no ancient rhetorician could have failed to identify as metaphor. The neat distinctions of the metaphor, its easy division into tenor and vehicle—"in the sea of life enisled": "we mortal millions live *alone*"—are such that we might be tempted to describe the figure as a simile in everything but syntax. But the confident descriptive elaboration of the vehicle in the succeeding stanzas proceeds in a manner which recalls and develops the social and philosophical tenor without, as it were, requiring even its silent articulation. A linguistic analogy might help. The difference between the status of the image in the first and the succeeding stanzas is like that between a language in which we are inexpert and which we therefore have to translate into English as we go, and a language in which we are so expert that we think in it without translation. It is of course the same language, and the poet drills us in our paradigms before making us free of thé literature.

The success of the poem—and it is Arnold's most perfect poem—depends partly on the inevitable rightness of its diction. Practically every line yields a special felicity of assonance, alliteration, or vowel variation of which even Tennyson need not have been ashamed. Of many riches, two may be cited: the concluding lines of the third and fourth stanzas:

Oh might our marges meet again!

The unplumb'd, salt, estranging sea.

The yearning for unity in the first line is intensified by the repeated labial closures, and is focused, unalterably, in "marges," sounding of *merges* as it announces *boundaries.* The second line, as decisive, if not as moving, as the final line of *The Scholar-Gipsy,* swallows its consonants in its long, open vowels, and emphasizes division by its sequence of distinct attributes, each separated from each by a heavy pause. The regular iambic rhythm of the poem's tetrameters, varied elsewhere only by an initial reversed foot, drives against the five heavy beats of the line, and almost conquers them, only to fall back, its forces divided by that hard, uncompromising "salt."

The diction intensifies, through a vocabulary of landscape, the emotion rather than the thought of the poem. The thought, indeed, is simple without being slight. The poem's preoccupation with division and unity, multiplicity and oneness, an idyllic dream of the past and a sad confrontation of the present, is of the kind which is easily transcended by the emotions it excites. And in Arnold's poetry the landscape is usually more fully accommodated to the emotion than to the thought. Because, then, thought is almost lost in emotion, because thought and emotion are here almost one, the landscape is fully adequate to its task of conveying, shall we say? emotion tinged with morality. From what has been said, it follows, I think, that we should resist any temptation to spell out the possible conceptual equivalents of the landscape. This is a language in which we think naturally, or of which we are ignorant.

That we can think in it without conceptualizing is certainly due in large measure to the way the poem recalls so many literary parallels without repeating any one of them at all precisely—apart, perhaps, from two or three lines of Horace. From its very first line, turning to the most familiar page in every man's commonplace book, the poem moves confidently through its new synthesis of some of the great, primary images. What the poem asks of us is to be conscious of possible glosses without fully articulating them. This request is best defined by contrast with *The Youth of Man,* also from the volume of 1852. In that curiously unrealized poem, the speaker comments on the past and present feelings and beliefs of a pair of now aging lovers, who are standing in a garden. "Well I know what they feel!" the speaker says,

> They gaze, and the evening wind
> Plays on their faces; they gaze—
> Airs from the Eden of youth
> Awake and stir in their soul;
> The past returns. . . .   (ll. 88–93)

And the scales of habit,
Fall away from their eyes;
And they see, for a moment,
Stretching out, like the desert
In its weary, unprofitable length,
Their faded, ignoble lives.   (ll. 106–11)

The reference to Eden releases the potential allusion of "desert" to that wilderness which the chosen were so long in crossing. In the second stanza of *To Marguerite—Continued* we have the balmy breezes of spring at night, while the faintly musical "airs" of *The Youth of Man* are represented by the divine harmonies of the night-ingales' song. But Eden itself, and the garden in which the pair stand, are represented in *To Marguerite—Continued* by the quite unlocalized "glens, on starry nights." Similarly, the saltness of the estranging sea is evidently as thirst-inducing as the desert of *The Youth of Man*. But, if the sea is at all biblical, it is because it is ordained by a god, and the God of the Jews once commanded the dry land to be covered by water. This imprecise allusiveness is characteristic of the poem. We can say that, while no one gloss is especially pertinent, the whole complex of glosses—analogues, sources, allusions, reminiscences—greatly contributes to the almost majestic inevitability of a poem which ends exactly as it begins. In between, we move from the rhetorician's figure of metaphor to a fully achieved image, whose descriptive coherence is such that, while suggesting "meanings," it forbids their articulation. It is tempting, indeed, to rest in a *symbol,* the *O, altitudo!* of an imagistic critic.

iv

To Marguerite—Continued is exceptional in its complete ade-quacy of landscape to thought and feeling. Quite often, the land-scape evidently struck Arnold as inadequate, as leaving unconveyed some important part of his feelings which was then supplied by ex-plicit utterance: "what heart knows another? / Ah! who knows his own?" It is possible that the frequency with which such questions have been asked in the past hundred years leads us to find them more commonplace than Arnold's contemporaries may have done. Whatever the reason, the portentousness which often accompanies the direct posing of these questions is usually embarrassing. For their proper expression they require a vehicle: a landscape or a human situation. When this vehicle is lacking or inadequate, the deficiency is likely to be supplied by exclamations which disquiet whether we find them in the work of Arnold or of Dickens:

A wonderful fact to reflect upon that every human creature is constituted to be that profound secret and mystery to every other. A solemn consideration, when I enter a great city by night, that every one of those darkly clustered houses encloses its own secret; that every room in every one of them encloses its own secret; that every beating heart in the hundreds of thousands of breasts there, is, in some its imaginings, a secret to the heart nearest it! . . . In any of the burial-places in this city through which I pass, is there a sleeper more inscrutable than its busy inhabitants are, in their innermost personality, to me, or than I am to them?[13]

Arnold, of course, was stirred more by a rural than an urban landscape. But this passage from *A Tale of Two Cities* makes use of a recurrent situation in Arnold's poems of 1852 and after: a speaker outside gazing at the blank façades or enigmatically lit windows of the houses that surround him. Where Dickens finds more than enough to work with in city streets, Arnold usually finds it necessary to amplify or gloss his city experience by imaginative excursions into the country, domestic or exotic. *Consolation* affords an instructive example of how this process manifests itself in poems where the imagination is not noticeably concentrated. The first stanza places the speaker in urban streets, presumably those of London:

Mist clogs the sunshine.
Smoky dwarf houses
Hem me round everywhere;
A vague dejection
Weighs down my soul.

The succeeding forty-five lines are devoted to a series of vignettes offering pictorial exempla of that characteristically vague dejection. Arnold later classified *Consolation* as an "early poem," and both the quality and content of the vignettes are reminiscent of the 1849 volume, especially *The Strayed Reveller* and *The Sick King in Bokhara*. The first three vignettes serve to annotate Arnold's London malaise by implicitly contrasting or paralleling it with life in

---

[13] *A Tale of Two Cities*, I, iii. For further images of alienation, Victorian and earlier, see Kathleen Tillotson, " 'Yes: In The Sea Of Life,' " *Review of English Studies*, New Series, III (1952), 346–64.

other cities: the serenity of religion in "holy Lassa," the serenity of
art in Rome surrounded by mid-nineteenth-century clamor, and the
harsh consequences of the battle for life in a desert city pictured in
a sand-blind beggar who had once been a robber. The beggar's pain
is then contrasted with the present joy of two lovers in a summer
field, and Arnold is ready for a concluding twenty-five lines of
philosophy. The same hour in which one man suffers is "pass'd by
others / In warmth, light, joy" (ll. 66–70); time "brings round to
all men / Some undimm'd hours" (ll. 71–75). These final, unobtrusive metaphors evidently constitute an attempt to recall the
earlier vignettes: the overcast sun of London, sun-drenched Lhasa,
the umbrageous alleys of the desert city, and the "warm June-wind"
that blows on the lovers. It is an attempt, indeed, to unite the syntax of reflection with the syntax of description. But the final metaphors are so commonplace as to be dead, and beyond resurrection
by their context. By the end of the poem, it is clear that the vignettes serve as illustrative analogies to a meditation, and the association of one with another is even more tenuous, less intensely imagined, than those which illustrate the discourse of *Epilogue to Lessing's Laocoön.*

Successive readings of *Consolation* suggest, indeed, that Arnold
began with the end of the poem, began, that is, with the commonplace little metaphors of the last two stanzas, and then invented a
series of pictorial glosses upon them. By contrast, a poem like *A
Summer Night* is successful just because it gives the impression of
beginning with the beginning, of beginning with the landscape and
proceeding to press into its moral and psychological significance for
the observer as representative man. This impression comes from the
evident concentration of the eye on the object, both the physical
eye and the memorial eye. I said earlier that merely to describe
accurately an object in itself means nothing; if anything it inter-
feres with the process of finding metaphors, analogies, or allegories
in landscape features. It means nothing, but it assists the process of
imaginatively renewing the object. Wordsworth insisted, in a familiar passage, that poetry "takes its origin from emotion recollected in
tranquillity: the emotion is contemplated till, by a species of reaction, the tranquillity gradually disappears, and an emotion, kindred to that which was before the subject of contemplation, is
gradually produced, and does itself actually exist in the mind."[14]

[14] *Poetical Works,* ed. de Selincourt, II, 400–401.

The choice of words is unfortunate to the extent that it implies a sharp disjunction between tranquillity and emotion; as if the difference were one of relative turbulence. What Wordsworth appears to be reaching for is a distinction between the detachment with which we customarily review our memories and the concentration or intensity with which we relive them, the strain of remembering precisely and yet with significance. This strain, this concentration, becomes possible and declares itself in the careful attention to detail. Hence the criterion of the eye on the object. It is not that the details of an object are sufficiently interesting in themselves to justify careful enumeration (the fallacy or weakness of much eighteenth-century landscape poetry). It is instead a question of the details being a prompter or objectification of a mood or a perception of the observer. The significance is not then located exclusively in the object, but between the object and the perceiver, thus facilitating the movement between reflection and description. Something of this kind is true of *A Summer Night*.

A Summer Night begins with Arnold's finest use of a reflective observer alone and outside in the streets at night:

In the deserted, moon-blanch'd street,
How lonely rings the echo of my feet!
Those windows, which I gaze at, frown,
Silent and white, unopening down,
Repellent as the world;—but see,
A break between the housetops shows
The moon! and, lost behind her, fading dim
Into the dewy dark obscurity
Down at the far horizon's rim,
Doth a whole tract of heaven disclose!

The notes of nightingales in *To Marguerite—Continued*, like the echoing hoofbeats of *A Farewell*, implied a possibility (admittedly delusive) of human communion. In *A Summer Night* the footfalls' echo insists immediately upon the speaker's isolation in a "repellent" world which drives him from it. But the suggestions are as much of constriction, of being shut in, as they are of being shut out. The frowning windows have implicitly the qualities given explicitly to the "smoky dwarf houses" which "hem . . . round everywhere" the speaker of *Consolation*. These implications are brought closer to the surface by the "break between the housetops" opening upon a wide vista of heaven and offering escape from the constriction of streets. Immediately, the combination of restriction and expansion facilitates, makes natural, the move to "a past night, and a far different scene":

> Headlands stood out into the moonlit deep
> As clearly as at noon;
> The spring-tide's brimming flow
> Heaved dazzlingly between;
> Houses, with long white sweep,
> Girdled the glistening bay;
> Behind, through the soft air,
> The blue haze-cradled mountains spread away.   (ll. 14–21)

The repellent constriction of the urban landscape modulates into the comforting enclosure of the coastal scene: the spring tide held between headlands, houses girdling the bay, the mountains haze-cradled. Despite this difference, important as it is, the ordonnance of the two scenes is sufficiently similar to justify their association. In both there is enclosure by dwellings; in both there is an opening out and up to a vista of heaven or a vista of mountains; both are brilliantly lit by the moon "as clearly as at noon." The second scene, however, contains an additional opening, out into "the moonlit deep." The similarity of the scenes is further marked by the observer's experiencing identical emotions in the different settings. The earlier night "was far more fair" than the night of the poem's immediate occasion, but in both there were

> the same restless pacings to and fro,
> And the same vainly throbbing heart was there,
> And the same bright, calm moon.

> And the calm moonlight seems to say:
> *Hast thou then still the old unquiet breast,*
> *Which neither deadens into rest,*
> *Nor ever feels the fiery glow*
> *That whirls the spirit from itself away,*
> *But fluctuates to and fro,*
> *Never by passion quite possess'd*
> *And never quite benumb'd by the world's sway?—*
> And I, I know not if to pray
> Still to be what I am, or yield and be
> Like all the other men I see.   (ll. 23–36)

In terms of what has preceded, this passage adopts an almost completely different syntax, and may therefore jar upon a reader endeavoring to perceive the coherence of the poem. In fact, the last two lines of the moon's speech refer clearly enough to important features of the two scenes. *"The world's sway"* recalls the windows frowning down "repellent as the world," while the passionate alternative recalls (less strongly, it is true) the brimming tide "heaved dazzlingly between" the headlands: the full flood of emotion. Much of the earlier part of the moon's speech will be allusively recalled in the remainder of the poem.

This tripartite opening sequence establishes, then, the speaker's troubled situation in terms of landscapes he observes or remembers to have observed and in terms of an explicit, if generalized, statement of his psychological condition. The sequence accounts for rather more than a third of the poem. The middle section contemplates the situation of "all the other men" with a reference to whom the opening sequence ended. The opening section described literal landscapes with moral and psychological implications or suggestions, and made these suggestions separately explicit. The two-part middle section draws on each of the opening scenes in turn, converting literal landscapes into landscape metaphors whose meanings are spelled out in the moment of description by recalling the terms of the third part of the opening sequence. The urban scene of the poem's occasion becomes the "brazen prison" of daily life, and we should certainly remember that the association of cities and prisons was not only Arnoldian but a *donnée* of his age which received its fullest and finest expression in *Little Dorrit*. The remembered coastal scene becomes, through its suggestive opening on to the moonlit deep, "the wide ocean of life" upon which a few escaped convicts set sail when they substitute the emotional life for the daily round.

While the two metaphoric scenes of the middle section generalize the conflicting impulses of the speaker in the first section into their significance for all men, they also define more precisely the speaker's situation itself, for he too is imprisoned in city streets and has gazed at the flood tide of emotion. The meaningless labor until death in the brazen prison recalls not only the heart which *"deadens into rest"* of the moon's speech but also the windows of the opening scene, "silent and white, unopening," with their evident sepulchral suggestions. The passion-given escaped convicts initially find the

ocean of life as free and enspiriting as the moonlit deep appeared
to be when gazed at from the security of the house-girdled shore
line. But they quickly learn the repeated lesson of the 1852 volume:
that moonlit waters are delusive in their temporary calm; the
tempest is always ready to blow in this world. They strive for that
passionately *"fiery glow"* of the moon's speech, which *"whirls the
spirit from itself away."* Having escaped the "unmeaning task-work"
of *"the world's sway,"* they now find themselves subject to the
despotism of fate (ll. 57–58). The danger of an emotional going-
out of the self, of sending *"the spirit from itself away,"* is that the
cross accidents of life deny the certainty of securely locating the
heart somewhere else, presumably in another person. The tempest-
driven mariner is last seen "still bent to make some port he knows
not where, / Still standing for some false, impossible shore" (ll. 68–
69), and then he disappears. By following out their manifestations
in "all the other men," we, and the speaker, have come to know
more precisely the nature of those conflicting impulses which so
trouble him that he cannot find joy in his past or present nocturnal
musings: the impulse to an apathetic acceptance of the daily round;
the impulse to a dangerous emotional outgoing; the impulse to a
dull acquiescence in constriction; the impulse to frantic escape.

> Is there no life, but these alone?
> Madman or slave, must man be one?   (ll. 74–75)

The final, and shortest, section of the poem poses against these unattractive possibilities the common term of the urban and coastal
scenes which open the poem: the way out and up to the moon and
the heavens. The moon's speech earlier in the poem had been a
tacit reproach, reminiscent of the "mild reproof / Sigh'd out" to
Mycerinus "by winter's sad tranquillity" (ll. 114–15). The clear
heavens of *A Summer Night* are now understood by the speaker to
teach the lessons of *Quiet Work* and, as in the sonnet, to offer in
their self-reliant industry a superior alternative to the deadening
toil of the brazen prison. They even offer a superior alternative to
the passion-driven mariner on the ocean of life by their suggestion
of controlled sorrow for some past love, as hopeless as it was intense.
Arnold is rightly hesitant about ascribing so much to the heavens,
about allotting them the "sad lucidity of soul" he allotted the poet
in *Resignation* (l. 198):

> I will not say that your mild deeps retain
> A tinge, it may be, of their silent pain
> Who have long'd deeply once, and long'd in vain.　　(ll. 83–85)

But in saying he will not say it, he of course says it. And by finding "mild deeps" in the sky he further associates it with the moonlit deep of the wide ocean of life.

A Summer Night is a poetic spiritual exercise, working from an initial composition of place through an analysis of the *acedia* consequent upon an imperfect understanding of the meaning of the place to an affirmation of spiritual regeneration when the true significance of the scene is grasped: the heavens remain

> A world above man's head, to let him see
> How boundless might his soul's horizons be,
> How vast, yet of what clear transparency!
> How it were good to abide there, and breathe free;
> How fair a lot to fill
> Is left to each man still!　　(ll. 87–92)

It it true that the poem contains rather more local infelicities than can be comfortably contained in a work of this length. The vaguely directed exhortation of the opening scene: "but see . . . the moon," sorts ill with the immediately preceding account of the speaker's solitude. The moon's speech is too evidently an act of rhetorical ventriloquism to follow comfortably from the naturalistic description of the two scenes. The description of the tempest-driven mariner is over-indulged for an overtly metaphorical scene: this emotionally-charged pictorialism is more appropriate to literal landscape with subdued significances than it is to a metaphorical vehicle the point of whose tenor is not in doubt. The final effort to make the moonlit heavens both contain and transcend the conditions of the sea as well as the prison leads to an awkwardly negative ascription of qualities inappropriate to the sky. Such infelicities cannot be dismissed with a comfortable "despite this." They are an inescapable diminution of the poem's achievement: the satisfying air of completeness that comes from attending scrupulously to all the details of the opening scenes, from the clear line of its meditation, from the evolution of metaphorical out of literal landscapes, and from the tight integrity of reflection and descriptive detail. They inescapably limit the achievement because part of the achieved integrity depends upon their presence. It is a question, perhaps, of Arnold's sinews cracking rather too loudly under the strain to unite matter.[15]

v

Part of the strain comes, it seems, from the difficulty of finding a single landscape sufficiently comprehensive to provide a complex analogy for the distinctions of thought, feeling, and human situation Arnold wished to express. This difficulty expresses itself both in the frequent move into commentary upon the issues represented by landscape and in the almost equally common association of a poem's immediate setting with other and often exotic landscapes. The associated landscapes can provide equivalents for issues only vaguely or not at all represented by the immediate setting. Arnold's own criterion of naturalness is most likely to be violated by such association, for it is difficult to avoid the arbitrary effect of a series of vignettes illustrative of some discourse. Such, certainly, is the effect of *Consolation,* in which the perfunctory description of the immediate setting demands, if the poem is to proceed, either the associational vignettes the poem actually uses or the movement of a poem like *A Farewell* into social and psychological commentary after an equally sparse opening description. But the technique of associated landscapes occurs even in poems which successfully present an immediate setting with wide possibilities as analogy. The technique is operative in the opening of *Resignation,* the close of *The Scholar-Gipsy,* or the songs of Callicles.

It is worth insisting that the associational technique is not necessarily poor or unnatural. Its value and its felicity depend to a large extent upon the way the poet uses or reacts to landscape. Wordsworth's association of the reaper's song with the cuckoo and nightingale in exotic settings is altogether different in effect from Arnold's association of "London" with Lhasa, Rome, and a desert city in *Consolation.* Wordsworth is endeavoring properly to know and therefore properly to experience the song of the reaper. His exotic associations define the song in terms of materials drawn from his own imaginative experience, and therefore the song becomes his, belongs in his heart instead of, as was initially the case, outside of him in the deep valley. In making a poem the poet has identified a

<hr/>
[15] *Clough Letters,* p. 65; [Dec., 1847–early 1848].

song which was not previously identified. Wordsworth is engaged in understanding an object in a landscape, and to do so he must express the object in terms of his own imaginative experience; the whole significance of the poem lies in the resultant process of understanding or experiencing. But Arnold is not engaged in understanding the urban setting of *Consolation*. He is engaged in explaining why he feels a "vague dejection" in such a place at such a time. The movement, then, is not to identify an object, but to identify the thoughts and feelings of the subject. In such a process the object, the setting, is principally useful in providing metaphors and terms with which to identify the situation of the subject. In poems in which the poet himself speaks, Arnold is normally given neither to thinking about landscape, to pressing into its significance, nor to thinking in landscape, to internal musings in a pastoral or urban scene, but to thinking in terms of landscape, to trying to understand or trying to explain why he thinks and feels as he does in such a setting. The movement is thus one of discourse or explanation, and the poet's task is to make the discourse emerge naturally from the objects and descriptive terms of his setting. When his setting is inadequately detailed or comprehensive, Arnold is prone to amplify it with brief and overt landscape metaphors, whose function as illustrative analogies for a discourse declares itself most clearly when they are imperfectly or insufficiently related to the natural scene of the poem's occasion: metaphors for the sea of life, the summit of excellence, or the prison house of urban life are usually most satisfactory when Arnold begins with a literal sea, mountain, or city.

The association of landscapes is often natural when they are the setting for the previous activities of figures seen in the immediate landscape or of characters in poems with some element of narrative. The gipsy nomads of *Resignation* and the much-traveled Ulysses of *The Strayed Reveller* permit the unforced amplification of the immediate scene in terms of other sites they have visited. This natural association is strikingly evident in *Tristram and Iseult,* for the focus in the first two parts upon Tristram's last night in a castle on the Breton coast is continually enlarged by retrospect to his earlier adventures across Europe from Ireland to Italy. As in the reflective, first-person poems, Tristram's situation, his feelings in such a place at such a time are to be explained by means of the retrospect; although the explanation is more in terms of narrative than discourse.

Narrative in *Tristram and Iseult* is in fact devoted principally to the description of places in which only minimal activity occurs. Action is largely replaced by tableaux of landscapes in which figures adopt significant poses. The tapestry huntsman in Part II and the story of Merlin and Vivian in Part III are simply the most striking of these tableaux. Part II also contains the description of Iseult of Ireland stretched across the bed of Tristam (II, 101–11), a scene which Professor Allott judiciously notes as "a subject for a Pre-Raphaelite painting." Early in Part I the narrator poses for us both Tristram and Iseult of Brittany in his sick chamber (I, 9–55). We are later to see Tristram and Iseult of Ireland becalmed on the Irish Sea and drinking the love potion (I, 94–160), and Tristram bending over a moonlit fountain in an Italian wood (I, 276–87). The life of Iseult of Brittany after Tristram's death freezes into the "exact repeated effigy" of the previous day's round (III, 95). Consequently, the significance of speech and gesture emerges primarily from the setting in which they take place. The landscape provides external equivalents to inner qualities and moods and to human situations. The poem functions through the orchestration of settings, landscape themes with variations.

We are prepared for this mode in the opening of Part I, where, as so often in Arnold's poems, Tristram's inner turbulence is mimicked by the winter winds beating upon the window. While the storm blows hard throughout most of Part I, the narrative is more broken and discontinuous than in any other part of the poem. When, finally, "the wind is down" (I, 300), we are ready to move, by way of the dream calm of the children, into the antiphonic formality of the *Liebestod* in Part II. The rise and fall of the winter wind is further a reminder that two major motifs in the poem are those of seasonal opposition: spring and winter, and of hot and cold.

All the present action of the poem takes place in winter: Tristram's last night in the first two parts and the winter excursion of Iseult of Ireland and her children a year later. Part of the retrospective action takes place, like the story of Merlin and Vivian, in spring, for Tristram brings the first Iseult from Ireland to Cornwall in May (I, 96, 156). Tristram's Italian campaign and vision in the glade are, like the tapestry huntsman, not assigned to a specific season, but—from the greenness of the huntsman's wood (II, 154) and the mildness of the night on which Tristram sees Iseult of Ireland's face mirrored in the fountain (I, 286)—they appear to be associated with spring or summer. One important part of the retrospective action, the parting of Tristram and Iseult of Ireland at Tyntagel, takes place in early winter (I, 179–80). This seasonal opposition is given its conventional association with human vicissitudes:

All the spring-time of his love
Is already gone and past,
And instead thereof is seen
Its winter, which endureth still.   (I, 173–76)

We have already been told that

There were two Iseults who did sway
Each her hour of Tristram's day;
But one possess'd his waning time,
The other his resplendent prime.   (I, 68–71)

The youth and age of the year find, indeed, a continuous counterpart in the youth and age of man. Both Tristram and Iseult of Ireland are prematurely aged (I, 304–5, II, 22), and the youth of Iseult of Brittany is insisted upon throughout the poem, not only by direct statement but by her close association with her children. She shares their pleasure, and, although with the death of Tristram "she seems one dying in a mask of youth" (III, 75), she still loves the Breton tales which delighted her when a child (III, 106–11). Exposed as she is to the winter of Tristram's despair, Iseult of Brittany is appropriately called by the narrator a "snowdrop by the sea" (I, 49, 196), the frail first flower of the year, the promise of spring in the time of winter. When she comes to renew her childhood pleasure in old tales for the delight of her children, she chooses a grassy hollow in the heath and the shelter of three holly trees, evergreen in the dead season, just as Iseult and her two children are three representatives of youth and life in a winter of dead love and dead lovers.

As they listen to the story, the children are warmed by fur mantles and their faces are still flushed from their exuberant games. Sheltered by the trees of the grassy hollow, the children find a landscape equivalent to "the warm nest" of their bed "on the castle's southern side," where the "buffeting wind and surging tide" sound but feebly "through many a room and corridor" (I, 327–32), and where they may dream securely of childish pleasures. They come by the healthy color of their cheeks in a way similar to that of the tapestry huntsman (II, 162) and of Vivian when "the spirit of the woods was in her face" (III, 169, 180). The healthy coursing of their blood contrasts with the "spiced magic draught" of the love potion which "for ever rolls" through the blood of Tristram and Iseult of Ireland (I, 64–66), which sets a fever in the blood of Tristram (I, 172), which dulls his blood (I, 248) beyond the aid of medicine (I, 290–93), which makes the cheeks of both of them flame (I, 148), and which sets a hectic flush in Iseult of Ireland's face as she struggles to act the queen in Tyntagel (II, 117). Tristram's feverishly hot brow, which cannot be cooled in the forest fountain (I, 280–82), reveals a man who has such blood and such dreams that he will burn himself out twenty years before his time (I, 304–6). As the man named for sorrow, Tristram will come, after brief joy, to find his *locus amoenus* to be "the drear forest" in which his mother died (II, 85–88). Ignoring Burton's short precept and shunning the life of the tapestry huntsman, Tristram passes his solitary days in the forest as "idle as a mossy stone" (I, 223). The dull melancholy he inevitably finds there, the sluggish blood (I, 247–48), is a drear alternative to the furious blood-letting, the river "red with blood" of the battle before Rome (I, 234). Those, like Vivian, who have the disdainful self-sufficiency of Urania will not pass unscathed along the hard road of life. But the "tangled wilderness" she travels with Merlin leaves only a superficial scratch on her hand (III, 172–75).

The feverish heat of Tristram and Iseult of Ireland is an inner malaise particularly susceptible to

> the gradual furnace of the world,
> In whose hot air our spirits are upcurl'd
> Until they crumble, or else grow like steel—
> Which kills in us the bloom, the youth, the spring.   (III, 119–22)

It is a sickness which consumed Iseult of Ireland's "beauty like a flame, / And dimm'd it like the desert-blast" (II, 134–35). It is a fire in Tristram's brain to drive him to wander (I, 187–88). Tristram's romantic passion is, for the narrator, an "unnatural overheat" comparable to the passion for conquest of Caesar and Alexander (III, 134–50), whose kind of life Tristram saw before Rome but could no longer share in. It is a restless drive that will burn out Tristram before his time as it burnt out Alexander, and will leave him with Iseult of Ireland as cold as monumental marble (II,

167), as cold as the "vein'd white-gleaming quartz" (III, 17) which lies in fragments, the broken emblems of death, about the evergreen hollies which shelter the second Iseult and her children. It is a death heat promising cold, just as "the red glow" of the setting sun "on the sea grew cold," reminding Iseult to end the tale of Merlin and Vivian and take her children home (III, 58–63).

It is worth describing in some detail the way in which human qualities and actions are constantly associated with landscape features and the seasonal cycle. To do so draws attention to the connection of human experience and the reflections it prompts with the details of landscape description. The landscape can, moreover, at any time in the poem, economically suggest other ways of life than the way immediately considered. The plains before Rome are suggestively present in the open heath surrounding the hollow in which Iseult and her children shelter from the harshness of winter. The sea which drives loudly with Tristram's sorrow is also the work place of fishermen and the trade route by which fur mantles are brought from Egypt to Brittany (III, 40–41). The wood is the place of healthful hunting, children's games (I, 350–61), melancholy solitude, Merlin's imprisonment, and of the death of Tristram's mother. Such suggestions and connections make clear that the poem is an examination of life from the viewpoint of passion, principally the passion of love, but with relevance also for the passions of remorse and ambition (III, 130). It should also be clear that the landscape is here principally a vehicle of psychological definition and objectification rather than, as is sometimes the case in Arnold's poems, of moral sanctions.

Perhaps the most beguiling temptation for a reader of *Tristram and Iseult* is to seek evidence for moral judgment upon the life of the chief characters. Such evidence is very hard to find in the poem itself and must, indeed, be tacitly or openly imported from Arnold's other poems. Tristram, for example, has obvious similarities with the "madman" of *A Summer Night,* the storm-tossed mariner; yet the moon does not bring for Tristram's world the tacit reproach of quiet work it brought the madman of *A Summer Night.* Instead, it brings yet more dreams and delusions: Iseult's face mirrored in the fountain, the "fairy sight" of the children's moonlit haunts (I, 353–54). Even more tempting is to build upon the poem's evident concern with youth and age. The places of security: the forest glade and its variants in the pleasure gardens of Tyntagel, the green fields of Wales, or the grassy hollow in the heath, offer their unalloyed pleasures only to the young, the innocent, and the unthinking. In such places and in such conditions a man can safely live his dreams, whether he be like the children of Tristram and Iseult, like the puzzled and simple-seeming huntsman of the tapestry, like Merlin, whose "best wits took flight" when he looked at Vivian, or like Tristram and Iseult of Ireland when with youthful insouciance they pledged each other in the love potion. But for the man who thinks hard and feels strongly, the man of Tristram's blood or Iseult of Ireland's imperious beauty, the man, indeed, of deep experience, the *locus amoenus* loses its pleasures—the wind drives through the "pleasaunce-walks" of Tyntagel—but it does not lose its enticement. Instead of living his dreams in the forest, he is haunted by them. The temptation, then, is to say that he should accept the conditions of experience and leave the forest behind. But the poem does not say so. Even when the narrator declares himself irritated by the way men allow themselves to be burnt out by a master passion (III, 133–50), he has no alternative to offer. Tristram asks Iseult of Ireland to sit silently beside him so he may think "we've lived so / In the green wood, all our lives, alone" (II, 35–36). Not only have they not done so, not only is this an attempt to regain the conditions of innocence, it is also an attempt to escape the ineluctable. A forest idyll for Tristram and Iseult of Ireland would not be reprehensible, it would simply be impossible, as impossible as for Antony to live the retired life in Athens for which he petitioned Octavius. Tristram and Iseult of Ireland have their destinies to live out: they must drink the magic potion, Iseult must marry Marc, her "deep-wrong'd husband" (II, 45), Tristram must be the man of sorrow for which he was named. Moreover, as Hardy, after Novalis, would say, "Character is Fate." The "proud Iseult" (II, 19) and the man of such blood as Tristram's could not live it any other way. They cannot live their dreams, they can only die into them, with the "flooding moonlight" (II, 71) pouring into their death chamber and the tapestry huntsman bringing the spirit of the woods all about them.

The high tragic destiny of Tristram and Iseult of Ireland, the sense that this cannot be and yet this must be, is further defined by the other lives. It is defined by Iseult of Brittany's pliant domesticity, by the evident truth of the narrator's assertion that, "weak as she is," she would find it "ill to bear" a "noisier life" than the one she leads after Tristram's death, a life, indeed, like Iseult of

Ireland's at the court of King Marc (III, 100–1). Unlike Tristram and Iseult of Ireland, she accepts what life brings her and does not dispute her destiny. As innocent as her children, she "can divine / A grief, and sympathise" (I, 322–26), but she does not, and apparently cannot, act within the realm of experience: an Ismene, not an Antigone. Her situation is imbued with pathos, with the quiet, indeed passive, acceptance of sorrow, but she is too innocent to be tragic. Iseult of Brittany shares with the narrator her ability to sympathize, although her character, unlike his, is presented consistently. The consistency of the narrator's characterization suffers more than any other element in the poem from Arnold's variation of rhyme, meter, and, especially, diction. In passages where the narrator engages in moral reflection upon the story (as distinct from his more usual office of describing the various settings of the story), Arnold "medievalizes" his diction with archaisms (I, 256–68, III, 112–50). The chief consequence of Arnold's efforts is to dissociate the narrator from an authorial point of view. With his common-sense, his occasional moralizing, his Burtonian prescription of exercise as a cure for melancholy, the narrator is reminiscent of Pausanias in *Empedocles on Etna*. He describes the situation without fully understanding or perhaps fully feeling it; hence his outburst against "this fool passion" (III, 133–50). Interestingly, Arnold omitted from the three editions after 1852 the passage containing the narrator's most explicit moral commentary (III, 112–50). Professor Allott suggests that Arnold may have thought "the digression" too long.[16] We can, of course, only speculate, but I do not find Professor Allott's proposal very winning in the context of so "digressive" a poem as *Tristram and Iseult,* and offer as an alternative the supposition that Arnold was not satisfied that he had sufficiently dissociated the narrator from himself, and thought that the passage might be read, as, indeed, Professor Allott reads it, as "clearly autobiographical." In the orchestration of voices and landscapes which is *Tristram and Iseult,* no one voice and no one landscape is "right," and none is "wrong." They simply are the voices and landscapes, points of view and settings, of the passionate life, which is sometimes tragic, sometimes nearly comic. For the major effect of the Merlin and Vivian story is not, as it were, to present

[16] Allott, p. 220. Arnold told Clough that if he republished *Tristram and Iseult* he would "try to make it more intelligible. . . . The whole affair is by no means thoroughly successful," *Clough Letters,* pp. 135–36; May 1, 1853.

Iseult of Ireland from the point of view of Iseult of Brittany. Its
effect is rather to evaporate the sorrow, the pathos and tragedy,
from the love situation, and to leave it charmingly remote, faintly
ridiculous, and not at all the kind of dream to haunt one's sleeping
or one's waking hours. The story of Merlin and Vivian depends,
indeed, upon the old joke of January and May, a joke that cap-
italizes upon the incongruity between youth and age and the attempt of age to be young in spite of itself. Merlin, that "learned
wight" whose "best wits took flight" when he became the "stately
prize" of the gay enchantress, is sufficiently absurd to neutralize any
feelings of pity or sympathy for him (III, 178–82). The charmed
circle in which Merlin is imprisoned glances back through the poem
not only to the sheltered hollow in which Iseult tells his story, to
the forest settings of the tapestry, of Tristram's melancholy and the
chapel with the fountain, but also to the persistent concern with
magic, dreams and enchantment: to the love potion, the dream
haunts of the children, the huntsman's suspicion that *"some glam-
our"* has made him sleep (II, 175), the vision of Iseult of Ireland in
the battle and the forest glade. The story of Merlin and Vivian
captures and refocuses the poem's attention to landscape, enchantment, youth and age. But it does not, any more than the narrator's
earlier remarks, provide a definitive commentary upon the main
action: Tristram is not Merlin, nor is Vivian either of the Iseults,
although they have points in common. Merlin and Vivian are
another perspective, similar to that of the tapestry huntsman, which
distances and fades out the high passion and sorrow of the main
action. At the end of the poem Vivian is surpassingly weary of
Merlin's love, and with her we pass on to other matters. The story
of Merlin and Vivian is, no more than the whole third part, an
"epilogue." It is instead the last voice to be orchestrated, the last
variation upon a theme.

vi

Although *Tristram and Iseult* presents points of view on love, its
primary concern with the pain of feeling and the difficulty of com-
prehending the passion of love leaves out of account the possibility
of meaningful communion in love, which is touched upon in some
of the lyrics of 1852 and most fully considered in *The Buried Life*.

The delusively temporary harmony of calm nights in *To Mar-guerite—Continued* and *A Farewell* becomes in *The Buried Life* the goal and final affirmation. The harmonious calm is still temporary, but by insisting upon its validity and concluding with that insistence Arnold sounds a note of qualified optimism more in accord with *A Summer Night* and *Kensington Gardens* than with the Marguerite lyrics.

The Buried Life is a difficult poem to understand and a difficult poem to describe accurately. Its concluding metaphor ranks high in the roster of memorable endings to Arnold's poems, and the whole piece is a widely used example of a doctrine or belief central to Arnold's work in both verse and prose: the Stoic and Socratic know thyself. But it is an unsettling and finally unsatisfactory poem, partly, it seems, because it differs from most of Arnold's other early pieces of comparable or greater length in making no use of literal landscape and substituting explicit discourse with incidental landscape metaphors. It is likely to be reminiscent at first of *Epilogue to Lessing's Laocoön*. But such a reminiscence is misleading, because the landscape metaphors of *The Buried Life* are not really analogies illustrating an argument. Instead they are attempts to render an imperfectly understood perception and, at the same time, to convey a sense of meditation upon the conditions of life and the world that can generalize the introspection and the spiritual exercise.

It was possibly misleading to speak of attempts "to render" something imperfectly understood, for the poem is quite evidently an attempt to explain a confused situation. We begin with a "nameless sadness," "a something in this breast" (ll. 3–6), and "the mystery of this heart" (l. 52). We end with the metaphorical life stream, clearly defined by its origin and end. The body of the poem, we may say, is an attempt to validate the assurance of the final consolation. The method is to use brief and discontinuous metaphors, principally of water, as glosses upon the emotional and intellectual disturbance, and then to gather them together into an extended metaphor which both contains and transcends the tenor of the earlier metaphors. At first it may seem that we should look for topographical consistency in the use of water imagery, and it is true that consistency of this kind would facilitate the association of the early metaphors with the final metaphor. But, as commentators have noticed, the river image is applied in different and topographically incompatible ways. Its function is to distinguish the surface of life, our quotidian sayings and doings, from the concealed truth of our nature, that sense of coherence and purpose which is presumed to come from knowing what it is to be man and a particular man. In pursuit of this function the river emerges as subterranean (ll. 38–40, 55–56, 72–76), as comprising the purposeful currents of the depth and the confused eddies of the surface (ll. 41–44), and, finally, as defined horizontally, from source to sea, instead of vertically (ll. 88–98). To harmonize these metaphors it is necessary to suppose something like Coleridge's sacred river. But such a supposition violates the mode of the poem by assuming that its meanings are principally established through the vehicle of its recurrent metaphor, rather than through the tenor.

What, strictly, the vehicles establish is the mood of the poem, the kinds of feeling associated with the intellectual endeavor to know oneself as a man. They are necessary to the poem because the intellectual endeavor issues constantly in vaguely defined emotion rather than philosophical precision. Indeed, the poem's weakness seems in part to inhere in its mistaking of the appropriate mode for its purpose. The fact that the river metaphors are discontinuous, that they make no coherent topographical scene, and that most of the lines are devoted to explicit utterance, to an attempted explanation of a human situation, requires for success a clarity of thought at odds with the poem's rendering of vaguely defined emotion. The poem requires, in fact, a preponderance of landscape vehicle in the manner of *A Summer Night*. What *The Buried Life* offers is an attempt at clarity through the separation of the earlier metaphors into the distinct objects of the final landscape.

While the life stream in its various guises provides the most clearly marked of the landscape settings, it is complemented throughout by a series of largely unobtrusive metaphors drawn from a favorite Arnoldian, indeed Victorian, cluster: burning plains, hot cities, brazen prisons, pointless battles. These metaphors provide us with locked hearts (l. 13), a bolt in the breast (l. 84), and chained lips (l. 28). They take us into "the din of strife" "in the world's most crowded streets" (ll. 45–46), and involve us in "the hot race" for the "elusive shadow, rest" (ll. 91–93). They explain part of the discontinuity of the river metaphors, for the life stream is presented in different relationships to the metaphor of the city as prison house. Since the pointlessness of quotidian living is represented, as elsewhere in Arnold, both by imprisonment on land and aimless wandering on the water, the stream of buried life emerges both as subterranean and as the purposeful current of water depths, driving below the cross-currents of the surface. The association of land and water metaphors commences, in fact, if elliptically, in the first line of the poem: "light flows our war of mocking words." The lack of true communion in this verbal sparring is pointed by the metaphoric war, which looks forward to the socially more inclusive "din of strife." But the war "flows" metaphorically like a river, and this metaphor for a metaphor fixes in the opening situation the identity of land and water experience. The poem proceeds by separating out land and water into their due associations with heat and thirst and with tears, limpid eyes, coolness, and refreshment. With the final lovers' communion land and water are recombined, but now as distinct objects in a composed landscape, which involves the speaker in turning from the land war, now a hot race, to contemplate the truth of water.

This "process" resolves the emotion, the inexplicable feeling of the opening situation. But to describe it as a "process" involves the extrapolation of incidental images from the meditation as if they alone constituted the poem. And the meditation is principally conveyed through philosophizing. It is the philosophy, the thought of the poem, which is left unresolved at the end, which remains as much a mystery as it was at the beginning. The mystery is darkest in lines 16–44, whose confusion is signaled most obviously by the shifting pronouns they employ. At first, what is concealed are "thoughts" whose expression would leave their speaker vulnerable to the scorn of others (ll. 16–19). Such thoughts are evidently those large ideas of universal brotherhood, the sense that "the same heart beats in every human breast" (l. 23), which are so difficult to express without pomposity or sentimental mawkishness. But it is left unclear whether the buried life is our common humanity or only our sense of common humanity, whether there is only one river in whose depths or on whose surface or by whose banks all men exercise themselves, or whether each individual has his own private river, identical, it may be, with the private rivers of other men, but nonetheless his exclusive property. The confusion is marked, I said, by the shifting pronouns, for there is the "we" of the two (presumably representative) lovers in lines 24–29, the generic "man" with "his being's law" of lines 30–37, and the "we" of all men

together possessed of "the unregarded river of our life" in lines 38–
44. The difference between a private and a communal river is one
between ethical and social problems of unreserved communion with
others or at least with one other and metaphysical problems involving an answer to the question, "whence our lives come and
where they go" (l. 54). The underlying assumption of this ambiguity is that unreserved communion will answer the metaphysical
question. But it does not. Communion merely conveys the feeling
that the problem is understood. A man (now an indubitable individual) "thinks he knows" the origin and the end of life, but his
"knowing" consists in contemplating landscape features, the hills
and the sea, for which the poem provides no conceptual equivalents. There is, therefore, nothing to check the obvious and commonplace association of the source and issue of a river with birth
and death. Communion is evidence of common humanity in the
most banal of senses: all men are born, live awhile, and die; the
strife of emulation, the hot race of life, the confusing cross-currents
of the world are finally to be defined by the ancient acceptance of
the natural cycle. Rest in a wise passivity. What remains unclear
is how such an unexceptional consolation follows from the earlier
difficult search for a hidden self. The spiritual exercise confronted
problems of full communion and the metaphysical definition of life
in terms other than those of life itself. The final consolation is
wholly in terms of the life cycle from birth to death. Because the
discontinuous metaphors used to express part of the problems
finally emerge as a triumphantly clear metaphor, it seems, superficially, that the problems have been solved. But only the emotions
excited by the problems have been soothed and resolved; the conceptual issues are, if anything, even more nebulous than they were
at the beginning. It was not only in *Culture and Anarchy* that
Arnold showed himself an unsystematic philosopher.[17]

vii

Unquestionably, much of the weakness of *The Buried Life* derives from its attempt at a discourse on the value of communion
and self-knowledge. Success in Arnold's poems comes usually from
finding and rendering an adequate landscape equivalent for the
feelings excited by his thoughts. Such, at least, is the foundation

[17] *Complete Prose*, V, 88–89, e.g.

for Arnold's finest lyric, *Dover Beach,* whose movement from literal
to metaphoric landscape and many of whose motifs are reminiscent
of *A Summer Night.* Nor is *A Summer Night* the only poem in
1852 of which *Dover Beach* is reminiscent, and it is on this basis
that I would justify treating the poem out of the chronological order of its publication. *Dover Beach,* of course, was not published
until 1867, but a composition date in 1851 is generally accepted,[18]
and like other pieces of evidently delayed publication—*Calais Sands*
and *Stanzas from the Grande Chartreuse*—it has an obvious place in
the European "itinerary" of the 1852 volume.

Most of Arnold's better poems are suggestive through expansion;
they are usually of at least medium length, and work slowly to
establish the landscape as an objective equivalent to the emotions
they inspire in the observer. *Dover Beach,* by contrast, is suggestive
through concentration, as if it were a distillation of moods and
landscape motifs Arnold had worked out more fully elsewhere. It
seems to capture, indeed, in its thirty-seven lines, the burden of
Empedocles on Etna, Tristram and Iseult, and *The Buried Life,*
to combine with an economy rare in Arnold his preoccupation with
a lovers' communion, the difference between epochs, the wistful delusions of moonlit scenes, the disappearance of religious certitude,
the anarchy of modern life. More strongly than with any other of
Arnold's poems we are likely to feel the relevance to *Dover Beach*
of Professor Wimsatt's definition of poetry as "a feat of style by
which a complex of meaning is handled all at once." The relevance
may strike us because we seem never fully to know or at least to
account for *Dover Beach,* even if we are able to resist the temptation to circumambulate the poem in ever-widening circles seeking
analogues in the collective history of western man.

Dover Beach begins with a striking parallel to the remembered
scene of *A Summer Night;* it ends with a parallel to Tristram on
the plains before Rome. It begins, that is, with security, and ends
with vulnerable exposure; begins in silence and ends in alarms.
As in *A Summer Night,* the sense of security is established by movement in from the sea to the land, each detail in the scene adding to
the protection of the speaker and his companion. Much of the work
is performed by adjectives: calm, fair, tranquil, sweet. But the adjectives only deepen the suggestions of security which come from
the successive images of enclosure: the sea held between the straits,

[18] Allott, pp. 239–40.

the French and English coasts, the bay between the cliffs, and, finally, the window through which the speaker looks, framing the scene. The pictorial impression is so strong that the poem's descriptive order is readily reversible into two people standing in a room, looking out through a window upon a bay with headlands on either side and beyond to the sea held between coasts. The emphasis falls upon stasis: the vast cliffs, the full tide, the moon lying fair upon the English channel, a Cynthia couched upon the waters. Even the one touch of change and movement, the light on the French coast which "gleams and is gone," implies a going to rest, Iseult of Brittany, it may be, dousing the light which showed like a star to the Channel fishermen. Without recourse to such explicit words as *rest* and *bed*, Arnold evokes the sense of secure sleep, and so strongly that the window through which the speaker looks appears a bedroom window, at which the two people stand for a moment before retiring. But before they can do so, sound breaks in upon the silent contemplation, not only disturbing the peace with a "grating roar" but also shattering the stasis into movement, a restless, if measured, to-and-fro which is the antithesis of deep sleep. Implicit in the much-admired description of water breaking on the shore, implicit in the studied onomatopoeia, is the strong suggestion of hostility. The waves which "draw back, and fling" the pebbles "up the high strand" are like so many Davids pelting the giant land, prefiguring the clash of ignorant armies with which the poem ends, moving us from peace to war.

But the waves also bring "the eternal note of sadness in," that "ground-tone / Of human agony" which sobbed "through the hum" of the mountain stream and mountain bee in 'Obermann' (ll. 33–36). "Eternal" is not, it may be, a theologically precise gloss on things human, but it does facilitate the geographical and historical expansion to "Sophocles long ago" beside a distant southern sea. Sophocles exemplifies the enduring truth of a mood generated in one time and place. He also makes appropriate the muted classical references of the last two verse paragraphs, the least important of which is the long-recognized "source" of the concluding night battle in Thucydides, awareness of which does not deepen our sense of the poem. Much more important is the description of the "Sea of Faith" in terms of the ancient Ocean Stream encircling the land mass of the known world. We need to take this reference in order to feel the metaphorical force of the contrast between epochs. The age of faith is as obsolete as an antique map; a map of modern sensibility must chart the ever-retreating horizons of discovery.[19] The spatial ordonnance of the opening scene is transformed into temporal sequence by way of implied cartography. The vastness of the English cliffs had the security of massive guardians. The vastness of the world's edges has only the frightening vulnerability of almost limitless emptiness. The Sea of Faith, moreover, emerges as Ocean Stream by way of simile: it "lay like the folds of a bright girdle furl'd." Arnold first wrote "a bright garment,"[20] a phrase providing a neater contrast than "girdle" to the "naked shingles" of modern coasts. But the girdle does provide a more precise image of encirclement without altogether losing the sense of clothing.[21] For it is evident that in the images of clothing and nakedness we have a continuation of the implied humanizing of the scene begun by the moon lying on the straits and the threatening gestures of the waves.

It is also clear that the pictorial movement of the poem is almost complete. We began with the sea out in the Channel and moved in to the shoreline. Contemplation of the sea generated a security and tranquillity gradually destroyed by the thoughts and sounds of the beach. Now the sea has retreated, leaving the beaches open and unprotected. We are ready for the final move inland on to the darkling plain. The light gleamed and disappeared on the French coast. The bright girdle was withdrawn, and now, it seems, the moon has also gone. More accurately, it acquires its usual association in Arnold with delusive dreams of the kind which may appropriately be dreamt in the full, calm sleep of the poem's opening. In fact, the whole poem has about it the air of a waking dream by virtue of the heavy deliberation which always makes the poem feel so much longer than it is. As so often happens in dreams, the sense of protective security gives place to the nightmare of exposure and vaguely defined threat. Tristram's children may dream happily and

[19] This point is made by Culler, p. 40.
[20] *Commentary*, p. 174.
[21] The change to "girdle" may also recall in this context of muted and explicit classical reference the embroidered cestus of Venus, which brings with it associations of love, emotion, and enchantment so appropriate to the whole poem. But this is a possible gloss not sufficiently demanded or realized by the terms of the poem. It is also possible that "girdle" permits a muted etymological pun on "shingles." The collective "shingle" is evidently pluralized as a synecdoche for "beaches," but the plural may permit allusion to the different derivation from the classical word for girdle, now the exclusive property of dermatologists. But such a pun is not, to my knowledge, in accord with Arnold's usual handling of language.

securely of innocent pleasure; they may be entranced by a fairy tale, but Tristram himself has only a fitful and haunted rest. In such a condition support can only come from one who has shared the dream, one who has known both the delusive harmony and the nightmare threat, both "the world which seems" and the world which is, the joy of being and the pain of becoming.

If Arnold really did write *Dover Beach* in 1851, it is no doubt fruitless to speculate on his reasons for delaying its publication. The delay, if delay it were, is particularly puzzling in view of the way the 1852 volume requires the poem for completeness. There is no poem in the volume which unites, as *Dover Beach* unites, the Empedoclean experience of changing epochs with the dreams and frustrations of Tristram. *Empedocles on Etna* shares with such poems as *The Future, 'Obermann,' Memorial Verses,* and *The Youth of Nature* a concern with the role of the sage and poet in bad times of doubt, despair, and confused individualism. This group is linked with the 1852 poems dealing with the trials of love by the attribution of unhappiness to the cross circumstances of a vaguely conceived destiny. What may be called the Empedocles group occupies itself with the destiny of nations as it affects the general plight of individuals, while the Tristram group deals with the destiny of individuals in love. Only in *Dover Beach* is the fate of individual love clearly associated with the destiny of nations and the evolution of European civilization.

Dover Beach succeeds, moreover, in just that point where poems of 1852 concerning themselves to some degree with historicism are usually at their weakest. The poem succeeds, that is, in expressing its philosophical tenor through a fully adequate landscape vehicle. As always, the critical use of "tenor and vehicle" requires modification and explanation. They are a useful pair of words which yet deceptively imply a clear separation between concept and concrete embodiment. Such a separation may be evident in a poem like *The Future,* where the river of time serves as a rather more successful link for the various historical vignettes than the associational principle of *Consolation.* Despite the descriptive charm of the vignettes, the function of the river as analogy for a preconceived discourse is evident from the careful explanation of "as is the world on the banks / So is the mind of man" (ll. 17–18). We have to deal, that is, with a largely excogitated landscape, a landscape thought up and thought out to fit the discourse. Typically enough, the imaginative concentration needed to make landscape detail fit the discourse takes charge as the river nears the sea. The historicist tenor is submerged beneath the waves of emotion Arnold seemed always to feel when contemplating moving water. The time stream is tacitly converted into an individual life stream and the conceptual precision of the bulk of the poem is quite lost. But in *Dover Beach* only critical custom requires that we speak of landscape vehicle and conceptual tenor. A more accurate description would identify the way in which ideas are a vehicle for the emotions excited by and located in the landscape setting. Since ideas explain landscape and the emotional response to it, the poem avoids the disjunction which occurs elsewhere in Arnold when a landscape vehicle for a conceptual tenor is elaborated upon for the sake of descriptive charm and emotions of only slight relevance to the tenor. *Dover Beach*, moreover, avoids another kind of disjunction by the economy with which explanatory ideas are presented. *The Youth of Nature* also begins with a present scene in its evocation of Wordsworth country, and moves to a historical parallel in the vignette of Tiresias (ll. 34–47) which serves a purpose similar to that of Sophocles in *Dover Beach*. But Wordsworth and Tiresias account for only the first third of *The Youth of Nature;* thereafter the poem pursues the philosophical issues of nature, historicism, poet, and prophet. It never returns, other than allusively, to the initial occasion, which consequently functions in the poem as an emotional exordium to a discourse. *Dover Beach* avoids this sort of disjunction, partly through brevity, but also because the final battlefield is explicitly "here" and implicitly-now, the same night after the moon has set. *Dover Beach* just succeeds, as relatively few of Arnold's poems succeed, in not thinking and feeling by turns. But T. S. Eliot would probably not have approved this application of his famous phrase.

EMPEDOCLES ON ETNA is Arnold's greatest poem. It is
more ambitious, more complex, and more inclusive than anything else he wrote. It projects through its compound of history,
legend, and fiction a total myth of Victorian England as Arnold saw
it. Moreover, this is a myth whose separate elements—the value of
the active and contemplative lives, the function of poetry in its
lyrical and didactic modes, the nature of the heroic, the historical
consciousness, the sense of landscape—are fully congruent with each
other. But even those who have admired the poem have usually expressed at least moderate dissatisfaction with the long homily delivered by Empedocles to Pausanias in the second scene. Their dissatisfaction is with the homily's quality of expression and, less often,
with its quality of thought. The diction of this long speech has
been variously described, but perhaps the usefully imprecise adjective "prosaic" best sums up what most readers feel when they compare this speech with the rest of the poem. It is not difficult to explain why, if it is to perform its proper function in the whole work,
this speech must be comparatively prosaic in expression. But even
after such an explanation there is residual dissatisfaction with a
speech which is so consistently prosaic and which comprises, moreover, almost a third of the poem's lines. For evaluative purposes, we
can say that the speech accords with the standard of conspicuous
holism advocated by Pope in his *Essay on Criticism*: the speech,
while more than a slight fault, plainly contributes to the joint force
and full result of all. But the speech fails to accord with the more

exacting standard of uninsistent holism advocated by Coleridge in the fourteenth chapter of *Biographia Literaria*: however much it contributes to the delight of the whole, the speech does not offer distinct gratification as a component part.

There are, in fact, several overlapping explanations of why the speech must be comparatively prosaic if it is to make its proper contribution to the whole work. If properly phrased, these explanations will confirm the sense we should have that *Empedocles on Etna* differs in kind as well as degree from Arnold's other poems. Unquestionably, each of the poem's elements recalls, when taken separately, a similar element in another of Arnold's poems. We can trace the lines of the Strayed Reveller in Callicles, or of Obermann in Empedocles. The brief descriptions of Catana in the hot plain recall Bokhara; the glen of Callicles recalls the haunts of the Scholar Gipsy and the palace of Circe. Typho is an Arnoldian Byron; Cadmus and Harmonia rest as peacefully after a painful life as the Duke and Duchess of Savoy in *The Church of Brou*. Empedocles' homily against hedonism inverts the arguments of Mycerinus, and the place where he delivers it to his disciple may remind us that *Progress* in the 1852 volume deals with the Sermon on the Mount. The persistent concern with good and bad times, with the difference between epochs, is reminiscent of both the Strayed Reveller's paired vignettes and the historicism of *The Future, The Youth of Nature,* and *The Youth of Man.* The association of Wordsworth in *The Youth of Nature* with Tiresias by "the spring of Tilphusa" could have made another song by Callicles. Even the prosaic quality of the homily to Pausanias finds a parallel of sorts in Arnold's frequent use of a section of fairly straightforward discourse to precede or follow a section of imaginative absorption into landscape. But a full explanation of the homily involves matters which cannot be paralleled elsewhere in Arnold, and thus helps us determine in what way *Empedocles on Etna* differs from the poems it recalls; why so many of the same parts should make a different whole. One reason is that *Empedocles on Etna* has a crucially different subject.

i

Unlike Matthew Arnold, Empedocles of Agrigentum had a developed metaphysic, a theory of noumenon informing and making comprehensible the confusing multiplicity of phenomena. Arnold's

Empedocles is sufficiently Arnoldian to have learned to doubt his metaphysic, but sufficiently un-Arnoldian to be capable of a final assertion that his metaphysic still has validity. Empedocles of Agrigentum had also an ethic of sorts; at least there are in his fragments some gnomic rules of conduct based upon his view of the delusive partiality of phenomena and of mortality as a painful exile from immortal bliss. Arnold's Empedocles expands those gnomic rules into a developed ethic with the aid of large accessions from Lucretius and the Stoics.[1] Arnold's Empedocles is an Arnoldian man distinguished from his fellows by some important traces of the antique Sicilian. The conjunction of the two figures makes to some extent explicable a spectacular suicide which appears in the records as a highly suppositious story.[2]

Arnold discounted in later life the identity of his Empedocles and himself, pointing out that Empedocles incontestably fails to produce a creed for himself to live by. He admitted, however, to "a sympathy with the figure Empedocles presents to the imagination," and explained that, being "greatly impressed" by Empedocles, he "desired to gather up and draw out as a whole the hints which his remains offered."[3] Authorial comment fifteen years after the fact should not be received without question: in his homily to Pausanias Empedocles does, after all, offer a creed for men to live by, a creed, moreover, obviously similar to that given elsewhere in Arnold's poems. But in several important ways this late letter accurately describes what happens in the poem. Arnold draws upon the leading Empedoclean doctrine of four elements forever combining and dissolving into warring antinomies under the contrary influences of love and strife, of the whole as an eternally adjusted relationship between elements and influences, and of the part as a temporary mixture of elements into a particular form. Certainly there are differences. The attractive and harmonizing influence of love largely disappears from Arnold's poem to be replaced by a Romantic joy in the oneness of all things. Joy, indeed, is a due

[1] For detailed parallels see *Commentary*, pp. 294–96, and Allott, notes *passim*.
[2] Simon Karsten, ed., *Philosophorum Graecorum Veterum . . . Operum Reliquiae*, II (Amsterdam, 1838), 36–37: "haec narratio [of the suicide on Etna] . . . nec ab ullo facile sano judice credita." Karsten's edition of the pre-Socratics, with the introductory life of Empedocles, was Arnold's main source, as we know from his extant notes on Karsten (see *Commentary*, p. 289). For the possibility of an additional "Empedoclean" source for Arnold's poem in Hölderlin's fragmentary drama, *Empedokles auf dem Ätna*, see Fred L. Burwick, "Hölderlin and Arnold: Empedocles on Etna," *Comparative Literature*, XVII (1965), 24–42.
[3] *Commentary*, p. 288.

sense of the activities and manifestations of Empedoclean love. The influence of strife emerges in the poem as anything which tends to dissociation and disintegration: hate, emulation, an over-busy mind, or an over-indulged appetite. But behind these differences, important as they are, there is still something of the original metaphysic, showing itself in allusive references to metempsychosis and especially in the exultant suicide carried out in the belief that something may still be salvaged from a wrecked life. For Empedocles of Agrigentum each mortal existence is a purgatorial probation either for immortal bliss[4] or, if the conditions are not met, for still another existence as "boy, girl, plant, bird, and dumb sea-fish."[5] Death is not an end, "but only a mixing and exchange of what has been mixed."[6] Arnold's Empedocles is principally in the condition set out in the first fragment of the edition used by Arnold: an exile from bliss because he trusted in furious strife.[7] In such a condition he is evidently far from the highest state of mortality which the original Empedocles elsewhere claims for himself, that state of prophet, bard, physician, prince which is the prelude to deification.[8] Arnold's Empedocles, indeed, disclaims his role as physician and lays down the insignia of bard, prophet and prince. He commits suicide to avoid dying in "despondency and gloom" (II, 414). He commits suicide while he can still feel at one with himself and "with the whole world" (II, 371–72), while he can still hope to escape the dreary cycle of metempsychosis through ever more fruitless lives (II, 373–90, 404–16).

It is reasonable to assume that Arnold did not reproduce the Empedoclean doctrine of metempsychosis as a "magister vitae" for himself and his public. It is also reasonable to enquire into the presumed relevance of such a doctrine for Arnold's generation. Arnold described himself as impressed by Empedocles and possessed of an imaginative sympathy with his figure. We have to deal once more, in fact, with an emotional and imaginative response to a human situation. That is the primary concern, the tenor. The Empedoclean metaphysic is to a large extent present in the poem as a vehicle for the emotion, as an explanation and motivation of

---

[4] Karsten, II, 140–43.
[5] Karsten, II, 140–41. I use the trans. of Kathleen Freeman, *Ancilla to the Pre-Socratic Philosophers* (Cambridge, Mass., 1957), p. 65.
[6] Karsten, II, 96–97; Freeman, p. 52.
[7] Karsten, II, 85–86.
[8] Karsten, II, 140–43.

human response and action. We may apply, indeed, at least to the second act, in which the metaphysic is concentrated, the judgment of Arnold's own Empedocles on Callicles' song of Typho: "he fables, yet speaks truth" (II, 89). The "truth," as Arnold insisted in the 1853 preface, is the modernity, the relevance, of Empedocles' feelings, when doubt and discouragement have replaced calm and cheerfulness.[9] The "fable" is the conceptual system through which he expresses those feelings. Empedocles did not have to believe literally in the story of Typho's revolt in order to find in it a widely applicable truth. Arnold's readers do not have to swallow metempsychosis in order to see the validity and relevance of Empedocles' situation and feelings.

That is not to say the metaphysic is some curious, antiquarian appendix irrelevant to the working of the poem. Its status is quite otherwise. The metaphysic "explains" existence; it identifies a single process working through all things, human and non-human. If it holds, and it is of course at the point of breaking, it makes for a symbolic world, in which all phenomena are part of the truth they signify, in which the glow of the volcano, the swell of the sea, and the light of the stars (II, 323–25) point, like the succession of human feelings, to the same process of combining and resolving elements. If, then, this is so, the natural setting and the philosophical reflections are united. The reflections are at least in part, and an important part, about the setting, as well as being delivered in it. Herein lies the difference between *Empedocles on Etna* and Arnold's other poems.

ii

Characteristically, it will be recalled, landscape functions in Arnold's poems as an analogy for emotion and sometimes for a way of life. Spiritual aridity is rendered by geographical aridity; calm seas and tempests render the voyage of life. Suggestiveness in such a mode comes principally through the accretion of descriptive detail, the emotion revealing and objectifying itself in the elaboration of a scene. When a conceptual point is to be made, the scene usually becomes or begins as overt metaphor: a sea of life or faith, a river of life or time, a summit of truth. Such a procedure implies

[9] *Complete Prose,* I, 1.

the separateness of man and the natural world, the distinction insisted upon by Arnold in the early sonnets, *In Harmony with
Nature* and *Religious Isolation*. Because the conditions for man
and the natural world are different, any connection between them
becomes one of analogy. For the analogy to be evident, it is usually
necessary to adopt a reasonably explicit syntax: we can scarcely
mistake the association of the fell walk in *Resignation* with a way
of life because the opening lines had clearly associated travel with
a world view. Such explicitness is limiting, of course; and expansiveness is nearly always in the area of generalized emotion
prompted by the scene.

But *Empedocles on Etna* differs materially by being about a man
who has, or had, a philosophy of the oneness of man and natural
phenomena. The "charr'd and quaking crust" (II, 307), the cool
glade of Etna, are, like man, part of the one life, products of "our
mother earth's miraculous womb" (II, 340). Because all things are
part of the same truth, they will be analogous to each other, and
associations between them will often be expressed by simile, the
characteristic syntax of analogy. But the analogies derive from a
metaphysic, not a rhetoric; they belong to a manner of looking at
the world, not a manner of discourse. They have, accordingly, a
far wider range of conceptual application than is usual in Arnold.
Empedocles on Etna is a conceptually rich poem, not only because
it has much philosophy—so has *Resignation*—but because the phenomena of the natural setting are included in the concepts and are
not only an objectification of the emotions prompted by the ideas.

Like man, Mount Etna is composed of, and in touch with, the
elements. Like man, it exemplifies the perpetually shifting relationship between harmony and strife. Callicles opens the drama by
asking of Apollo "what mortal could be sick or sorry here?" (I, i,
20). He closes the drama by assuring Apollo that this is no place
for the god of poetry when "Etna heaves fiercely / Her forest-clothed
frame" (II, 419–20). There is no Typho beneath Etna, except in
the fables of poets, but the mountain embeds its "roots of stone" in
the sea (II, 43–44), and permits at its summit a closer communion
with the stars. It exemplifies in its various regions the shift from
fertility to barrenness whose human manifestations preoccupy
Empedocles. The clarity with which the elements may be identified
on Etna makes of it an epitome of the natural world and hence a
fitting place for the meditations of a man seeking oneness with all

life. Empedocles wishes to glow like the mountain, swell with the sea, to be as "full of light as the stars," to brood "over the world like the air" (II, 323–26). And the syntax suggests the analogies of rhetoric. But the similes derive from a physics:

> To the elements it came from
> Everything will return—
> Our bodies to earth,
> Our blood to water,
> Heat to fire,
> Breath to air.   (II, 331–36)

One may reasonably speculate that a major attraction of the Empedocles story to Arnold, an attraction sufficient to divert him from his projected play about Lucretius,[10] was the curious legend of the philosopher's end on the mountain, which receives such sceptical mention in the lives by Diogenes Laertius and Karsten. Lucretius was to have been treated with all the panoply of historical action.[11] It was a sound if temporary instinct for his own poetic strengths which led Arnold to substitute a poetic drama with little action but with the most richly suggestive natural feature in all his poetry.

Professor Allott properly points out that the poem implies a "journey from youth to middle age" by setting its three scenes in the mountain's forest region in early morning, on the bare upper slopes at noon, and the summit in the evening.[12] The suggestions for the human cycle of this diurnal and geographical progress are intensified by the fact that the three characters, Callicles, Pausanias, and Empedocles, represent youth, maturity, and age, and that each moves only so far up the mountain as he has progressed in life: Callicles stops in the forest, Pausanias goes on to the upper slopes, Empedocles alone stands on the summit. Professor Culler rightly observes that Pausanias is associated with the hot cities of the plain, with, that is, the dustily unpleasant conditions of the active life.[13] And we may add that Pausanias receives from Empedocles a sermon on proper active living in a most appropriate place, for the upper slopes at noon have all the heat and unattractiveness of the city: in

[10] Karsten, II, 57, links Empedocles and Lucretius as unquestionably pre-eminent among the Greek and Roman didactic poets who celebrated the nature of things.

[11] *Commentary*, pp. 342–45.

[12] Allott, p. 149.

[13] Culler, p. 161.

both places success comes from loving the sun, from shining like the yellow gentian in those Arnoldian cities which are nearly always burning hot (I, ii, 4–6). The active life is a contest in the sun, as Callicles reminds us with almost the last lines of the poem:

> The day in his hotness,
> The strife with the palm.

Professor Allott finds also in the progress "from youth to middle age" a journey "from elasticity of spirit to world-weariness, from a proper balance of man's mental powers to his 'enslavement' by thought."[14] Callicles unquestionably possesses the "pure natural joy" which Empedocles shared with Parmenides when young and whose loss he now laments (II, 235–49). Between them, Pausanias is evidently flirting with that undue intellectual curiosity, that pressing for news "of the last miracle" (I, ii, 106), whose longer operation in Empedocles we must presume to have, at least in part, substituted doubt and anxiety for the earlier joyful contentment. The homily of the second scene is accordingly anti-intellectualist to the extent that Empedocles endeavors to reprove the curiosity of Pausanias and thus save him from falling into the condition of Empedocles himself. We may find, indeed, a further extension of the distinctions between settings and between times of day and life. The philosophies of the active and contemplative lives expressed on the upper slopes and at the summit concentrate respectively on the heart and the head.

It is not the head-heart opposition of *The New Sirens*. The feelings that concern Empedocles in his homily are those of "hate, and awe, and shame" (I, ii, 112), and envy (I, ii, 118). He is concerned also with the desire for riches and for inward peace, with the impulse to sin (I, ii, 227–36), and, even, briefly, with the desire for sensory pleasure (I, ii, 352–66). He is concerned at large with everything that makes for unease and impatience, and so he includes the drive for theological and metaphysical assurance that a predictable divine plan exists or that there are definable natural rights. The ethic which emerges from this chastisement of man's pride and fretfulness is, once again, that of *Quiet Work,* with Empedocles teaching the lessons of nature. Man should base his conduct on the assumption that he has no special importance and distinction in the world:

[14] Allott, p. 149.

Nature, with equal mind,
Sees all her sons at play;
Sees man control the wind,
The wind sweep man away;
Allows the proudly-riding and the foundering bark. (I, ii, 257–61)

In such conditions "the wise man's plan" is "to work as best he can, / And win what's won by strife" (I, ii, 267–70). It makes for a familiar variant on the age-old consolation of philosophy. Empedocles claims not to be offering a rule of life which degrades the dignity of man (I, ii, 97–101). But in addressing himself to eradicating the chief ill of man: the restless desire for change and impatience with a present lot (I, ii, 149–51), he inevitably tends to recommend the unthinking life as that in which the heart's affections best flourish and in which man most readily feels the simple joys of the sun and the spring (II, i, 397–401), those other manifestations of the "one stuff" from which all things are spun (I, ii, 287–88). His exemplary man is accordingly some "village churl" who clings to a life which has brought him much toil and small but definable pleasures (I, ii, 411–16). The drift of his counsel is summed up in the immediately following song of Callicles, the song of Cadmus and Harmonia, who, after a life of such strife and ills as beset Pausanias and Empedocles, are translated by the gods to a pastoral retreat where they pass the remainder of their days, "two bright and aged snakes," "placid and dumb" (I, ii, 435, 460).[15]

If the second song of Callicles sums up the homily of Empedocles, his first song prepares for it. The parallel between the counseling of Achilles by Chiron and the counseling of Pausanias by Empedocles is too evident to have gone unremarked. It is usual to add, in Professor Allott's words, that "the traditional lore taught to Achilles contrasts with the philosophical instruction about to be given to Pausanias."[16] Professor Culler explains the significance of the contrast: Callicles is a poet of Keatsian natural magic deficient in the moral profundity Empedocles so obviously possesses. This is a partial view of things which must be left regretfully, but firmly, in the last glen where it belongs, among the trees and streams about

[15] For this parallel between the second song of Callicles and the counseling of Pausanias see Donald J. Gray, "Arthur, Roland, Empedocles, Sigurd, and the Despair of Heroes in Victorian Poetry," *Boston University Studies in English*, V (1961), 11.
[16] Allott, p. 158.

which he sings.[17] Callicles is offering in fabular form a picture of counseling in which the life of man is fully consonant with the cycles of nature and supernature. Achilles learns not only the ways of the woods and mountains, but

> of the Gods, the stars,
> The tides;—and then of mortal wars,
> And of the life which heroes lead
> Before they reach the Elysian place
> And rest in the immortal mead.   (I, ii, 71–75)

From the last glen to the Elysian fields Achilles sees life unroll before him a continuous if not entirely placid whole.[18] So too Empedocles once saw it in the days when he was young with Parmenides. What has broken the sense of continuity for him is evidently long reflection upon and exposure to those "mortal wars" which make such a comfortable item in Chiron's schedule of living.

In his homily Empedocles urged Pausanias to understand and come to terms with the impulse to restlessness he possessed by virtue of being man. He urged Pausanias to live with men but not as most men live. He asked of Pausanias "why are men ill at ease?" why "man with his lot thus fights?" and answered it is because man "believes Nature outraged if his will's gainsaid" (I, ii, 147–56). This is an explanation in terms of final cause: restlessness is a consequence of seeking to rest in a resting place not natural to man. The counsel on active living accordingly addressed itself to identifying the natural resting place: an acceptance that man is part of a whole which, being but part, he cannot fully comprehend. Attempts to do so lead only to dissatisfaction and discontent. But in addition to the explanation in terms of final cause there is the explanation in terms of formal cause: what is it in the constitution of man which leads him to have such impulses to restlessness? The contemplative life at the summit accepts, as did the earlier homily on active life, that man is composed of the elements; they constitute his matter. But his particular constitution involves the imposition of form upon matter. When man returns to the elements at death he loses his form, that shape or organizing principle which distinguishes man from other combinations of the same matter. It is this aspect of man which Empedocles calls "mind" (II, 345–63) :

[17] Culler, pp. 158–59.
[18] See *Resignation*, l. 190.

homo sapiens indeed. Empedocles confronts at the summit the dreary circumstance that it is the major defining principle of man, his mind, which works to separate man from that wished-for harmony with the one nature with which he is materially identical. Empedocles finds in this reflection none of the suggestions of human dignity which upheld Arnold in the sonnets *In Harmony with Nature* and *Religious Isolation.* The ethical injunctions of the active life on the upper slopes give place to a depressed acceptance of the metaphysically ineluctable at the summit.

Achilles learned in the glen "of the life which heroes lead," an apparently glorious probation for their "rest in the immortal mead" of Elysium. Empedocles at the summit understands the story of Typho to exemplify the passing of the age of heroes:

> The brave, impetuous heart yields everywhere
> To the subtle, contriving head;
> Great qualities are trodden down,
> And littleness united
> Is become invincible. (II, 90–94)

Chiron could teach the receptive Achilles "all the wisdom of his race" (I, ii, 76). Empedocles finds in contrast that the people who thronged about him asked not for wisdom "but drugs to charm with, / But spells to mutter" (II, 115–17). He finds that men use their minds not to understand their place in the universe and work out their personal salvation (I, ii, 27–29), but to impose their will upon others. Once the process of selfish depredation has begun, it necessarily continues and increases, removing ever further from men the possibility of "rest in the immortal mead" and substituting the dreary cycle of metempsychosis, in which

> we shall unwillingly return
> Back to this meadow of calamity,
> This uncongenial place, this human life;
> And in our individual human state
> Go through the sad probation all again. (II, 364–68)

Because Empedocles sees what he thinks necessary for man and also sees that most men are disinclined to pursue it, he almost inevitably has become "fierce, disputatious, ever at war with man" (II, 395). A consciousness of the superiority of his perception leads him, as it led Gulliver, to be "too scornful, too high-wrought, too bitter" (I, i, 149). Gulliver observed in the Houyhnhnms, "the perfection of nature," the practice of individual and social virtues by a race without original sin. When he returned to the human race, he knew his fellow men were such that the social virtues of the Houyhnhnms were impossible to exercise and, shunning the virtues appropriate to a fallen Christian community, created for himself an artificial solitude in which to keep pure his own mind, if by somewhat bizarre methods. Empedocles felt in his youth and perceives in his age the oneness of all things, the fullest sense of community. But other men now act so counter to his feeling and perception that he can no longer live with them. And yet other men are, like Empedocles, the rocks and the stars, part of the one life, and failure to live with them means the practical failure of his philosophy. The truths Empedocles can only feel and perceive in solitude are not really true if they can only be felt and perceived in solitude. Well might Arnold record in his notes for the poem that Empedocles "sees things as they are—the world as it is—God as he is: in their stern simplicity. The sight is a severe and mind-tasking one."[19]

The overbearing sense of solitude comes upon Empedocles in his reflections upon the fourth song of Callicles, the song of Apollo and Marsyas. Professor Culler asks of the song "what can Empedocles see in this but the flaying of his own joyous former self by his present cold, man-hating mood?"[20] Empedocles does not make so precise an application, but it is implicit in his rejection of the laurel and his succeeding reminiscences of his youth. Marsyas has the song of woods and lakes, a simple and convivial song, able to please

> The red-snooded Phrygian girls,
> Whom the summer evening sees
> Flashing in the dance's whirls
> Underneath the starlit trees
> In the mountain villages. (II, 180–84)

It is those same Phrygian girls, his friends, who vainly intercede with scornful Apollo for the hapless Marsyas. When Empedocles was young with Parmenides and "received the shock of mighty thoughts / On simple minds with a pure natural joy," they could find pleasure in the "smallest thing":

[19] *Commentary*, p. 291.
[20] Culler, pp. 169–70.

> The sports of the country-people,
> A flute-note from the woods,
> Sunset over the sea;
> Seed-time and harvest,
> The reapers in the corn,
> The vinedresser in his vineyard,
> The village-girl at her wheel. (II, 242–57)

No doubt it was Marsyas who sent the "flute-note from the woods."

But Apollo is the one true god of poetry. His rule is recognized even by Callicles, who has more than a touch of Marsyas in his penchant for "country-festivals" (I, ii, 15) and in his convivial songs at feasts (I, i, 31–35). In his adherence to Apollo, however, Callicles has already come, like the Strayed Reveller he so obviously resembles, to relish solitude, to wander "far among the glens" away from the "gay revelling band" he accompanied to the hills (I, ii, 16–17). No more than the Strayed Reveller has Callicles come to accept the need of poetry to constitute a "magister vitae." He sings, like the Muses of Apollo, "the action of men" (II, 464), but not of men's needs. It is the sixth interpolated poem in *Empedocles on Etna* which is, if in a special sense, the most fully Apolline: the poem recited by Empedocles to Pausanias on the upper slopes of Etna. As he delivers his homily, Empedocles accompanies *"himself in a solemn manner on his harp,"* and the stage direction makes sense only if we understand the homily to constitute a didactic poem similar, for all its accessions from later philosophy, to the didactic verses *On Nature* which Empedocles of Agrigentum addressed to a pupil called Pausanias, son of Anchites, and fragments of which form the largest part of his remains. The poem of the upper slopes, in fact, conflates, in both purpose and specific allusion, the *On Nature* of the original Empedocles with the *Katharmoi* or *Purifications,* which comprise the remainder of his canonical fragments. The *Katharmoi,* Karsten notes, were the lustral songs of poets and priests who, by almost divine, especially Apolline inspiration, saw the causes of woes and the means to expiate them.[21] For Arnold's Empedocles such a combination leads to a discourse similar in some but by no means all respects to what might be produced by the poet of *Resignation.* In particular, it offers a view of the general life and the many pains but small pleasures of active living by virtue of its detachment from active engagement. The upper slopes at noon may

[21] Karsten, II, 67.

be appropriately like the hot place of public life, but they are none-theless isolated from it. The poet of *Resignation* is self-justifying: his "sad lucidity of soul" is not anatomized for symptoms of de-spondency. But Empedocles confronts the pain of isolation visited upon the man who is a poet of impartial detachment. The poet may benefit from the detachment, but the man suffers from isola-tion, a condition in which he is not only excluded from the "life" which is his subject, but is particularly prey to the doubts which feed upon lonely contemplation. The price the gods exacted for the gift of song in *The Strayed Reveller* was small in comparison with the conditions laid upon Apollo's votary in *Empedocles on Etna*. The sympathetic imagination of Callicles can draw from him the pain-filled cry of "ah, poor Faun, poor Faun! ah, poor Faun!" But Empedocles has learned that to follow Apollo leads in the end to an adoption of Apollo's own scorn, a quality he already possesses by over-much reflection upon the insufficiency of men. These songs of Apollo sound harsher even than the words of Mercury.

But some of Apollo's songs still sound sweet. Arnold's Em-pedocles rejects poetry; his Callicles clings to it. And it was Em-pedocles whom Arnold himself came to reject, not Callicles, if on what he thought poetical rather than philosophical grounds. Pau-sanias ascends to a region analogous to active life; Empedocles pro-ceeds to the summit of contemplation; Callicles stays in the region of imagination, the cool glen which is so often in Arnold's poetry the realm of image-making and dream-weaving. But his voice carries up, and is heard both on the upper slopes and at the sum-mit; it is the last voice we hear. Callicles himself claims that

> The lyre's voice is lovely everywhere;
> In the court of Gods, in the city of men,
> And in the lonely rock-strewn mountain-glen,
> In the still mountain air.   (II, 37–40)

If the songs of Callicles are important in emphasizing the poem's vertical movement, they are also important in supplying a measure of geographical expansiveness. The settings in the Eastern Mediter-ranean are associated with Sicily because the events of Callicles' songs take place in mountainous areas and sometimes among trees. Usually, moreover, Callicles supplies some such associative link as "in such a glen," "far, far from here," or "not here, O Apollo." Etna is the dominant feature of the poem: it is the major landscape exemplification of the reflections upon the nature of man and all phenomena. Its exemplary role is greatly supported by the songs of Callicles, in which mountainous areas are settings for a variety of human actions: the giving of counsel, the pastoral retreat, the treachery and strife of men, the pains and triumphs of poetry, the keeping of sheep. The songs are pictorial examples of many of the things Empedocles discourses upon. The poem's philosophical subject is the efficacy of the active, the contemplative, and the imaginative lives as means to individual salvation. Etna and the settings of Callicles' songs are an objectification of that subject and at the same time an intimate part of it. For the poem is about man and his environment; the landscape is his environment.

The songs of Callicles also have a temporal function in their large contribution to the poem's historicism. Callicles himself has the youthful capacity for joy which is lost to Empedocles. But if Callicles is the youth of man, his songs are of the youth of nature, when gods and men engaged in active commerce, when heroes flourished, and when Achilles listened to all the wisdom of Chiron. The lore of the woods was continuous with the science of all phenomena and an assurance of a blissful hereafter. It was an untroubled journey for the Muses from "the still vale of Thisbe" to "Olympus, / Their endless abode," and on the way they sang of the night and stars, of the gods and the strife of men (II, 425–68). One syntax expresses this one, unified view of life. Love of nature is identical with love of man. But Empedocles, born into such a life, has lived out of it into a time when knowledge and the strife of men have so increased that coherence is scarcely possible any longer (II, 261–75). It is difficult to hold all things together, to speak at once of the social life in towns and the solitary life in the country. The lessons of the country are simple; the demands of the town are highly complex.

iii

This difference partly explains the prosaic quality of Empedocles' homily on the upper slopes. The songs of Callicles record a time when man was completely in harmony with nature, when human existence was definable in terms of such large fundamentals as martial and poetic contest, triumph and failure, the lore of the woods, the peace of glens. The task of the bard was then to hymn "what will be for ever; / What was from of old" (II, 459–60). But the complications of human life are now such that it cannot any longer be presented as in harmony with nature. Large fundamentals may satisfactorily account for the life of heroes, but they do not account for the life of lesser men; and the Victorian was, for Arnold, an age marked by the absence of great natures and the presence of millions of small ones.[22] It is irrelevant to urge these small men "to be like Nature strong, like Nature cool!" Natural strength and a natural ability to abide steadfastly will not do men's business in the world, will not assuage men's fear of the grave, nor satisfy men's need for a "safe conscience" and for an assurance that there exists something men may properly adore.[23] And so the homily adopts only a limited and generalized analogy between man and nature. The analogy persists throughout the poem, but its limited application in the homily means that the terms appropriate to nature will be subordinated to the terms appropriate to man. Nature is represented in the homily only generally by such words as heaven and earth, rivers, winds, lightning-fires, stones, sea, the "one stuff," tides and sands, a flood, flowers and fields. None of these words leads to descriptive elaboration. Such an elaboration would distract from the *unum necessarium* contained in the ethical injunctions of the homily. The lesson must come through clearly and simply; hence the stanzaic pattern of the homily, with its four declarative trimeters followed by a frequently summarizing alexandrine, approximate, it may be, to the hexameter line of the original Empedocles; hence, too, its reliance on unobtrusive simile and metaphor which will not distract from moral content by striking image. A Calliclean poetry, charming though it may be in its descriptiveness, enspiriting though it may be in its accounts of heroic life, is now irrelevant to the life of all those small men in towns, troubled by fear and contentiousness. The only relevant poetry now is the unadorned didacticism of Empedocles' homily to Pausanias.

Within weeks of the publication of the 1852 volume, Arnold was writing to Clough of his desiderata for modern poetry, and it is worth quoting in full a passage I have already quoted in part.

And now what shall I say? First as to the poems. Write me from America concerning them, but do not read them in the hurry of this week. Keep them, as the Solitary did his Bible, for the silent deep.

[22] *Clough Letters*, p. 111; Sept. 23 [1849]. This outburst to Clough constitutes, despite a few Victorian particulars, a schedule of social woes similar to that drawn up by Empedocles in his homily and his solitary reflections.
[23] The terms and quotations in this and the previous sentence are drawn from the 1849 sonnet, *In Harmony with Nature*.

More and more I feel that the difference between a mature and a youthful age of the world compels the poetry of the former to use great plainness of speech as compared with that of the latter: and that Keats and Shelley were on a false track when they set themselves to reproduce the exuberance of expression, the charm, the richness of images, and the felicity, of the Elizabethan poets. Yet critics cannot get to learn this, because the Elizabethan poets are our greatest, and our canons of poetry are founded on their works. They still think that the object of poetry is to produce exquisite bits and images—such as Shelley's *clouds shepherded by the slow unwilling wind,* and Keats passim: whereas modern poetry can only subsist by its *contents*: by becoming a complete magister vitae as the poetry of the ancients did: by including, as theirs did, religion with poetry, instead of existing as poetry only, and leaving religious wants to be supplied by the Christian religion, as a power existing independent of the poetical power. But the language, style and general proceedings of a poetry which has such an immense task to perform, must be very plain direct and severe: and it must not lose itself in parts and episodes and ornamental work, but must press forwards to the whole.[24]

We can see from *Empedocles on Etna* that there is less of a break in thought between these two paragraphs than might superficially appear. The contrast between Elizabethanizing Romantics and the plain severity of a "magister vitae" follows naturally from Arnold's reference to his 1852 volume. This is precisely the contrast which is exemplified by the songs of Callicles and the homily of the upper slopes in the title poem of the 1852 volume. *Empedocles on Etna* is not only about the quality of life in different epochs, it is also about the kinds of poetry appropriate to different epochs. And if the kind of poetry appropriate to a mature age of the world reads as prosaic or unpoetical, then it is evidence that Arnold has indeed analysed "the modern situation in its true *blankness* and *barrenness,* and *unpoetrylessness.*"[25] Professor Culler insists that the homily is intended to be disliked by readers for its "harsh, crabbed style," because its dramatic function is to deliver a "practical, *ad hominem*" lesson whose import even the simple and credulous Pausanias could not mistake.[26] Empedocles himself says as much, when he is alone at the summit (II, 7–10). But a further function of the homily's *unpoetrylessness* is to exemplify one aspect of the poem's dominant

[24] *Clough Letters,* p. 124; Oct. 28, 1852.
[25] *Clough Letters,* p. 126; Dec. 14, 1852. This letter immediately follows that advocating a "magister vitae." The quotation here is drawn from a paragraph discussing the 1852 volume.
[26] Culler, pp. 163–64.

historicism. Whether we stress the dramatic or thematic function of the homily, its bleakness is evidently deliberate. Arnold could certainly write this kind of verse more pleasingly. He was to do so in *The Scholar-Gipsy,* and had already done so in *Resignation,* of which Swinburne remarked that "it excels in beauty and in charm the kindred song of Empedocles."[27]

Swinburne's witness is particularly relevant to an evaluation of the homily, which he, alone of critics, has admired almost without qualification. He called the homily "the largest if not the brightest jewel" of the poem.[28] But he admitted later in his essay that "a poem throughout so flowerless and pallid [as the homily] would miss much of the common charm of poetry."[29] We can see what he means without going outside Arnold's work. Poems like *In Harmony with Nature* and many of the sonnets and short lyrics of the 1867 volume are indeed "flowerless and pallid" throughout; so much so that it would be a temperate estimate to say that they "miss much of the common charm of poetry." Swinburne's "flowerless and pallid" is a fair description of the homily, which is by no means as unreadable as I have so far implied. Indeed, it is the section of the poem which seems most to improve on rereading, as we respond more attentively to its muted rendering of tones which sound strongly elsewhere in *Empedocles on Etna.* A true estimate of its quality probably lies somewhere between Swinburne's praise for its "grave, clear, solemn verse" and one of Professor Culler's epithets, "uncouth."[30] The chief weakness of the homily is not that it is at times syntactically or metrically clumsy, but that its meter is almost intolerably monotonous, especially when read aloud. This monotony is in fact emphasized by the very alexandrines which ought to vary the dominant rhythm of the trimeters. For the overwhelming majority of the alexandrines have a strong caesura after the third foot (the caesura often coinciding with a punctuation mark). Inevitably, then, the alexandrines break into two trimeters, and thus repeat the rhythm they should vary. It is equally of note

[27] Swinburne, "Matthew Arnold's New Poems [of 1867]," in *Complete Works* (1926), XV, 86–87. Swinburne's review essay was first published in 1867.
[28] Swinburne, *Complete Works,* XV, 65.
[29] Swinburne, *Complete Works,* XV, 75–76.
[30] Swinburne, *Complete Works,* XV, 65; Culler, p. 163. Culler's evident wish is to be at once fair to the homily and honest with the readers of it. A similar wish informs Walter E. Houghton's assessment of the homily as "not a failure by any means, but the one serious flaw in a fine poem," "Arnold's 'Empedocles on Etna,' " *Victorian Studies,* I (1957–58), 333.

that the short lines have an inevitably straitening effect on the diction. We need not pass the poem through a computer to be struck by the great paucity of adjectives in the homily by contrast with their frequency in other parts of the poem. Since adjectives always play an important role in descriptive poetry as the conveyers of attributes, it is easy to see why their paucity in the homily should render it thin and colorless; and appropriately so. When the life of heroes is replaced by the life of the unheroic, complete harmony with nature is no longer possible, and the first sign of a disjunction between man and nature is the virtual disappearance of adjectives, and with them the disappearance of distinguishing attributes.

Ruskin's discussion in *The Stones of Venice* of musical and scenic monotony provides the terms for an estimate of the homily:

There is a sublimity and majesty in monotony, which there is not in rapid or frequent variation. This is true throughout all nature. The greater part of the sublimity of the sea depends on its monotony; so also that of desolate moor and mountain scenery. . . .

[But] monotony after a certain time, or beyond a certain degree, becomes either uninteresting or intolerable, and the musician is obliged to break it in one of two ways: either while the air or passage is perpetually repeated, its notes are variously enriched and harmonized; or else, after a certain number of repeated passages, an entirely new passage is introduced, which is more or less delightful according to the length of the previous monotony. Nature, of course, uses both these kinds of variation perpetually. The seawaves, resembling each other in general mass, but none like its brother in minor divisions and curves, are a monotony of the first kind; the great plain, broken by an emergent rock or clump of trees, is a monotony of the second.

Farther: in order to the enjoyment of the change in either case, a certain degree of patience is required from the hearer or observer. In the first case, he must be satisfied to endure with patience the recurrence of the great masses of sound or form, and to seek for entertainment in a careful watchfulness of the minor details. In the second case, he must bear patiently the infliction of the monotony for some moments, in order to feel the full refreshment of the change. This is true even of the shortest musical passage in which the element of monotony is employed. In cases of more majestic monotony, the patience required is so considerable that it becomes a kind of pain,—a price paid for the future pleasure.[31]

[31] Ruskin, *The Stones of Venice*, II, vi, paras. 33–35, in *Complete Works* (1904), X, 209–10. Volume II of *The Stones of Venice* was first published in July, 1853.

We can say that the monotony of the homily is prolonged rather beyond the point at which it becomes intolerable, and that it is principally broken, in a manner appropriate to mountain and desert scenery, by the "emergent . . . clump of trees" of Callicles' immediately following song of Cadmus and Harmonia. But the monotony is sufficiently prolonged for it to require relief, to a far greater extent than it receives, by a various enrichment and harmony of its notes in the manner of sea waves. As it stands, the homily exacts too exquisite a pain, too high a price for the future pleasure.

If the bleakness of the homily is appropriate to Pausanias as a representative of the millions of small natures in a mature age of the world, there is still one last possibility of a heroic act. It is this act which Empedocles seeks to identify and finally performs when alone at the summit. The songs of Callicles have presented the old heroic life as an instinctive accord with the vital principles of nature. The homily has abundantly demonstrated that such heroism is no longer possible. The heroism which remains is to achieve harmony with nature in full consciousness. Since mind and consciousness are the qualities which most sharply divide man from nature, a conscious endeavor to achieve harmony with nature is a high and difficult undertaking. Its difficulty is rendered by the syntax of Empedocles' solitary reflections at the summit. For these reflections unite, as it were, the assured lyricism of Callicles and the bleak didacticism of the homily. Swinburne said that "the special crown and praise" of *Empedocles on Etna* "is its fine and gentle alternation of tone and colour."[32] "Gentle" is certainly an ill-chosen epithet, but the praise is otherwise just. It is especially appropriate to the reflections at the summit, which are the one component part of the poem which fully epitomizes the major achievement of the whole. The reflections modulate between the lyrical descriptiveness of a youthful age of the world and the harsh necessities of a mature age. There is the sad recollection of those long-gone days when Empedocles was young with Parmenides, a moving *viximus* which appropriately swells into the lyrical assurance of "sunset over the sea; / Seed-time and harvest" (II, 253–54). There is the apostrophe to the stars, terminating with a statement of absolute separateness:

[32] Swinburne, *Complete Works*, XV, 76.

No, no, ye stars! there is no death with you,

. . . .

I alone
Am dead to life and joy, therefore I read
In all things my own deadness.   (II, 301, 320–22)

Thereafter, Empedocles endeavors to think himself back into a oneness with all things, back into the kind of life which heroes once led
without thinking about the matter at all. The strenuousness of the
endeavor is rendered, enacted indeed, in that section of the final
meditation (II, 345–90) of which J. D. Jump has written so well:

This is Arnold's finest passage of blank verse; and it is a genuinely
dramatic speech. The repetitive sequences of harassed and despairing utterances, each one receiving very much the same degree of
emphasis as its neighbours, convey insidiously the bewilderment of
men driven hither and thither by "thought and mind"; and the
larger rhythm which unites the sequences carries us on, unrestingly
and dizzily, to the desolate silence which follows the words "And
be astray for ever."[33]

What the passage vividly conveys in both rhythm and specific allusion is the sense of the intellectual life as heroic battle, with buffet-
ings and retaliation, with peril and faintheartedness, with the nagging impulse to fly the field. As the lines near their climax, so the
image of battle becomes dominant:

And we shall struggle awhile, gasp and rebel—
And we shall fly for refuge to past times,
Their soul of unworn youth, their breath of greatness;
And the reality will pluck us back,
Knead us in its hot hand, and change our nature
And we shall feel our powers of effort flag,
And rally them for one last fight—and fail;
And we shall sink in the impossible strife,
And be astray for ever.   (II, 382–90)

The last hero takes his last stand, and, like other heroes before
him, in the moment of defeat, he sees and snatches the victory. He
is not a hero of "past times" with "their breath of greatness." The
assurance of past heroes, their instinctive harmony with nature, is

[33] J. D. Jump, *Matthew Arnold* (1955), p. 93.

denied him by his strong consciousness of separation from nature. The only true modern heroism is to strive strenuously with the mind to feel a harmony with all things, while accepting, at every moment of the struggle, that the paths of intellection, if followed honestly, lead ever farther from the wished-for harmony:

> Yea, I take myself to witness,
> That I have loved no darkness,
> Sophisticated no truth,
> Nursed no delusion,
> Allow'd no fear!   (II, 399–403)

Such tough, demanding existentialism is of course exhausting. It cannot be endlessly repeated. Indeed, once Empedocles has glimpsed the truth of his own heroism, the battle is won, and to continue living is simply to risk losing the fruits of a victory which can only be confirmed by his instant death:

> Is it but for a moment?
> —Ah, boil up, ye vapours!
> Leap and roar, thou sea of fire!
> My soul glows to meet you.
> Ere it flag, ere the mists
> Of despondency and gloom
> Rush over it again,
> Receive me, save me!   (II, 409–16)

In a bleaker climate and mythology Empedocles would have leaped to his death clutching his sword before him and calling on Odin. As it is, we may catch in his last words a faint *victoria!* The tired cliché of moral earnestness that life is a battle to be fought manfully provided many a Victorian poem with matter to feed upon. Pieces like Browning's *Prospice*, Clough's *Say Not the Struggle Naught Availeth*, or Arnold's own *Palladium* and *The Last Word* simply retail the cliché; and of these only *Palladium* succeeds in decorating it at all attractively. But in the last stand of Empedocles the sense of cliché is quite lost by the new application and the new substance that Arnold gives to the image.

With the passing of Empedocles and the stilling of "the dialogue of the mind with itself," we are granted one last display of "the calm, the cheerfulness, the disinterested objectivity" of "the great

monuments of early Greek genius."[34] The concluding hymn of
Callicles is not, of course, an adverse reflection on Empedocles:
quite the contrary. Empedocles had laid aside the insignia of both
bard and leader, had stripped himself for the last, lonely heroism of
his intellectual struggle at the summit. Callicles could not understand such a heroism, and could not therefore make a song specifically about it. But he can, and splendidly, make a song about the
heroism of old. And this is the heroism which Empedocles has
approximated in the only way open to a man in a mature age of
the world. The last song of Callicles repeats part of the burden of
his first—"the life which heroes lead"—but now treats it as the subject of bardic praise. The whole thrust of the poem makes for an
inclusion of Empedocles himself among the subjects of praise.
Appropriately, his identity and individuality are lost in the summary enumeration of all the things hymned by the Muses, just as
he strove, and succeeded in losing himself in all things:

—Whose praise do they mention
Of what is it told?—
What will be for ever;
What was from of old.

First hymn they the Father
Of all things; and then,
The rest of immortals,
The action of men.

The day in his hotness,
The strife with the palm;
The night in her silence,
The stars in their calm.

Within two months of the publication of the 1852 volume,
Arnold was writing to Clough that he believed he had analysed in
his poems the *unpoetrylessness* of "the modern situation." But he
admitted in the same letter that he now felt the 1852 poems to be
"all wrong," apparently because he doubted that they would give

[34] Preface to *Poems* 1853 in *Complete Prose*, I, 1. The Greek analogues of Callicles' last song are enumerated and discussed by Warren D. Anderson, *Matthew
Arnold and the Classical Tradition* (Ann Arbor, 1965), pp. 44–45, and by Allott,
pp. 192–94.

pleasure to a reader.[35] By the time he came to prepare the 1853 volume, the doubt had grown sufficiently for Arnold not only to omit *Empedocles on Etna,* but to rehearse his reasons for doing so. The volume of 1853 is not, in any sense, a collected works, any more than it is a gathering of new work. Of its thirty-five poems only nine were new, and the twenty-six which had been previously published in some form represent a selection from the sixty-two poems contained in the volumes of 1849 and 1852. *Empedocles on Etna,* then, was only one of thirty-six poems which Arnold decided not to use in the 1853 volume.[36] Arnold's decision to explain the omission of *Empedocles on Etna* indicates that it was pre-eminently the poem in terms of which he was defining and redefining during these years his idea of poetry and the social function of poetry. Quite simply, he came, at least for a time, to reject the naked "magister vitae" of the homily and the heroic self-destruction of the intellectual struggle, because he felt they were not what men needed after all. By the end of 1853 he could assure Clough that what "the complaining millions of men" need is to be animated and ennobled.[37] Such a poetry will tell of the life which heroes lead, or, rather, of the life which heroes led of old. And so we have *Sohrab and Rustum, Balder Dead, Merope,* and—all that was salvaged from *Empedocles on Etna* until Browning successfully petitioned for its republication in 1867—the songs of Callicles printed separately as "The Harp-player on Etna" together with the least melancholy portion of Empedocles' apostrophe to the stars, the portion associating them with long-gone heroes.

But the objection of the "magister vitae" letter still stands. Such a poetry is inappropriate, perhaps irrelevant, to a mature age of the world.[38] The three new works are all, in various degrees, tinged

[35] *Clough Letters,* p. 126; Dec. 14, 1852.
[36] Among the thirty-six omitted were such considerable pieces from 1849 as *The Sick King in Bokhara, The New Sirens, To a Gipsy Child by the Sea-Shore,* and *Resignation;* the omissions from 1852 include *Memorial Verses, The Youth of Nature, A Summer Night, The Buried Life,* and *'Obermann.'* After a second edition of the *Poems* of 1853 in the following year, Arnold published *Poems: Second Series* in 1855, to which the *Poems* of 1853 and 1854 became the *First Series. Second Series* includes all the major poems of 1849 and 1852 omitted from 1853, except for *The New Sirens,* together with many of the minor pieces omitted from 1853. The two series together thus constituted Arnold's idea of his collected works in 1855.
[37] *Clough Letters,* p. 146; Nov. 30 [1853].
[38] The "magister vitae" letter's reproval of Keats and Shelley for inappropriately trying to reproduce Elizabethan exuberance may be combined with Arnold's later description of Keats as "an Elizabethan born too late," *Complete Prose,* I, 143. Callicles and his poetry are just as much "come too late" as Empedocles

with a self-indulgent antiquarianism. Divorced from their context, the songs of Callicles are not less charming; they are not less enspiriting, but they are unquestionably less interesting. Stripped of their significant contribution to the historicism of the whole poem, they are of note in themselves principally as finely realized exercises. One of them, *Cadmus and Harmonia,* was included on its own in the 1853 volume (the others were reissued in 1855), and, by itself, *Cadmus and Harmonia* emerges as a charmingly mythic rendering of that recurrent Victorian nostalgia for a paradise lost. By themselves, then, the songs have charm, but little or no significance. Conversely, by itself the homily has significance, or relevance, but virtually no charm. Empedocles' reflections at the summit are certainly elevated, if not charming, poetry; and they have significance, but not—unlike the homily's—the kind of significance which can be fully or almost fully grasped without reference to the other parts of the poem. The three main components of *Empedocles on Etna* are the songs of Callicles, Empedocles' solitary reflections, and the homily to Pausanias. The homily depends on the other components to justify it— however imperfectly—as poetry. It also depends a little, as the other components do completely, on the presence of the other parts to justify its significance. Only in the whole poem does each component make its historicist point about the different quality of life in different epochs, and about the necessarily different poetry which must record and respond to that quality of life. Only when we read the poem whole are we aware of its massive relevance to Arnold's idea of his own time.

Arnold is engaged in chronicling the shift from his idea of Romanticism—the joy of glens and lakes—to the "blacken'd, melancholy waste" of his idea of the Victorian age. And it is of capital importance that he chooses as his exemplary modern man "a Sicilian Greek born between two and three thousand years ago."[39] Empedocles of Agrigentum not only had a metaphysic, he was also, complain as he might, in touch with a social life far less complex than that to which Matthew Arnold was subject. Callicles can sup late with Peisianax, then slip home to saddle his mule and ride through the night to Mount Etna. The people of Catana throng about Empedocles, asking the secret of his magic: how did he raise

---

with his philosophy (II, 16). The difference is that Empedocles knows he is "too late"; Callicles does not know that he is also.
[39] *Complete Prose,* I, 1.

Pantheia, purify streams, stop up chinks in a mountain? Because
the social life was simpler, Empedocles can still just hold town and
country together, can use one syntax in telling Pausanias of the elements and of active living, although at the summit his syntax is
breaking under the pressure of cognition. It is indeed the antiquity
of Empedocles which enables Arnold to use one syntax to express
the breakdown of syntax into terms for man and terms for nature,
and thus to parallel the achievement of Wordsworth and Coleridge
in writing highly imaginative odes about the loss of imagination.
Empedocles on Etna may be used to illustrate that Arnold had a
cyclical view of history, of conditions repeating themselves, of processes coming to maturity and passing away. But the poem is also a
grand historical analogy by means of which we view a lost, idealized
Romanticism from a Victorian desert. We also view the fifth century
B.C. from the industrial bustle of the nineteenth; and from the fifth
century we view the prehistoric times of those gods and heroes who
people the songs of Callicles. The poem is a long regression of
nostalgia for conditions that are presumed once to have been, and
certainly are no longer.

The Cumnor Hills

THE REASONS FOR THE CUSTOMARY critical pairing of *The Scholar-Gipsy* and *Thyrsis* are obvious. The poems are linked through their use of the same setting and through the later poem's explicit allusion to the earlier. The means by which description and reflection are presented in the two poems differ sufficiently to provide grounds for a comparative judgment. Indeed, it seems at times that by declaring a preference for one or the other, or by resting *in utrumque paratus,* a critic betrays just what kind of Arnoldian he is. (Those who like neither are probably not Arnoldians, at least of the poems.) I might as well announce at the start that I think *The Scholar-Gipsy* by far the better poem.

i

"I am glad you like the Gipsy Scholar—but what," Arnold once enquired of Clough, "does it *do* for you?" The poem, he went on, "at best awakens a pleasing melancholy. But this is not what we want"; what men want "is something to *animate* and *ennoble* them—not merely to add zest to their melancholy or grace to their dreams.—I believe a feeling of this kind is the basis of my nature— and of my poetics."[1] From the perspective of modern scholarship and critical elucidation, Arnold's question is at least as interesting as his self-deprecatory answer. If we put aside his answer for the moment, we must agree that the Gipsy Scholar has done a great deal

[1] *Clough Letters,* p. 146; Nov. 30 [1853].

209

for later readers, or at least they have made a great deal of him. G. Wilson Knight, for example, finds him to be a repository of the intuitive wisdom of the East, especially as it confronts the intellectual legacy of Greece and its practical application by Rome.[2] On his Scholar side Professor Knight sees in him "the eternal undergraduate" and therefore the true "presiding deity of a great university" because, unlike the dons, he has not yet learned enough to lose his youthful "wonder," his "intuition of fields unexplored."[3] Quite evidently, such a deity is very different from the undergraduates Arnold characterized a decade later with a witty adaptation of Byron as "our young barbarians, all at play,"[4] although a recognizably similar donnish sentiment plays about both portraits. A strong sense of this discrepancy informs A. E. Dyson's rebuttal of Professor Knight.[5] The Scholar Gipsy, Mr. Dyson insists, "is a creature of superstition and credulity: a kindly creature, not a dark one, it is true, but when all is said, Arnold's own sympathies were with knowledge."[6] The Scholar Gipsy does not meet the requirements of *Culture and Anarchy, Literature and Dogma, God and the Bible*; he is the mythical embodiment of a lost innocence which must be recognized and rejected by the head, however much the heart may yearn for him. Arnold was on the side of those "light-hearted" Greeks, "the bearers of culture," rather than the side of the Tyrian trader who flees before them.

Professor Culler notes that the readings of Mr. Dyson and Professor Knight are "diametrically opposed," but each reading is, Professor Culler feels, "half right," a consequence of Professor Knight's exclusive emphasis on the Scholar Gipsy and the Tyrian trader and Mr. Dyson's exclusive emphasis on "the central statement of the Gipsy's unfitness for the modern world." The whole truth resides in a due synthesis of Professor Knight and Mr. Dyson into a recognition that the poem consists "of the vision, the repudiation of the vision, and its recovery in a different mode."[7] This Hegelian progress takes place in the three main settings of what Professor Culler calls Arnold's symbolic world: the forest glade of the Cum-

[2] G. Wilson Knight, *"The Scholar Gipsy:* An Interpretation," *Review of English Studies, New Series,* VI (1955), 53–62.
[3] *RES,* NS, VI, 56.
[4] Preface to *Essays in Criticism* (1865) in *Complete Prose,* III, 290.
[5] A. E. Dyson, "The Last Enchantments," *Review of English Studies, New Series,* VIII (1957), 257–65.
[6] *RES,* NS, VIII, 264.
[7] Culler, p. 185.

nor hills, the burning plain of mid-Victorian life, represented not by an actual desert or hot city but, briefly, by the Hades in which Dido shunned Aeneas and, more extensively, by the aridity and barrenness of language which "speaks directly and abstractly . . . of the modern world"; the final setting is the wide-glimmering sea across which the Tyrian trader sails in order to pass "through the 'straits' which separate one realm from another."[8] The three settings usually represent in Arnold youthful innocence, active maturity, and the peaceful acquiescence of old age or death; in the historicist poems they are past, present, and future. In *The Scholar-Gipsy* Professor Culler feels that the wide-glimmering sea is also the realm of culture: when the Tyrian trader undoes his corded bales they are found to contain, symbolically speaking, the alphabet, the *Bhagavad-Gita* and "other instruments of learning," along with, literally speaking, "rich brocades, silks, and gold."[9] Professor Knight, on the other hand, by implication associates the "secret goods" of the bales with the mysteries of *atman* and Dionysus.[10]

If we ask again what the Gipsy Scholar has done for these three readers, we must say that Professor Knight has been animated, Professor Culler has been ennobled, and Mr. Dyson awakened to a rejection of melancholy. Not so F. R. Leavis, from whose brief notice of the poem the readings of Professor Knight, Mr. Dyson and Professor Culler ultimately derive. All three, the first two explicitly, deal with Dr. Leavis' charge that the poem displays "weak confusion" and "intellectual debility." All Arnold knows about the Scholar Gipsy is that he had "what we, alas, have not"; "he exhibits the Scholar as drifting about the Oxford countryside in an eternal week-end."[11] Professors Knight and Culler contend that there is much more to the Scholar than Dr. Leavis allows, while Mr. Dyson feels that Arnold in effect anticipated Dr. Leavis by not exhibiting the Scholar for our unqualified approval.

It is not axiomatic, but it is often the case that when a poem yields for four different and intelligent readers such dissimilar interpretive and evaluative experiences it is because each has a sense

[8] Culler, pp. 186, 191.
[9] Culler, p. 192.
[10] Strictly speaking, Knight associates the Scholar rather than the Tyrian with *atman* and Dionysus, but he does so as a consequence of searching "within the main body of the poem for qualities roughly corresponding to the oriental powers symbolized by the Tyrian trader," *RES*, NS, VI, 55.
[11] I quote from the brief discussion by F. R. Leavis, *The Common Pursuit* (1953), pp. 29–31, but his slightly fuller account in *Revaluation* (1936), pp. 186–91, is also relevant.

that something worthwhile is happening in it. That "worthwhile" may be as small as the charm and representativeness Dr. Leavis finds in *The Scholar-Gipsy*; it may be as large as Professor Culler's feeling that here is Arnold's best poem and therefore, by implication, a very good poem indeed. What accounts for the differences between the critics is their shared sense that the Scholar Gipsy is a symbol; that is to say, he implies a truth or truths more extensive than what is explicitly said of him. Dr. Leavis's complaint, if I understand him rightly, is that the extended truths are, so far from being implied, simply and explicitly asserted by Arnold in the section Professor Culler calls "the repudiation of the vision." For Dr. Leavis the assertion is, moreover, both uninteresting and strictly discontinuous from the earlier description in a way which works against symbolic effectiveness. The Scholar Gipsy is described as "drifting about the Oxford countryside"; we are told he had "*one* aim, *one* business, *one* desire." In noting the same disjunction, Professor Culler defends it on the grounds that it is a necessary part of the poem's dialectic, its movement from "the flimsiness of seventeenth-century superstition and Romantic imagination" to the "toughness" required "for survival in the real world."[12]

The word *symbol* is often a sign of something which is happening or is going to happen in the critical discourse which uses it; rather less frequently it is an indication of something which happens in the literary work to which it is applied. *Symbol* often marks a critic's release from what is said in a work to what a work suggests by way of natural association with the object called symbolic. The three main sources of association are the writer's other works, the postulates, especially written postulates, of his contemporaries, and the general cultural tradition to which the writer belongs. Unless the work is short and simple, the number of possible associations is likely to be very large, and not all of them can be comfortably and coherently accommodated in a single reading of the poem. Discrimination between possible associations involves the critic in the use of tact and the arts of persuasion.

We may take as exemplary of this critical situation what Professor Culler calls the "end-symbol" of the Tyrian trader, and apply Arnold's question to it: "what does the Tyrian trader *do* for you?" The answer appears to depend on whether you associate culture and wisdom with the Tyrian or with the Greeks. Mr. Dyson's case

[12] Culler, pp. 187–88.

for the Greeks would be supported almost everywhere but in the poem, where they are bearing figs and tunnies, not culture. The difference in the cases of Professors Knight and Culler for the Tyrian depends upon how much of the Scholar Gipsy you feel he contains. Professor Knight finds him a final underlining of the "oriental powers" of intuitive wisdom possessed by the Scholar. Professor Culler finds him a transmogrification of the superstitious Scholar into the bearer of such oriental wisdom as the *Bhagavad-Gita*. Both are responding to the eastern possibilities of the Tyrian, but if we try to combine them we get the curious picture of the trader's corded bales yielding Dionysus proferring the alphabet to those shy (and no doubt startled) traffickers, the dark Iberians. Professor Culler gives us the clue and, indeed, exemplifies the critical method in epitome:

Whereas the cargo of the Greeks was the Sybaritic one of "amber grapes and Chian wine, / Green, bursting figs, and tunnies steep'd in brine," that of the Tyrians was "corded bales," whose contents are wisely not specified but which our imagination fills with rich brocades, silks, and gold—and perhaps also with the alphabet and other instruments of learning. It is sometimes complained that Arnold's hero does not, as he promised to do, impart his knowledge to the world, but surely this is what is meant by the last line of the poem, where the trader "on the beach undid his corded bales." In Arnold's bale would have been the *Bhagavad-Gita,* his personal treasure from the East, which, though it was "foolishness to the Greeks" when he offered it to Clough, was to him a wisdom most deeply to be desired.[13]

The persuasion works here through a sequence of insinuations, beginning with the suggestive adjective "Sybaritic." The inhabitants of Sybaris no doubt relished figs and wine, just as they relished brocades, silks and gold. But it is the Greeks alone who are associated with that notoriously decadent city because, it is quite clear, Professor Culler's (or, rather, *our*) imagination only fills the Tyrian's bales with cloth as an indication that it is quite aware of the literal possibilities and by no means given to ungovernable fancy. After quietening the fears of the literalists, Professor Culler is ready to ease us, by way of an undogmatic dash and "perhaps also" to the alphabet, and it would certainly be niggling to remark that the alphabet is more usually described as Tyrian property under

[13] Culler, p. 192.

their other name of Phoenicians. Even if—a large condition—we set aside the fact that the Phoenician alphabet was transmitted to western culture by way of the Greeks, we have to admit that, in itself, it is not suggestive of advanced knowledge, and converts, as it were, the Scholar Gipsy's Oxford into an Iberian Kindergarten. And so we move on to those vaguely apprehended "other instruments of learning" and thence to the indisputable wisdom of the *Bhagavad-Gita*. Between them lies that body of the imperceptive who complain that "Arnold's hero" does not impart his knowledge to the world. This taciturn hero is, of course, the Scholar Gipsy, not the Tyrian trader, whom Professor Culler sees, and rightly, as to some extent different from the Scholar. But, waiving the distinction, if only the imperceptive had thought to investigate those corded bales, they could scarcely have failed to find the *Bhagavad-Gita*. Professor Culler does not put it quite like that. It is Arnold's "bale" which has the *Bhagavad-Gita,* and of course it did, as Professor Culler can show by apt quotation from the Clough letters. Arnold's metaphoric bale is offered as a valid gloss on the Tyrian's literal bale, because the Tyrian came from the Eastern Mediterranean while the *Bhagavad-Gita* also came from out east, and because *The Scholar-Gipsy* was by Arnold. But Professor Culler is not, it seems, offering the *Bhagavad-Gita* as a private, wholly esoteric association of Arnold and perhaps Clough, for we must not forget that it is our imagination which is responsible for this impressive inventory. And yet to say "in the Tyrian's bale would have been the *Bhagavad-Gita*" must surely move even our docile imagination to protest. It is a question, perhaps, of which bale has the *Bhagavad*. The clue to what is going on here is embodied in that phrase about the corded bales, "whose contents are wisely not specified." Arnold's wisdom consists in not telling us that there was wisdom in the bales; if he had, we plainly would not believe him. But Arnold, and here is the excellence of his wisdom, does not prohibit "our" putting wisdom in the bales: and if we do so and still do not believe in it, we have only "ourselves" to blame. If this is, more or less, Professor Culler's point, I think he is being very unfair, and wish to enter a protest on behalf of those of us less perceptive or less imaginative than he.

Each of the four critics I have cited responds in his own way to a central fact of *The Scholar-Gipsy*: its lack of conceptual depth and its evocation of moods appropriate to ways of life presented in wholly general terms. Professors Knight and Culler and Mr. Dyson respond by endowing the poem with conceptual riches drawn from one or more of the three main sources for "symbolic" association. Dr. Leavis responds by expressing dissatisfaction with the poem's conceptual vagueness and what he feels its sole compensation in sonorous diction. He finds the poem self-indulgently relaxing, a holiday from serious cares. A value judgment of this kind is, as Dr. Leavis would himself insist, a personal matter; but it is not necessary to agree with all his requirements for the proper substance of poetry to see that he is responding far more accurately to the mode of *The Scholar-Gipsy* than are the critics who, directly or indirectly, attempt to controvert him.

ii

The Scholar-Gipsy, like *Resignation* and *Lines Written in Kensington Gardens,* concerns itself with the contrast between the active and reflective lives. As with the two earlier poems, the reflective life is first rendered by absorption in landscape detail and then identified in discourse. *The Scholar-Gipsy* differs most obviously from the other two in its use of the title figure, among other things, to assist the process of absorption and identification, but also in its greater scepticism about the useful relevance of the reflective for the active life.

The poem begins, as it ends, with dismissal and untying: "Go, for they call you, shepherd, from the hill; / Go, shepherd, and untie the wattled cotes!" and this opening dismissal is plainly to the pastoral care of active life. The very plainness is important. We cannot mistake the human suggestions of "No longer leave thy *wistful* flock unfed, / Nor let thy bawling *fellows* rack their throats." The unfed sheep calling their shepherd fellow to his duty keep us from substituting a Theocritean poet for a biblical guardian of his people. The language of the poem, that is, discriminates among available associations by recalling, as it were, the middle rather than the opening section of *Lycidas.* It is also important that the associations are priest-like rather than specifically priestly; whether or not Arnold knows the worldly equivalent of feeding sheep and not letting the grass grow too long, he certainly does not say, any more than he elaborates upon the "quest" which the shepherd is summoned to recommence at night when the day's duties are done.

Arnold is rendering the quality of a kind of life rather than the programs it entails. It is in its way, moreover, an integrated life, even though it involves valley work by day and hill quest by night. For it is evidently the night quest which justifies the pastoral metaphor of sheep and shepherd as fellows: the shepherd is a man able to help other men, to liberate and give them sustenance, because of the superior endowments which he exercises in the night quest.

The opening stanza establishes the moral norm of the poem; appropriately, it is couched in a series of ethical imperatives as well as conveyed in terms of the rural setting and pastoral convention. The second and third stanzas apply this norm to the speaker himself and make clear his divergence from it. He tells the shepherd he will sit and wait "till sun-down" "in this high field's dark corner." What scene should we, as Professor Knight bids us, stage or dramatize for ourselves? Evidently the speaker was accompanied by the shepherd on the hill until the cries of the sheep were heard. The speaker promises to wait for the shepherd to rejoin him at sundown in the high field for the renewal of their night quest. The speaker's dissociation from the active life of the day is emphasized by practically every detail in the second stanza. He chooses a corner where the day-laboring reaper repairs for brief refreshment, a place out of the sun where the sounds of sheep and reapers bring but distant reminders of daily tasks while, closer at hand, the field before him is as yet "half-reap'd," the work incomplete. The drowsiness which "all the live murmur of a summer's day" may be supposed to induce is already operative by the early lines of the third stanza, where the speaker gives his attention to small details of flowers and roots. It is no surprise to find that he has slipped from a sitting position and now lies on the bent grass, while all this time, it will be remembered, the shepherd is below, ensuring that "the cropp'd herbage" does not "shoot another head." Well may the eye travel "down to Oxford's towers," instead of merely gazing at them: traveling, after all, is the slowest of all movements performed by the eyes. By the end of the third stanza the poem has rendered three or perhaps four activities: day labor, day reverie, and night quest; the fourth activity obtains if we distinguish between the work of the reaper and the shepherd's care of his flock. The reapers participate only in the first activity, for they must presumably be numbered among the tired men who rest at night (l. 7). The speaker participates in the second and will apparently participate in the third; the shepherd in the first (or fourth) and third.

The traveling of the speaker's eye to Oxford's towers, in addition to emphasizing the note of drowsy reverie, facilitates the transition to Glanvill's "story of the Oxford scholar poor" (l. 33) , which the speaker has carried with him to his retreat. In telling the "oft-read tale," the speaker naturally uses and expands upon those parts which interest him (much as Arnold proposed to gather up the hints of Empedocles' fragments) . The Scholar was not only, as in Glanvill, of "pregnant parts" but also of "quick inventive brain." We learn, moreover, as we do not from Glanvill, that he "roam'd the world" with the gipsies. In Arnold's paraphrase of Glanvill which served as note to the poem, we are told that the gipsies imposed their will on others by the power of imagination. But this power is rendered in the poem only as "arts" and a "skill." The modification should serve to check an emphatic association of the Scholar with poetry, the poet, or poetic inspiration:[14] "the secret" of the gipsies' "art" is unlikely to consist in this. "The secret of their art" is no more precise than the "quest" which the shepherd was earlier summoned to renew at nightfall.[15] The point of a secret is, precisely, that it is secret, unknown "to the world" if half-known to the Scholar. In view of what is going to happen in the poem, Arnold's most important additions to Glanvill are the Scholar's assertion that "it needs heaven-sent moments" for the practice of the gipsies' skill and that after the Scholar had met two of his college acquaintances "rumours hung about the countryside / That the lost Scholar long was seen to stray" (ll. 52–53) .[16] The rumors will permit the speaker in his succeeding reverie to project the Scholar into the speaker's own day.

The sixth stanza completes a two-part induction in which the first two stanzas and part of the third are addressed to the shepherd while the remainder exhibit the speaker talking to himself, musing

[14] Thus Allott, p. 334, and J. P. Curgenven, "*The Scholar Gipsy:* A Study of the Growth, Meaning and Integration of a Poem," *Litera,* II (1955), 41–58, III (1956), 1–13, especially II, 52–53.

[15] I partly agree with David L. Eggenschwiler, "Arnold's Passive Questers," *Victorian Poetry,* V (1967), 1–11, that "Arnold seems hardly interested in the nature of the [Scholar's] quest, which serves him as little more than a vague symbol for single-minded activity," but feel he makes a common mistake in assuming that the Scholar actually has a quest as such. The Scholar's one aim, business, and desire is to *wait* for the spark; his only purposeful movement is to run for cover. The Scholar has a quest in *Thyrsis,* but not in his own poem, and if we may, with caution, gloss the later poem with the earlier, we should not reverse the process.

[16] Arnold played fair by abstracting from Glanvill into a note everything he used in the poem; anything in the poem but not in the note is Arnold's addition to Glanvill: see *The Vanity of Dogmatizing* (1661), pp. 196–98.

aloud. The rest of the poem will be addressed to the Scholar. The induction distinguishes the active life and two versions of the contemplative life: the night quest and the day reverie. The two versions are syntactically related:

Come, shepherd, and again begin the quest!   (l. 10)

Come, let me read the oft-read tale again!   (l. 32)

The original reading of the first line, "again renew the quest," is pointedly pleonastic, heavily emphasizing the endlessly repeated task. If the day reverie and the night quest are similar in some respects, they differ in others. In the day reverie the speaker will "sit and wait" for the renewal of the quest, which is, presumably, both energetic and purposeful. It will be a major function of the poem to bring together the product of the reverie and the object of the quest with a view to testing the validity of the contemplative life in its relation to the active life of mid-Victorian England.

As is common in dreams, or at least the literary convention of dreams, it is the details of the last waking moments which are worked, transmuted, into the substance of the reverie. The Scholar is introduced as an item in the speaker's retreat; he is there in Glanvill's book, and it is as a projection of the speaker that he commences in the reverie. When the Scholar runs from the shepherds at the inn, the speaker observes, in his first direct address to the Scholar, "and I myself seem half to know thy looks, / And put the shepherds, wanderer! on thy trace" (ll. 62–63). Just why the speaker thinks he half knows the Scholar's looks is perhaps easier to understand than to express accurately. It is a question of sympathy, of the speaker's saying he knows why the Scholar ran, because he had done the same thing himself. He had done so already within the poem by withdrawing to a nook far from the cries of sheep and the reapers. Because, moreover, he withdrew from noise to await the renewal of the quest with his shepherd companion, he associates the Scholar with that quest by putting the shepherds on his trace, even though the shepherds in the inn had hitherto shown no inclination to pursue him. The process here is one of creating the Scholar out of the mood and significant posture of the speaker in his reverie. The process is rendered clear, if not quite explicit, in the seventh and eighth stanzas. In the seventh the speaker lies in a boat wondering if the Scholar haunts the "shy retreats" of the Cumnor hills.

"For most, I know," the eighth stanza begins, "thou lov'st retired ground" (ll. 70–71). He knows it because the Scholar is a creation of himself, expressing at least part of himself. The connection is emphasized by the succeeding picture of the Scholar lying in a punt with a lap full of flowers, the emphasis falling upon the sameness of the speaker's and the Scholar's posture. The Scholar's "heap of flowers," similar to those he will later distribute to the maidens of the Fyfield elm (ll. 86–89), recalls the speaker's earlier absorption in the poppy and convolvulus as he slipped into his reverie.

In the seventh stanza, commencing the apostrophe, it is not only the Scholar but the speaker too who moves through the landscape, seeking the counterpart of his sequestered nook in "lone wheat-fields," "shy retreats," or a boat moored to a "cool bank." It is an obvious but necessary point that the Scholar frequents those parts of the Cumnor hills which have appealed to the speaker and which he, in effect, recalls from his nook in the high field by projecting the Scholar into them. Although in Glanvill the Scholar is alone when he encounters his college acquaintances, he has still, in the poem as well as in Glanvill, to return to the gipsies to complete his initiation. The speaker's imagination fixes him at the moment of his last recorded appearance alive, because, it is clear, this is the point which most fully corresponds to the speaker's mood in the work. So it is that, although the Scholar frequents "the skirts of Bagley Wood" (l. 111), where the gipsies pitch their tents, he has, as far as the poem is concerned, no more communication with them than he has with the haymakers, the housewife, or the children; we are not even told that he is seen by the gipsies. He is a scholar gipsy not only because he was a scholar and joined the gipsies, but because he wanders like the gipsies and is as solitary as a scholar.

The main function of the Scholar in that section of the poem Professor Culler calls "the vision," roughly lines 51 to 130, is to hypostatize the mood of the speaker in his nook. By means of the Scholar, indeed, that mood is rendered as a whole way of life, for such I take to be the point of reviewing the Scholar's haunts throughout the passage of seasons. Just as the speaker sits and waits for the renewal of the quest, so the Scholar waits "for the spark from heaven to fall" (l. 120). While the speaker waits, his mind wanders about the "shy retreats" of the Cumnor hills; so too the Scholar wanders as he waits. The speaker turned again to the Scholar's story when his eye traveled down to Oxford. He wakes from his "dream" when the Scholar looked toward Oxford before turning away into the night. The process, indeed, is in many respects typically Arnoldian: the rendering of a mood in terms of the landscape in which the mood is experienced. Often, it is true, rendering takes the form of "explaining" a generally described condition: the sickness of the King of Bokhara, the giddiness of the Strayed Reveller, the man-hating of Empedocles, the death fever of Tristram, or the vague dejection of *Consolation*. In *The Scholar-Gipsy*, however, the initial mood "explains" the succeeding rendering at least as much as it is "explained" by the rendering. This more fully reciprocal relationship ensures a tighter integrity between the two halves of the analogy, modal tenor and landscape vehicle, than is common in Arnold's poems. As is also frequent in Arnold's poems—*Parting* is an obvious case—the landscape rendering of a general condition is succeeded by a section primarily reflective and only incidentally recalling the landscape. But here the recall is more satisfactory than it often is because the landscape rendering had been effected through the figure of the Scholar, who persists into the section of reflection as the object of the speaker's apostrophe.

The dream ended with the speaker's recollection that the Scholar lived and died two hundred years before; he dreams, that is, because he thought he had seen the Scholar on "the wooden bridge" (l. 123), or could put the shepherds on his trace. The literal Scholar is appropriately laid to rest "in some quiet churchyard," "some country-nook" (ll. 137–38). But the dream has imaginative if not literal truth:

> And we imagine thee exempt from age
> And living as thou liv'st on Glanvil's page.　　　(ll. 158–59)

These lines identify the process by which the speaker was able to dream his dream. During the reverie the Scholar was so much a projection of the speaker as to be, for the duration of the reverie, almost identical with the speaker. But the speaker has also his waking moments, which differ from his dream life. They differ because, while in quiet nooks on warm summer days, a man may, imaginatively, live his dreams, at other times the most he can do is live for them. The reflective section accordingly addresses itself to determining what in the dream a man may live for. To do so, it must dissolve the near identity of speaker and Scholar which it was the function of the dream to establish. The dissolution is accomplished by confronting the imagined with the literal Scholar, by emphasizing the historical distance and the Scholar's "glad perennial youth" (l. 229) in contrast with the cycle of mortality in which the speaker is caught; by emphasizing, indeed, that the Scholar is a dream of being from the world of becoming.

The presentation of the world of becoming in which the speaker is caught with his contemporaries gives a measure of conceptual direction to the poem. Before, we had only an unidentified quest, the helpful day labor of a shepherd whose worldly equivalent is not indicated, mysterious arts involving the imposition of one man's will upon others, and a spark from heaven which has not fallen. These conditions, with all their imaginative and emotional accretions, are now associated with faith, hope, and purpose in order to make clear where, conceptually, the poem is pointing. And it is a pointing, not an analysis, a pointing toward a spiritual condition which was at best only suggested by the earlier part of the poem and is now overtly confirmed. But it is still a generally realized condition, without precise theological implications for either the active or contemplative lives. What the Scholar has and what the speaker and his contemporaries lack is faith in the existence of a supernatural power, something outside of and beyond men which can define their lives. Without such faith it is necessary to follow the Sophist and make man the measure of man. With such a measure the maximum contemporary wisdom consists in introspection, a melancholy self-analysis because man in himself is such a contradictory figure (ll. 182–90).

The happy "dream" (l. 131) of the Scholar's "unclouded joy" (l. 199) is drawn into "the long unhappy dream" (l. 192) of mid-nineteenth-century life where it is, by Gresham's law, in danger of extinction. Light belief inevitably destroys deep belief, but deep belief presents itself as the only way out of the debilitating consequences of light belief. It is a sad, ironic circle, and the maximum contribution of art is to arrest the process at a point just before the circle is completely drawn. The Scholar and what he stands for are the product of the day reverie, the substance of a dream. Literally, the Scholar is as dead as Dido in Hades, an "inviolable shade" of "unconquerable hope" (ll. 211–12) as long as the "light half-believers" (l. 172) do not catch up with him in their periodic endeavors to live their dreams. He accordingly becomes the object of the night quest, a quest which must be without end, the pursued forever eluding his pursuers. The only faith available to the mid-nineteenth century, as the poem sees it, is to believe in the possibility of belief; the imagined Scholar is that possibility. In a sense, then, the poem exists to provide an object for the quest of the shepherd and the speaker. The object is created in a daydream and is, perhaps, not very different from the ability to dream dreams of hope.

It is not a robust ideal, and a major function of the concluding simile is evidently to dissipate the languor and melancholy associated with the ideal without altering its general point. The heroic venture of the trader is a strikingly invigorating variation upon the flight of the hopeful Scholar before the blandishments of the faithless nineteenth century. The Tyrian's flight from trade competition to traffic with a simpler, less sophisticated society is reminiscent, not only of the Scholar's flight before the noisy shepherds in the inn, but also of the Scholar's original flight from Oxford, tired as he was "of knocking at preferment's door," to commerce with the gipsies (l. 35). But that metaphoric commerce is here rendered as literal commerce. The Greeks, those "young light-hearted masters of the waves" foreshadow other and later rulers of the waves, Adolescens Leo, it may be, proving Podsnappery on the pulse of the Stock Exchange.[17] The prosperity of Roebuck's England thinly disguises its spiritual emptiness but it has, nonetheless, its own deceptive allurement, the deceptiveness rendered by the stealthiness of the Grecian coaster—reminding us again to beware the Greeks bearing gifts, or goods—and the allurement rendered by the relish-filled inventory of goods, all of them, as it happens, perishables. Whatever it is that goes into "corded bales," it is unlikely to be perishables, and if we must exercise our imagination about their contents, it would be well not to think beyond purple cloth. But better still, because it permits the poem the suggestiveness it has worked for, we should not speculate. We do not know the secret of the gipsies' skill, nor the meaning and validity of the spark from heaven, nor the contents of

[17] If a reader objects that my mélange of *Friendship's Garland, The Function of Criticism,* and *Our Mutual Friend* is a product of the symbolic associationism I have reproved in others, I happily withdraw what was meant only as a convenient set of terms to describe the evident difference in crediting the age both with "sick hurry . . . divided aims" and friendly "speech and smiles," in extending by simile the "light half-believers of our casual creeds" into the "young light-hearted masters of the waves"; spiritual debility and material prosperity yield complementary glosses upon the lightweight quality of Victorian life.

the bales. If we did know the contents we would certainly, being what we are, prefer a good dinner of fish, figs and wine.

What helps make the concluding simile the finest ending by a poet of fine endings is the way it captures allusively so much of what has preceded it. The simile adds the suggestion of commercial vigor as a concomitant of the nineteenth century's spiritual debility. It also extends the scope of flight. When the speaker intruded in his reverie upon the ancient home of the Scholar in the Cumnor hills and then bade him "fly our paths" to protect himself (and to protect the dream for the dreamer), the speaker dismissed him to a remote corner of what are still recognizably the Cumnor hills. When the Greeks intrude upon the ancient home of the Tyrian trader, he sails far away, not only from them, but also from his home. The seascape begins as simile for the Cumnor landscape and ends by taking us right out of it, away from the place of reverie and quest alike, away from the place where the active and contemplative lives seem to meet. It might, after all, be only another place which seems, like the view from a window across the Channel at Dover. We do not know whether we can follow the trader and share his traffic with the Iberians, nor do we know whether the trader will ever return to his ancient home. We do not know because the poet, or his poem, does not. All it knows is that the age has lost hope and faith, however it may gloss over the fact. The age is, moreover, in a condition which precludes the recovery of hope and faith; it can at most, little as it is, hope to recover hope, but even that may be a delusion. It is a glum conviction, and unexceptional, for, as Arnold noted, it corresponds to men's dreams and melancholy; the dreams and melancholy of very many in the age, if we can trust Dickens:

Between Battle Bridge and that part of the Holloway district in which he dwelt, was a tract of suburban Sahara, where tiles and bricks were burnt, bones were boiled, carpets were beat, rubbish was shot, dogs were fought, and dust was heaped by contractors. Skirting the border of this desert, by the way he took, when the light of its kiln-fires made lurid smears on the fog, R. Wilfer sighed and shook his head.

"Ah me!" said he, "what might have been is not what is!"
With which commentary on human life, indicating an experience of it not exclusively his own, he made the best of his way to the end of his journey.[18]

[18] *Our Mutual Friend*, I, iv.

But Clough was right to like the Gipsy Scholar and Arnold was less than fair to the zest and grace he brought to men's melancholy and dreams. For the zest and grace come from the whole process by which the poem renders what it felt like in Victorian England to hold that "what might have been is not what is." It is a process in which the control scarcely falters, apart from an occasional infelicity of phrasing,[19] in which the quality of thought and work, dreams and hope is fully conveyed through landscape and reflection that are united by the figures of shepherd, speaker, trader and, above all, of the Gipsy Scholar, whose creation within the poem is perhaps its most important "meaning." As often as it is read, the poem confirms the possibility of good dreams in bad times; and if the poem also questions the validity of such dreams, it never quite commits itself against them: that, after all, is what the Gipsy Scholar does for you.

iii

The Scholar-Gipsy involves a dream of being from the world of becoming and leaves undetermined whether the dream was a delusion. *Thyrsis* devotes itself to recovering a vision of being from the world of becoming and insists that it is true. Both dream and vision derive from a response to the features of the landscape.

The Cumnor poems exemplify the frequently discussed move in Arnold from what may be called uncertainty whether his dreams pass through the gate of horn or of ivory to a conviction that his dreams are all of horn. Severely qualified though it was, the greater optimism of Arnold's later work is unquestionable: the two Obermann poems provide another clear example. The twentieth century has found, with Tennysonian authority, the expression of doubt more satisfyingly honest than the expression of assurance, however tentatively it may be offered. In itself this is a quite invalid criterion. We must allow a poet his faith or his doubt, and ask only that it be properly realized in his poem. Proper realization means in this context the due rendering of the Cumnor countryside so that it really seems, at least for the duration of the poem, to contain the truths it is said to contain.

The problem is the signal tree, not, certainly, whether it was oak or elm, truly solitary or near a clump of pines, on Cumnor Hurst or

[19] E.g., "but thou possessest an immortal lot" (l. 157).

just above Chilswell Farm, visible or not visible on the path from South or North Hinksey.[20] The problem is whether the tree can do the work the poem asks it to do. It is important to pay careful attention to what is first said of the tree, for on that saying the poem will depend. The main details are given in the third stanza after a brief mention of the tree in the second:

> That single elm-tree bright
> Against the west—I miss it! is it gone?
> We prized it dearly; while it stood, we said,
> Our friend, the Gipsy-Scholar, was not dead;
> While the tree lived, he in these fields lived on.   (ll. 26–30)

What, it is pertinent to ask, was their authority for this assurance? More accurately, it is impertinent to ask the question at this point; it only becomes pertinent in the subsequent development of the poem. Thus early, the assurance emerges as a youthful fancy, slightly whimsical perhaps, and therefore all the more amenable to that easy nostalgia for happiness past which the poem so largely exploits. If the poem proceeded merely to exploit that nostalgia, it would not matter that no authority is given for the assurance; it would, indeed, be quite proper. Quite proper, that is, if the eventual sight of the tree signaled only the memorial recovery in the evening of life of the joyous hopes of the morning.[21] Such a poem would have no doubt been as charming as the poem Arnold actually wrote; it would have hung together rather better, and have been quite commonplace. But that is not the poem which Arnold wrote.

The lines of what Arnold is about are clear enough, even if there are more of them than there are in *The Scholar-Gipsy*. *Thyrsis* extends the earlier poem's concern with the possibility of belief in unbelieving times into a search for confirmation that the possibility is well founded, for confirmation that the hopes and creative ability of youth are recoverable in age. The search is rendered in terms of literal passage through a landscape which shows almost everywhere the evidence of change, the cycle of becoming, and the evocation by way of pastoral convention of a changelessly immortal landscape.

[20] The various candidates are reviewed by Sir Francis Wylie in an essay on "The Scholar Gipsy Country" contributed to *Commentary*, pp. 351–73, esp. pp. 356–60.
[21] See J. P. Curgenven, " 'Thyrsis' V: Art and Signification," *Litera*, VI (1959), 2: the quest in the poem is "less a *recherche du temps perdu* than a *recherche de l'absolu.*"

The search is for evidence in the landscape of becoming that it is a copy, however imperfect, of the landscape of being. If the search is successful it will confirm the existence of what Arnold a few years later was to call the eternal not ourselves which makes for righteousness, something identifiably outside the cycle of mortality which makes it both bearable and meaningful.[22]

In the youth of man and nature the pastoral mode embodied an effortlessly meaningful communication between this world and another. The continuity between becoming and being was assured by the beneficent rule of Proserpine, queen of the dead, who "herself had trod Sicilian fields" (l. 93). Her head was crowned in the underworld with flowers which "first open'd on Sicilian air" (l. 89), and this persistence of the emblems of life into the time of death confirmed that Orpheus could indeed have brought back Eurydice and that "Moschus" was right to think he could emulate him on behalf of Bion (ll. 84–90). To this "boon southern country" Thyrsis has gone in death to hear Daphnis sing the perils of life and the consolations of heaven: "all the marvel of the golden skies" (ll. 175–90). As in the youth of man, so in the youth of Thyrsis and Corydon, rowing their skiff along "the shy Thames shore," where the mowers "stood with suspended scythe to see us pass," the emblems of arrested time in a world of time (ll. 126–29). But the Cumnor hills are not Sicilian fields; Proserpine does not know them, and instead of her crown of living flowers there are only "the coronals of that forgotten time," the long-gone flowers of "the loved hill-side" (ll. 112–17). The passage of the seasons marks itself as surely on the landscape as the passage of the years on Corydon. In the "winter-eve" of the poem's now (l. 16) only the primroses are left as "orphans of the flowery prime" (l. 120). The dying of the year and the day, the death of Thyrsis, the aging of Corydon, the passing of "Sibylla" (l. 4), and even of those mowers who once held still their scythes lead inevitably to the quiet despair of *ubi sunt?* (ll. 121–30). The haunts which once mediated between mortality and immortality, which once permitted a dream of "glad perennial youth," can no longer work their magic. Corydon picks his way cautiously through the landscape—"runs it not here, the track by Childsworth Farm?" (l. 11)—seeking the missing tree. If that too is gone, then Corydon's youth with Thyrsis and all its hopes are as

[22] The distinction between the immortal world of pastoral and the mortal world of Cumnor is recognized by Richard Giannone, "The Quest Motif in 'Thyrsis,'" *Victorian Poetry*, III (1965), 71–80, who sees its importance in different terms from mine.

irretrievably past as Proserpine in Sicilian fields and Daphnis singing the Lityerses song. The vision of being is irrecoverable, and if so, even the loved hillside confirms the sad experience of growing older in the world away from Cumnor. The "unbreachable" if "long-batter'd" fortress of the world interposes its wall between Corydon and his youthful vision of the mountain-top throne of truth, bright and bare in his morning's sun (ll. 141–50), the very "marvel of the golden skies" of which Daphnis now sings to Thyrsis in the "boon southern country." Of old there was "easy access" to the grace of Proserpine (l. 91), but now "long the way appears" to the airy throne of truth. The morning is long gone, and the night offers only repose, a cessation from earthly turmoil. From becoming to being involves passage across an "unpermitted ferry's flow" (l. 85), absolute discontinuity with no mediator between.

"Alack, for Corydon," indeed. But, in striving to emulate "Sicilian shepherds" by "piping a ditty sad" for a lost mate (ll. 81–84), he not only gives his "grief its hour" (l. 102), he also renders clearly the difference between becoming and being, their erstwhile continuity and present separateness. We are theologically prepared to appreciate epiphany. It comes when, after painful and unsuccessful striving to recover the past, he is suddenly startled by an unexpected repetition of the past into the instinctive move which renews it. "A troop of Oxford hunters going home, / As in old days" drives him to flight (ll. 153–54), just as, in those "old days," they had driven the Scholar Gipsy. And so the tree. It stands there in the world of becoming, "bare on its lonely ridge" (l. 160), backed by the sun which in "life's morning" had shone so brightly on the bare mountain top of truth. It is now an evening sun and night will soon follow, but between Corydon and the immortality after death, between becoming and being, there is the tree signaling that not all things change, that some things abide to body forth to the world of becoming the permanence of being. Such embodiment is no longer the bright, bare summit which presented itself to "the less practised eye of sanguine youth" (l. 142), but a tree backed by a sky which is "orange and pale violet" (l. 159), orange to remind of the bright sun of morning youth, and pale violet to foreshadow night and death. And then the vision is gone, a "fugitive and gracious light," indeed, which we are soon told the Scholar Gipsy also seeks in these hills, and so does Corydon, and so did Thyrsis (ll. 201–11). Their youthful poetry was right, after all; the "rustic flute" piped of permanent truths in a world of cross doubts and shifting cares. The "haunt beloved" which seemed so changed at first is now shown to yield a virtue still (l. 220), and the poem can end with a whispered assurance from Thyrsis to Corydon, the full establishment of communication between immortality and mortality, being and becoming, validated by the persistence of the tree and the Scholar, those mediators between the two realms.

But an elm is a tree, a vegetable, and no more than an oak or sequoia is it evidence of permanence. Longevity, it must be said, is not the same as immortality: it is not even a mortal approximation of immortality. We are insistently reminded of the discrepancy, if we are at all awake, by the poem's very emphasis upon the vegetable indices of impermanence. The poem buckles beneath the weight of its own philosophic pretensions. To hold together it must find something, preferably in the landscape, to mediate between the literal world of the Cumnor hills with all its emotional associations and the idyllically unchanging world of the antique pastoral. So a tree which begins as the unexplained fancy of youth ends as arbitrary sign, an allegorical object in a literal landscape,[23] but the "justification" for the sign remains the unexplained fancy. Arnold, it seems, had long forgotten the shite's oracle on the unpoetical attributes of the allegorical. If he had recalled it, he might have paused before exclaiming "I cannot reach the signal-tree to-night" (l. 165). We see what he means, of course. He has been afforded the maximum vision that mortal can look for in these bad times, and he rests content, for Arnold was never extravagant in his optimism. He has just devoted three stanzas to a careful reminder that morning is youth, evening is age, and night is death; indeed such an identification of the diurnal with the human cycle is central to the poem, and perhaps explains why, in contrast with *The Scholar-Gipsy*, there are no night pieces among the remembered scenes of youth. So the fact that he cannot reach the tree to-night "means" that he cannot reach it in this life: mediators between being and becoming can in their very nature only be glimpsed at moments and from a distance. But the exclamation also irresistibly reminds us that all this is a nostalgic outing commenced a little too late in the

[23] Wylie's own conviction, *Commentary*, pp. 356–57, endorsing the view of "generations of Oxford men," that the signal-elm was really an oak, which could not have looked "on Ilsley Downs," as Corydon thought, because Boars Hill would be in the way, is an ironic comment upon the obstacles created for topographical source-hunting by placing a symbolic object in a literal landscape. The probability that the signal-tree never existed in its Arnoldian guise and place makes it, as mediator between becoming and being, even more fanciful than the poem itself indicates.

day. If the tree still stands, it can be inspected the next morning or some other morning. But of course that would never do: the whole thrust of the poem makes the tree a symbol which is only complete when glimpsed against an "orange and pale violet evening-sky." The literal landscape very properly rebels against the symbolic burden it is forced to carry.

The poem's process is a familiar one in Arnold. The emotions associated with landscape seem satisfyingly resolved; the epicedium effects its due modulation from despair to consolatory hope. But the resolution depends upon a highly questionable metaphysics involving a fanciful association more expressive of feeling than thought and the arbitrary selection of one object from a literally rendered landscape as a symbolic sign. The poem's heart is stronger than its head. *Thyrsis* is a less successful poem than *The Scholar-Gipsy* because, while the earlier poem uses landscape in ways which accord with the poet's strength to render the emotional quality of generally presented kinds of life, the later poem does that and tries to do more, tries to use landscape to make precise distinctions between this world and another. *Thyrsis* is less successful because it fails to realize its greater philosophic ambitions.

A case might perhaps be made for preferring *Thyrsis* just because it does try to be "more important" than *The Scholar-Gipsy*. But usually, one suspects, a preference for *Thyrsis* signals a response to the strong heart it brings to the English countryside. The most strongly emotional portion of *The Scholar-Gipsy* is the five stanzas of dismissal with which it ends, only one of which evokes the Cumnor hills and that in general terms. In the earlier description of the Scholar's haunts the speaker's—Arnold's—undoubted rural nostalgia rarely becomes overt, because it is passed through the dream concentration upon a gradually created figure. But in *Thyrsis* the poet's nostalgia is overt and weighty, phrasing felicitously an experience which most have known, something charmingly commonplace. It tempts to hikes about "the Scholar-Gipsy country," more accurately named "the *Thyrsis* country," whose pleasures are to be set beside the search for Pickwickian inns or Wordsworth's tracks in the Lake District. The poem certainly asks more of us, is far from content merely to render the charmingly commonplace, but it is perhaps because it fails to be convincing in these endeavors that the track seems to run so clear from the Cumnor hills to the old vicarage at Grantchester.

A RNOLD WROTE TO HIS MOTHER in 1861 "I must finish off for the present my critical writings between this and forty, and give the next ten years earnestly to poetry. It is my last chance. It is not a bad ten years of one's life for poetry if one resolutely uses it, but it is a time in which, if one does not use it, one dries up and becomes prosaic altogether."[1] Arnold did not finish off his "critical writings" by his fortieth birthday at the end of 1862, and although he took time from his criticism for poetry, the results were, with the exception of *Thyrsis,* more or less and usually altogether prosaic.

It is probably useless to inquire what Arnold meant by "prosaic." As normally applied to poetry, the word is comfortably and imprecisely pejorative, performing a function similar, say, to "academic." It presumably does not include such things as the opening of *Bleak House,* and should be applied rather to uses of language in which the figurative element is both limited and obvious, and in which the coherence and additional suggestiveness which come from the repetition with differences of epithets, images, and key terms is minimal or non-existent. "Prosaic" poetry is strictly straightforward, making little or no use of that insistent retrospection which checks the tendency shared by all verbal discourse to an exclusively linear progress. The "prose" reference of "prosaic" is the essay, in which any sense of completeness and inevitability comes usually from satisfaction with matters of rhetoric: the working out of an argument,

[1] *Works,* XIII, 188; Aug. 15, 1861.

the establishment and manipulation of a tone of voice or stance, the skilful introduction of incidental felicities of phrasing.

When such "prosaic" poetry includes landscape, as it so often does in Arnold, the landscape is likely to emerge as simile illustrating a conceptual point but rarely enlarging upon it by conveying, for example, how it feels to hold such a philosophy. The syntax of simile of course insists upon a connection between description and reflection, but it is difficult to make the connection more than one of decorative set-off to an argument. Those few of Arnold's later poems which make use of actual landscape sites rarely succeed in deriving the thought from the description in the manner of *Resignation* or *Kensington Gardens*. The effect of such pieces is similar to what might be achieved from laying side by side the philosophizing of the Clough letters and the flower catalogues of Arnold's letters to his mother.

i

The evident fact that Arnold dried up more completely than most poets of similar stature has led, inevitably, to frequent speculations upon the reasons. The usual and most persuasive is that Arnold felt increasingly the need to treat subjects to which his own poetic talents were unsuited. The remark quoted at the beginning of this chapter should caution against an assumption that Arnold made at any time or over any period of time a clear commitment whose consequences he fully understood. It would be wrong, for example, to seek in *Empedocles on Etna* or its subsequent suppression evidence for Arnold's rejection of poetry. Certainly he passed through periods of dissatisfaction with his early work, but he continued to alter and republish it to the end of his life. He claimed for his poems, in a frequently quoted pronouncement, a large historical representativeness and a by no means modest aesthetic achievement.[2] We can perhaps account for the decision to publish those late elegies on sundry pets as the whimsical self-indulgence of a Great Man. But his expressed satisfaction with the poeticizing of *Westminster Abbey*[3] is explicable only if we assume that Arnold was not greatly gifted with critical self-awareness. He continued to write poetry because he thought he could still write it.

[2] *Works,* XIV, 195–96; June 5, 1869.
[3] *Works,* XV, 101; [1882].

From the vantage point afforded by a century the danger signs seem clear enough. Of the forty-six so-called *New Poems* of 1867, ten had been previously published in magazines or earlier volumes, two were extracts from longer poems already published,[4] four were apparently composed years before.[5] The remaining thirty pieces included some twenty-one sonnets and short poems whose only interest is that they are by the author of *Empedocles on Etna* and *The Scholar-Gipsy*. The pieces reprinted or of delayed publication comprise almost everything that is worthwhile in the volume of 1867. Although there is no reason to suppose that Arnold fully appreciated what processes were at work, there is in the 1867 volume an evident effort to rework or relive earlier poetic experiences. The qualified success of *Thyrsis* depends very much upon the prior existence of *The Scholar-Gipsy*. *A Southern Night* alludes explicitly to *A Summer Night*. *The Terrace at Berne* is a late epilogue to the *Switzerland* poems, and, most clearly of all, *Obermann Once More* is an attempt to repeat the modest success of *Stanzas in Memory of the Author of 'Obermann.'* These pieces, those of long-delayed publication and the poems reprinted, especially from the 1852 volume,[6] give to *New Poems* the air of a declining talent feeding parasitically upon its own youthful vigor.

The two Obermann poems exemplify the process most fully, as well as exhibiting that move from doubt to optimism, from regretful dream to enspiriting vision which distinguishes *Thyrsis* from *The Scholar-Gipsy*. 'Obermann' is one of the better early poems. It exhibits a control, characteristic of Arnold, over the relationship between the speaker and the person addressed by apostrophe. The relationship is established, also characteristically, through a landscape common to both persons. By finding analogues for the departed Obermann in a mountain setting which he himself experiences in the present, the speaker gains both the immediacy of meditation and a necessary point of contact between his subjective self and the object of his contemplation. The landscape, moreover, is sufficiently varied in its associations to convey the different aspects

---

[4] *Early Death and Fame* from *Haworth Churchyard* and *Youth and Calm* from *Lines Written by a Death-Bed.*
[5] *Fragment of . . . a 'Dejaneira'* (1847–48?), *Calais Sands* (1850), *Dover Beach* (1851), *A Caution to Poets* (before Dec., 1852). I follow the dating of Allott.
[6] *Empedocles on Etna, Human Life, Youth's Agitations, Lines Written in Kensington Gardens, The Second Best, Progress.* The pieces first published separately and then collected in *New Poems* were *Thyrsis* (1866), *St. Brandan* (1860), *A Southern Night* (1861), and *Stanzas from the Grande Chartreuse* (1855).

of Obermann, which are almost Petrarchist in their contradictions: cold languor and fevered pain, virgin freshness and human agony. The working out of the meditation is the process of resolving these light contradictions; by coming to identify Obermann the speaker comes to identify himself and his kind of life. When identification involves comparison, Wordsworth and Goethe come equipped with a locus, the place of burial. Indeed, the poem's persistent concern with death bed, grave and transfiguration make it very much an elegy in a country cemetery. The speaker apostrophizes and meditates upon shades who come and go through cloud and mist, sometimes gaining a "wide / And luminous view" (ll. 79–80), sometimes offering only "the dreams that but deceive" (l. 129), dreams, that is, of continuous calm and clarity in this life. *Stanzas in Memory of the Author of 'Obermann'* is a monody on the meaning of that memory for the speaker. Obermann and his Alpine retreat are a means of objectifying introspection; they make it possible for a private meditation to be properly overheard and experienced by another person. What the landscape provides is, once again, the source and correlative of the emotion attaching to a way of life. It conveys no ethical imperatives: that we should or should not be or strive to be like Obermann, Wordsworth, or Goethe. Instead it helps convey what it feels like to lead a life definable in terms of theirs, but different from theirs, following its own ineluctable permutation upon the desire for solitude and the desire for society.

The reasons that keep *'Obermann'* below *The Scholar-Gipsy* in achievement are no doubt attributable to its stanzaic form. Arnold certainly eliminates most of the sing-song hymnal effect of his variation upon common measure by the plentiful use of an initial reversed foot, but there is in his meter a large residual jauntiness which sorts oddly with the sober melancholy of the poem's utterance: *'Obermann'* goes well if startlingly to the tune of *All Things Bright and Beautiful*. The other tendency of common measure to settle into a rhythm of short declarative phrases is checked by the use of run-on lines. But even these cannot properly slow the fast-moving stanzas to the deliberation appropriate to reverie. The rapid, impressionistic sketching of the opening lines makes their scene-setting sound more perfunctory than it is. We have only to compare *The Scholar-Gipsy*'s slow making of a dream figure out of a mood in a landscape to appreciate what is missing from *'Obermann.'*

The inappropriateness between manner and matter which limits the achievement of 'Obermann' largely disappears in the use of the same stanza for Obermann Once More. The hymnal chant of common measure, breaking at moments of narrative into the related rhythms of ballad (ll. 85–140), sorts well with the spiritual uplift of the later poem. But, this aside, Obermann Once More is clearly inferior to 'Obermann.' The reason is not hard to see. In his early poems Arnold developed and at times came close to perfecting a talent for poetry to be overheard: a private meditation effecting its necessary communication with others by working out mood and thought in terms of landscapes which recall common experiences. Arnold came later to prefer a poetry to be heard, the rough equivalent in verse to his prose addresses to the English people. The wistfully equivocal dreams of the earlier poems give place to the authoritative visions of the later. Thyrsis whispers briefly but conclusively from the grave, and the shade of Obermann delivers a sermon complete with lengthy historical exemplum and assurance of a social millennium. Where Arnold once climbed a mountain to understand a mood and a way of life, he now ascends as a chosen vessel to be filled with the Word of Hope. Such mutations require changes in poetic mode which Arnold was seemingly unable to make. Especially do they require attention to the arts of rhetoric: the persuasive establishment and manipulation of an ethos. We know from his later strictures upon Dryden and Pope that Arnold thought these arts appropriate to prose not verse, and his own prose is a constant revelation of his mastery.[7] Epilogue to Lessing's Laocoön is lengthy testimony to his inability to effect a sastifactory adaptation of the manner of Pope in verse, while Obermann Once More marks a notable failure to unite the landscape of private mood with the discourse of public address.

Like much of Arnold's work, Obermann Once More is evidently a made poem, for the speaker's progress through a landscape in the opening and closing sections clearly corresponds to a spiritual progress whose details are set out in the visionary homily of the middle section. The valley and lower slopes evoked in the opening lines invite the traveler to pause for refreshment by indulging his nostalgia for the past. "The gentian-flower'd pass, its crown / With

[7] For an analysis of rhetorical effect in Arnold's prose see John Holloway, The Victorian Sage (1953), pp. 202–43.

yellow spires aflame" (ll. 21–22) marks the way out of random self-indulgence to purposeful and hopeful action. We are not told what program that action entails (Arnold was reluctant even in prose to make practical suggestions), but we are told why it is necessary to undertake that unspecified action: things are better than they were; there must be no more lolling in meadows with the cows, for it is time to be up and on.[8] Throughout the night on the mountain the ghost of Obermann insists that a new day is dawning, just as the day of Christianity once dawned. The tempests are past, the sun up and the ice melting. It is a lengthy sermon and with "the vision ended" (l. 325) there is not long to wait for testimony that it passed through the gate of horn. *"Dost thou ask proof?"* Thyrsis once whispered; well, it is available:

> And glorious there, without a sound,
> Across the glimmering lake,
> High in the Valais-depth profound,
> I saw the morning break. (ll. 345–48)

Arnold's assumption seems to be that if you repeat a cliché metaphor often enough—a new age is dawning—it is sufficient to describe a literal occurrence of its vehicle—a sunrise—to effect a strong symbolic charge. We are asked to accept, and it is difficult to do so, a continuous landscape in which some features are important as they set off moods and memories in the speaker while others are held to contain significances existing independently of the speaker. Arnold's own criterion of naturalness is most obviously violated by such a landscape, just as it was by the signal tree of *Thyrsis*.

The criterion of naturalness is also strained by the apparition of Obermann's ghost. The visionary homily is presumably offered, not as actual happening, but as a poetical version of the speaker's own nocturnal musing upon the mountain. The spirit is raised, rather abruptly, as a consequence of the speaker's nostalgic recollection of his "wandering youth" (l. 39), but it is raised in order to bridge the disjunctive gap between wistful memories and enspiriting prognostication. The ghost is a way of smoothing over the fact that the historicist meditation by night does not follow from the random

---

[8] See also the essay on Wordsworth, where Arnold approvingly quotes a passage from Epictetus (*Discourses*, II, xxiii) requiring men to leave the pleasant inn or meadow in which they would linger and make their way home to a sense of moral duty, *Works*, IV, 106–7.

reverie of the day. The ghost serves to join two landscape syntaxes: the "mountain-flower" and "shepherd's garb" of wistful emotion (ll. 64–65) and the daybreak of moral exhortation. To do so,
the ghost is assigned a speech he patently did not write himself.
The effect is painfully ventriloquial. Old Matthew takes young
Matthew by the scruff of the neck and makes him recant. The recantation is given a pseudo-objective authority by delivering it from
the lips of Umbra Obermann. But since we plainly cannot believe
literally in Umbra Obermann, he ought, for poetic validity, to
emerge as an extension of old Matthew just as he once emerged as
an extension of young Matthew. The poem seems to lack, indeed,
a section immediately before the appearance of the ghost in which
old Matthew himself makes the transition from "infinite desire /
For all that *might* have been" (ll. 51–52) to a conviction that
what might have been is now what is. Such a transition could have
made for a more satisfying unified poem, although it would certainly have diminished its effectiveness as prophecy, in which
Arnold, an English Moses, hands down the Word to a nation
running after false gods.

ii

False gods figure largely in an earlier and more successful elegy,
Stanzas from the Grande Chartreuse. The world is as committed
there to "pride of life" (l. 167) as was the haggard Roman of
Obermann Once More (l. 133). But in *The Grande Chartreuse*
men must wait longer than the next sunrise for a millennium. Indeed, the tentative hope that "years hence, perhaps, may dawn an
age, / More fortunate, alas! than we" (ll. 157–58) is severely ques-
tioned by its implicit association with the "emblems of hope" which
the Carthusians are said to find in the "yellow tapers" shining over
the high altar (ll. 200–202). It is a questioning not so much of
whether the hope will be realized as of the hope's spiritual validity.
For the yellow tapers play also against "the high, white star of
Truth" to which the speaker insists he is still committed (ll. 67–
78).[9] This is a truth of purged faith and trimmed fire,[10] and
although we are characteristically not told the constituents of such

[9] Although suggesting landscape, the star of truth is a metaphor outside the
literal setting of the Grande Chartreuse and thus does not jar in the manner of
the signal-tree or the daybreak of *Obermann Once More*.
[10] The *trimming* of faith's fire is perhaps recalled in the yellow tapers of hope.

a truth, we must assume from the purging of faith that it involves some restriction of supernatural sanctions upon man and the substitution of a pattern of life which will produce wisdom without tough cynicism and gaiety without frivolity (ll. 157–60) : joyful self-knowledge, perhaps. It is when we extrapolate this characteristic opposition between the clarity of natural light and an artificially lit gloom that we confront the central weakness of what is, in many respects, a highly impressive poem.

Stanzas from the Grande Chartreuse is impressive in ways which should now be familiar. It poses openly the question which serves implicitly as an organizing principle in many of Arnold's early works: "what am I, that I am here" (l. 66). The speaker proposes, that is, to understand himself, his present feelings, in terms of the landscape in which he finds himself. By the time the question is asked, in fact, the answer to it is already half-given. The ascent to the monastery and the tour of its buildings and precincts establish by repeated motifs the quality of life and kind of feeling which are to be explored. The tour gives us the context of the monks; the ascent, the context of the speaker in his emotional passage to their retreat. The evident similarity between the two contexts fixes a connection between speaker and monks even before he asks his question. The similarity is expressed in terms of the transmutation of rain-soaked meadows into humid corridors with splashing fountains, of the "spectral vapours white" of "the cloud-drift" to the "ghostlike . . . Cowl'd forms . . . in gleaming white," of the "strangled sound" of "the Dead Guier's stream" to the monks' kneeling and wrestling "with penitential cries" before retiring to "that wooden bed, / Which shall their coffin be, when dead," of the "boiling cauldron" of the Guiers Mort to "stone-carved basins cold." This repetition of motifs with differences not only prepares the speaker emotionally for identification with the monks, it also makes clear, before the move to reflection and comment, which are the elements of significance. Before the voice of conscience implanted in the speaker by the "rigorous teachers" of his youth upbraids him with *"what dost thou in this living tomb?"* (l. 72), it is plain that he has undertaken an emotional passage to forested retreat and stony death. Appropriately, retreat and death are associated with the past, both by recalling the pilgrim hosts who once thronged the halls of Grande Chartreuse and by the rather artificially forced question, "what pointed roofs are these advance?–/ A palace of the

Kings of France?" (ll. 23–24). The sense of historical survival, of a coelacanth in a sea of mackerel, is applied in reflection to outmoded faiths and outmoded melancholy. In the final assertion of the speaker's emotional identity with the Carthusians, landscape and figures are accorded a faintly medieval dress:

> We are like children rear'd in shade
> Beneath some old-world abbey wall,
> Forgotten in a forest-glade,
> And secret from the eyes of all.
> Deep, deep the greenwood round them waves,
> Their abbey, and its close of graves!   (ll. 169–74)

Stanzas from the Grande Chartreuse is the most consistently and overtly escapist poem in the Arnold canon. Escape is from the unattractive alternatives of the frivolous gaiety of hunters (ll. 160, 181–86) and the tough practicality, the big pomp of the life battle (ll. 159, 175–80) with its suggestive vulgarity (ll. 164–67). Escape is toward both aspects of the Scholar Gipsy: his literal death and his imagined "perennial youth," toward stones and spectres and the bowering wood. The final couplet of the poem originally read:

> —Pass, banners, pass, and bugles, cease;
> And leave our forest to its peace!

When he reprinted the poem in the volume of 1867 (it was first published separately in 1855), he changed *forest* to *desert,* changing, that is, the final impression of Grande Chartreuse as a historical survival to that of another place in the wilderness in which to die, having saluted the promised land from afar.[11]

What, then, is impressive about the poem is the way the setting provides a full objectification of the emotions associated with the speaker's meditation. But the setting is not the only operative analogy for the speaker; there are also the monks. The full success of the poem depends upon our accepting as true an analogy between the "last of the race of them who grieve" and the "last of the people who believe" (ll. 110–12). The speaker anticipates Yeats by numbering himself among the last Romantics; he sees the Carthusians as survivors from a medieval age of faith. But it is not the

---

[11] *The Function of Criticism at the Present Time,* in *Complete Prose,* III, 285.

medievalizing strain in the Romantics with which he identifies himself; instead he sees himself as the inheritor of a generally apprehended melancholy or agony (ll. 121–50), and he is justifiably vague about the causes of that Romantic melancholy, not identifying it as a loss of religious certitude. Revealingly, the fullest statement of an analogy between the speaker and the monks comes in the form of allusion, an analogy for an analogy:

> Not as their friend, or child, I speak!
> But as, on some far northern strand,
> Thinking of his own Gods, a Greek
> In pity and mournful awe might stand
> Before some fallen Runic stone—
> For both were faiths, and both are gone.   (ll. 79–84)

What is striking about this analogy is the extent to which it fails to express the relationship between speaker and monks. To a (presumably) modern Greek the disappearance of Teutonic paganism may well parallel the fall of the Olympians. But the Carthusians still believe, however the world may deride them for it (l. 89). The speaker may lament the loss of his personal Olympus, but the rock on which the monks fix themselves is no fallen stone. The true relationship between speaker and monks is in fact very close to the relationship between the speaker and the Scholar Gipsy: disjunction, not conjunction. In that poem Arnold can exclaim "thou hadst—what we, alas! have not," and be reasonably sure that no one will suspect him of desiring to rule "the workings of men's brains." The Scholar's ideas are important only for the general feelings they inspire. But the "ideas" of the Carthusians are less amenable to such treatment. Professor Culler's point is nicely taken: "Arnold is well aware that a young Oxford man visiting a continental monastery in 1851 might easily be queried about his intentions."[12]

Arnold is engaged in the delicate task of fashioning an analogy between himself and the monks, while at the same time making clear that he certainly does not share their convictions: "Not as their friend, or child, I speak!" The consequences are, inevitably, a damaging haziness. The world is condemned for crying that the Carthusians' "faith is now / But a dead time's exploded dream" (ll. 97–98). But the speaker had felt the same thing when contemplating the "fallen Runic stone" of the monastery, although—

[12] Culler, p. 92.

and the difference is certainly important—he expressed himself "in pity and mournful awe," not derision. The haziness is most apparent in the concluding stanzas, where Arnold strives for a full establishment of analogy between speaker and monks by way of a shifty use of personal pronouns reminiscent of *The Buried Life*. The "we" of line 156 are plainly the last Romantics, of whom the speaker is representative, addressing the shades of the first Romantics. But this "we" is tacitly associated with the monks, the last believers, in the medievalizing simile of lines 169–92, which finds in the monastery an appropriate setting for the last Romantics. When the warriors of action and the pleasure hunters bid the *"shy recluses, follow too!"* (l. 192), they address themselves to monks who, if the poem is working properly, are also representative of the last grievers.[13] In replying for themselves the monks should also be replying for such a last Romantic as the speaker. But they do not. Their kind of hope is different from the speaker's; it burns in yellow tapers not high, white stars. Unlike his, their hope is not for a "perhaps"; it is the hope that walks with faith. The one true point of contact between last believers and last grievers is the impulse to retreat from a furious and frivolous world. And so the last line applies to both, because landscape avoids the divisive consequences of concept.

The weakness of *Stanzas from the Grande Chartreuse* is that in answering the question "and what am I, that I am here?" it seemed necessary to deal explicitly with possible but incorrect reasons for the speaker's presence and thus to draw attention to the tenuousness of the analogy on which the poem is based. It may be, indeed, that the very posing of the question points to a failure prior to weakness in execution, a failure in invention. The question perhaps signals Arnold's uneasiness that the analogy he commits himself to working out is not truly viable.

iii

The weakness of analogy in *Stanzas from the Grande Chartreuse* is forced upon us by the overt presence of Arnoldian man, the "I" in the poem. He focuses, and damagingly, those areas in which the analogy will not hold. *Empedocles on Etna* gains, in contrast, by

---

[13] It is true that Arnold makes the distinction: *"we* are like children rear'd in shade," but "deep the greenwood round *them* waves." Of this pronominal shift we can only say that Arnold wants to use an analogy he knows will not hold.

the fact that its analogy with Arnoldian man in Victorian England is implicit, if unmistakable. Empedoclean metempsychosis, lying as it does conceptually outside the limits of analogy with the nineteenth century, is far more acceptable than the Carthusians' faith. Their faith is sufficiently unlike the speaker's view of things to weaken the analogy conceptually, and yet sufficiently similar to limit the possibility of using it, as the gipsies' strange art is used, to express the emotion, the feel, of looking at things in a way analogous to the speaker's.

The issue here is one of contemporary relevance; what Arnold was to call an adequate interpretation of the age. Whenever we feel that relevance is not properly achieved, we are likely to call the work "academic" or "escapist." Arnold's interest in the temporally and spatially remote has opened him to the charge of academicism, of rendering the materials of antiquarian research with only minimal relevance to his own age. Poems like *Empedocles on Etna, Tristram and Iseult,* or *The Sick King in Bokhara* are properly exempt from such a charge because so much of their total "meaning" is conveyed in terms of landscape. They benefit, in fact, from Hazlitt's principle that "the interest we feel in external nature is common and transferable from one object to all others of the same class." It is to the long poems of the mid-1850's, *Sohrab and Rustum, Balder Dead,* and *Merope,* that the charge of academicism seems, if in varying degrees, most appropriate. It seems so because, as we know from Arnold's comments in letters and prefaces, the main endeavor was to locate the significance in an action which embodied some fundamental human emotion or situation. And of course he does. We can describe these pieces in terms of other poems by saying that *Sohrab and Rustum* is a tragic rendering of enislement in the sea of life, *Balder Dead* is an epic version of the Empedoclean move from joy to strife, *Merope* is a tragedy about the buried life or, perhaps, the lament of *Parting*: "what heart knows another? / Ah! who knows his own?" But the crucial difference between embodying fundamental emotions or situations in landscapes and embodying them in historically remote actions is that, where the descriptive details of landscape are, at least potentially, a necessary part of the embodiment, the details of actions are quite incidental to the fundamental truths. Mount Etna is meaningful from the charred crust of its summit to the cool glen below, but Peran-Wisa's "sheep-skin cap" is an item principally of local or antiquarian color.

To mention the cap seems niggling. Obviously, a poem of some length can comfortably accommodate details of local color, just as a landscape poem can afford to indulge itself occasionally with scraps of lichen and rock fissures while primarily engaged in composing the scene into some morally or emotionally significant arrangement of objects. In fact, *Sohrab and Rustum* depends heavily upon the creation of a landscape to complement the central action and situation. The landscape is presented in terms of descriptions of the plain and river where the combat takes place, of the homes of Sohrab and Rustum, and in terms of frequent epic similes. The contribution of the landscape matter to the poem has been finely discussed by Professor Culler, who has pointed out the way it draws the single incident of the battle within a continuing cycle of life, seasonal, diurnal and human.[14] Despite the generalizing tendencies of the nature myth, that life cycle is specifically *ein Heldenleben,* from "high mountain-cradle" to marine grave and heroic stellification among "the new-bathed stars" which "shine upon the Aral Sea." *Sohrab and Rustum* is an obvious attempt to compensate Victorian England for its "absence of great *natures*" in contrast with the bulk of Arnold's poems, which constitute a lament at being surrounded by "millions of small ones."[15] It takes its place with the youthful prize poems on Alaric and Cromwell, or the early sonnet on Wellington, rather than with *Empedocles on Etna.*

I said that *Sohrab and Rustum* is tragic rather than epic.[16] It is so because, despite its heroic preoccupation and its Homeric imitation, the emphasis falls not upon the epic revelation of qualities needed to sustain a society subject to attack from without and emulation within, but upon a tragically fateful dichotomy between individual fulfillment—to find a father or a child of whom one can be proud—and the public obligation to be a great warrior. The sense of the situation is tragic, and is therefore, as Arnold later insisted, emancipated from "that which is local and transient." But the context of the situation is presented epically, giving us, in addition to "the thought and passion of man, . . . the forms of outward life, the fashion of manners, the aspects of nature, that which is local and transient." It gives us Peran-Wisa's cap and the "sugar'd mulberries" with which the "pedlars, from Cabool" "slake their parch'd throats" when crossing "the Indian Caucasus" (ll. 160–66). Now,

[14] Culler, pp. 209–14.
[15] *Clough Letters,* p. 111; Sept. 23 [1849].
[16] It is of note that the 1853 preface conducts its tacit endorsement of *Sohrab and Rustum* principally in terms of tragedies, not epics.

said Arnold in his inaugural lecture at Oxford, "in the *reconstruc-tion,* by learning and antiquarian ingenuity, of the local and tran-sient features of a past age, in their representation by one who is not a witness or contemporary, it is impossible to feel the liveliest kind of interest."[17]

Arnold's idea of the epic follows from the false premise that Homer was "representing contemporary or nearly contemporary events."[18] We have only to read Moses I. Finley's *World of Odys-seus* to appreciate the extent to which Homer was representing past events. More often than not an epic action is set in the quasi-legendary past of its author's society. It avoids antiquarianism by its sense of the relevance of the past for the present of its society. The virtues needed for the founding of Rome are relevant to its flourishing under Augustus. The idea of an Elizabethan gentleman can be embodied in adventures through Faerie. The earliest "Christian" community is of highest import for seventeenth-century Christians. The pastness of the action facilitates that introduction of the marvelous which permits the needed qualities to be shown in magnified form. Beowulf's fortitude appears far greater in Grendel's mere than it would if he tackled Unferth in single com-bat, but his conduct of himself is far from irrelevant to Brunan-burh and Maldon. When this kind of relevance is lacking, as it appears to be lacking to *Sohrab and Rustum,* the representation of "the local and transient" will appear antiquarian. Curiously, *Sohrab and Rustum* grew later in the century into a kind of rele-vance it scarcely possessed at its first publication. Khartoum and Omdurman, the North West Frontier of India and the Zulu War gave immediacy to the poem's portrayal of stoic death in the desert, and *Sohrab and Rustum* vied for a time with *The Scholar-Gipsy* as the poem by Arnold most frequently used as a school text. It prob-ably lost its brief relevance in Passchendaele, in company with much else.

But this quirk of literary history scarcely constituted a full and proper response to the poem. Too many elements in *Sohrab and Rustum* make it a closed and alien system for it to be a true Vic-torian (or Edwardian) myth. Most obviously is this true of its ani-mate view of nature: the "sympathetic" sand eddy which shrouds the father and son for the duration of their combat (ll. 480–85,

[17] *Complete Prose,* I, 35.
[18] *Complete Prose,* I, 34.

522–24), the curdling of the Oxus at the "dreadful cry" of "Ruksh, the horse" (ll. 501–8), and, most painfully of all, "the big warm tears" which "roll'd down" from the "dark, compassionate eyes" of Ruksh "and caked the sand" when his master wept for the son he had mortally wounded (ll. 730–36). If Ruksh were just another Victorian stag at bay or doleful dog mourning a lost master, he would simply be uncomfortably mawkish. But Ruksh is representative of a simple, homogeneous life, in which heroes are expressed in terms of the landscapes they traverse and the beasts of the field and air they so closely resemble in combat. It is a life completely in harmony with nature, neither passing nature nor resting "her slave." It is not a view of nature with which Arnold was ever comfortable and his uneasiness declares itself in the way he introduces his fullest statements of one nature and one life:

> And you would say that sun and stars took part
> In that unnatural conflict; for a cloud
> Grew suddenly in Heaven, and dark'd the sun
> Over the fighters' heads; and a wind rose
> Under their feet, and moaning swept the plain,
> And in a sandy whirlwind wrapp'd the pair. (ll. 480–85)

Who is the "you" responsible for this theory of chain reaction in nature? The conditional "would say" is an evident attempt to soften objections to the philosophical implications of that purposeful wind. So, too, when Ruksh moves downstage to weep over the father and son, he is presented "as if inquiring what their grief / Might mean" (ll. 734–35). But that is precisely what the poem makes Ruksh do: there is no "as if" about it.

It is difficult not to admire *Sohrab and Rustum;* and just as difficult not to feel uneasy about doing so. The last one hundred and fifty lines have a movingly sustained dignity in their gradual absorption of the life cycle of heroes into the life stream of the Oxus, compensating, as do so many other works, for the sense of tragic loss by epic affirmation. But the noble resolution unties an antiquarian knot. The sense of nature informing the close is established earlier in terms alien to Arnold and his England. It is a sense, moreover, which does not rise fully from the action itself and which must be supplied by similes occurring, at times, so closely together and illustrating such sparsely described gestures that they seem a parody,

not an imitation of the epic manner. Indeed, it is sometimes difficult to decide whether the similes illustrate the action or the action
the similes. But that is not altogether surprising in a poet whose
characteristic strength lay in the objectification of mood and emotion in natural phenomena and the representation of action by
means of tableaux in landscapes.

By contrast, it is comfortably unnecessary either to admire *Balder
Dead* and *Merope* or to feel uneasy about not doing so. *Balder
Dead,* indeed, contains a small kernel of meaningful relevance in a
thick shell of antiquarianism. Beneath the heavy characters of its
Teutonic myth there are discernible traces of a Christian significance. Balder, the mild spirit of joy, the miracle worker, the poet
of youth, family, and home is evidently Christlike, and like Arnold's
Christ he is lost to his fellows when the forces of strife and hate
have their way. There is a Dombeyish play with frozen landscapes
and the tearful thaw of love and joy. And lest we should think this
of importance only for Valhalla and Hell, we are assured that the
gods are, at least in some respects, like the sons of men (III, 426).
But it is indeed impossible to feel a lively interest in this careful
antiquarian reconstruction. The general significance of Hermod's
journey to the dead, the difficult and frozen passage to joylessness,
is not much affected by the details of the landscape through which
he passes, and the details accordingly "justify" themselves by the
extent to which they accurately recall the poem's sources. It is true
that Arnold takes such opportunities as he can to parallel by half
allusion the Teutonic myth with classical and biblical events and
situations.[19] The result is to make the poem read at times like an
exercise in comparative mythology, a kind of antiquarianism from
which *Merope* is at least reasonably free. Professor Culler has made
out the best possible case for the relevance of *Merope*'s concern with
a politics of self-justifying expediency and a politics of ethical principle to the Victorian concern with motive and authority.[20] In fact,
the play's action is grounded so firmly upon constitutional issues of
tyranny, usurpation, insurrection, and hereditary succession that its
investigation of the nature of public obligation makes it a suitable
subject for a seventeenth-century heroic play reflecting upon the
political troubles of the Stuarts. It is less clear what it has to offer
to the England of Victoria and Albert.

[19] See the notes to the poem in Allott.
[20] Culler, pp. 224–25.

iv

We are pointed toward the explanation for Arnold's poetic decline by Professor Culler's remarks upon the landscape of *Merope*.
Landscape in *Merope* is almost entirely restricted to descriptions of
Aepytus' Arcadian upbringing, especially the long, fictitious account
of his death while hunting which Aepytus gives Polyphontes (ll.
722–846). Professor Culler comments: "one feels that this passage,
almost alone in the drama, is vital and alive because in it Arnold
is returning to the source of his true poetic feeling."[21] For Professor Culler this means a largely fixed symbolic landscape of "idle
youth" in the glade, an underground river of the buried life, and a
mature acceptance of responsibility on the plain of public life. The
vitality of the passage is in fact referable to its using a landscape,
of forest, lake, and mountain, whose details are amenable to an attempted rendering of the quality of a life. By contrast, the plain
and its variants in hot or drab cities and brazen prisons seem not to
have moved Arnold imaginatively as, say, they moved Dickens.
Dickens again and again expressed his sense of Victorian life in detailed descriptions of chimney pots, dirty streets, factories, tottering
houses, dust heaps, or the Marshalsea.[22] But when Arnold came to
express his sense of the active life the urban details he found useful
were very few in comparison with his rural scenes. It is of note that
Arnold's best "London" poem is *Lines Written in Kensington
Gardens.*

A desert is hot and sandy, and there, for Arnold, you have it.
Three lines on the darkling plain with ignorant armies contrast
with twenty-eight on the shore-line in *Dover Beach. A Dream* devotes thirty-six lines to the details on the banks of "a green Alpine
stream" and a bare line to "burning plains / Bristled with cities."
Mycerinus only acquires an environment when he moves to the
glade. *Consolation*'s comment upon the pains and small pleasures
of active life requires for its landscape realization the brief description of four different cities. The topographical possibilities of the
bare upper slopes of Etna are soon exhausted, and so are the
topographical possibilities of Catana. The plain and its variants

[21] Culler, p. 227.
[22] By contrast—or compensation—when Dickens moved into Arnold territory in
the pastoral scenes of *Oliver Twist* or *The Old Curiosity Shop* the result was a
diminished imaginative intensity.

figure frequently in Arnold's poetry, but their qualitative and quantitative contribution is small beside that of glade and mountain, river, lake, and field. These rural settings are places of retreat, meditation, imagination, dream-weaving, and these are for Arnold all activities which derive from and find a counterpart in the details of the scene. But when Arnold has noted that public life is subject to hot sun, to metaphorical battles and prisons, the environment lets him down, and further rendering of active life must proceed in terms of explicit discourse with, perhaps, incidental metaphor. Bokhara is a seeming exception, but, when the poem is not reiterating the consequences of plague and drought, its rendering of environment is largely in terms of glades or glade surrogates. The late poem *Palladium* sums up in its brief compass the maximum topographical possibilities of the plain in order, once again, to contrast the active and contemplative lives. And *Palladium* is a superficial little poem, whose simple, indeed banal, declarations are no more than decorated by the Homeric setting. By contrast with *Kensington Gardens,* which creates a complete landscape image for the inner and outer life of a man, *Palladium* offers a landscape simile for the body and soul which not only distributes these properties about the landscape, but also leaves it quite uncertain what Arnold means by such crucial words as "soul" and "die."

Whatever the source of Arnold's poetic feeling, the source of his poetic strength was a by no means constant ability to objectify a mood, an emotion, a quality of life, more rarely an idea, in a landscape. There is certainly variety in his output, but his characteristic poem is *The Scholar-Gipsy,* in which the withdrawn life of contemplation and imagination is rendered in terms of a detailed landscape and is then tested against an active life conveyed by straightforward discourse and incidental metaphor. Such an active life might, in other poems, be associated, if briefly, with the plain and the city, although it is given no topographical context in *The Scholar-Gipsy.* Arnold's strength, which manifests itself even in lesser poems, is the sense he so often conveys of something evidently made. The making involves his own solution to the aesthetic problem of uniting reflection and description in landscape poems.

Increasingly, it is clear, Arnold was moved to treat the active life directly instead of from the vantage point of nook or mountain top. One consequence was a poetry of declarative discourse in which brief landscape similes enter to illustrate some straightforward point. Another consequence was the curious confusion of *Baccha-nalia,* in which an English rural scene is incongruously disturbed by "wild Mænads" in order to effect a not very compelling analogy with the ebullience and vulgarity of Victorian life as Arnold saw it. The neat division of the poem, juxtaposing the two halves of the analogy, declares the way in which it was excogitated, just as the rude importation of maenads into England signals an ill-advised attempt to use rural scene as illustration for, not contrast with, the life of cities and plains. But the most obvious consequence was an increasing tendency "to treat political, or religious, or social mat-ters, directly" in prose, instead of touching them "only so far as they can be touched through poetry."[23] Landscape still plays a part in Arnold's prose, most often as appropriately brief and discontinuous similes, although Arnold occasionally indulged himself with de-scriptive mood pieces rendering qualities of life or emotion through landscape. Such pieces are the memorial review of his first visit to George Sand, the crossing from Liverpool to Llandudno which opens *Celtic Literature,* the wistful recreation of the society at Great Tew in the essay on Falkland, and, most famous of all, the apostrophe to Oxford at the end of the preface to *Essays in Criticism.*

v

If we think, as we should, of the apostrophe to Oxford as a land-scape equivalent to a way of life, then we have, evidently, a parallel in Arnold's prose to one of the most frequent features of his poems. Nor is its concluding apostrophe the only point at which the preface to *Essays in Criticism* may remind us of Arnold's poetry. The preface has, in its first and fullest form of 1865, what might be called a double movement: a movement through a series of false images, of gods and edifices, towards the true image of Oxford as both the "beautiful city" and the "Queen of Romance"; and a movement through a series of mockingly defended positions in which the attention is drawn to ironic turns of phrase, to the estab-lishment of tone and personality. The second movement, which may fairly be called rhetorical, accounts for the topical satire in which the original preface is so rich as to make it, perhaps, another "prologomena of the *Dunciad,*"[24] complete with testimonies of

[23] *Works,* XIII, 308; May 24, 1864.
[24] *Pall Mall Gazette,* I, No. 16, Feb. 24, 1865, p. 127.

authors. The first movement, which may, with less assurance, be called poetic because it encourages retrospection to the terms of what has been previously established, mythologizes Arnold's skirmishes with the newspapers into an episode in a continuing holy war. The full success of the preface depends upon a proper confluence of the two movements into one stream. Such a success would be as a satiric apology for a life. It is as pertinent to recall the *Epistle to Arbuthnot* as *The Dunciad.*

Even if it is valid to distinguish rhetorical and poetic elements in the preface, it must be admitted at once that the poetic is by no means restricted to images of gods and edifices. These are not the only features which encourage retrospection and between which lie those implicit links which make for coherence and added suggestion. When reading the penultimate paragraph devoted to Müller the murderer and the transcendentalist consolations offered by Arnold to his fellow travelers on the Woodford Branch, we should recall the complaint earlier in the preface of the unlucky Mr. Wright that Arnold had "declared . . . there is not any proper reason for his existing."[25] Mr. Wright dated his complaint from Mapperley Hall, Nottingham,[26] and thus prompted Arnold to enquire whether he could report "what has become of that poor girl, Wragg?" (p. x) . Wragg, as no reader of *The Function of Criticism* can forget, was "in custody" at Nottingham after killing her illegitimate child "on Mapperly Hills," and thus delivering herself as mute witness against the thesis that "our old Anglo-Saxon breed [is] the best in the whole world."[27] By the chance of geography, then, Mr. Wright, the unfortunate translator of Homer, is associated with the vulgar Philistine assurance of Podsnappery.[28] Because he is so associated,

[25] *Essays in Criticism* (1865), p. ix. Subsequent references to the first edition will be shown in the text by page number. The preface is usually printed in the greatly shortened version of Arnold's later editions, which reduced the first edition by nearly a half. The cut passages are given in the textual notes of *Complete Prose*, III, 535–39.

[26] *Complete Prose*, III, 485.

[27] *Complete Prose*, III, 273. *The Function of Criticism* was first published separately in Nov., 1864, two or three months before *Essays in Criticism*.

[28] Arnold's "juxtaposition [of 'Wragg is in custody'] with the absolute eulogies of Sir Charles Adderley and Mr. Roebuck" on "our old Anglo-Saxon breed" is obviously similar to the unfortunate interposition of that "stray personage of a meek demeanour" into the after-dinner conversation of Mr. Podsnap. The meek man, it will be recalled, enacting his diffidence in indirect speech in contrast to Podsnap's self-assured direct speech, referred "to the circumstance that some half-dozen people had lately died in the streets, of starvation," and thus attracted to himself the angry incredulity of Podsnap (*Our Mutual Friend*, I, xi). The "Podsnappery" chapter of *Our Mutual Friend* appeared in the fourth number of the serial version in Aug., 1864.

and because Arnold had apparently declared there was not any proper reason for his existing, Mr. Wright is doubly connected with that "portly jeweller" on the Woodford Branch whose fear that he would be the next victim of a railway murder Arnold pretends to have assuaged with *"il n'y a pas d'homme nécessaire"* (p. xvii).[29]

This transcendentalist consolation contributes, moreover, to an important topic which runs through the preface, that of the brevity of human life and the permanence of certain verities. It is, of course, a topic which Arnold had frequently explored in his poems. Mr. Wright and his complaint account for its introduction into the preface. In his mock apology for declaring that Mr. Wright had no reason for existing Arnold confessed that his "phrase had, perhaps, too much vivacity: alas! vivacity is one of those faults which advancing years will only too certainly cure" (p. ix). But, he insisted later in the preface, "Mr. Wright would perhaps be more indulgent to my vivacity if he considered [that]. . . . it is but the last sparkle of flame before we are all in the dark. . . . the earnest, prosaic, practical, austerely literal future" of Philistinism (pp. xi, xii). The concern with epochs, which makes its first significant appearance in Arnold's work with the volume of 1852, was fully developed and articulated by the time of *Essays in Criticism* in 1865. It appears in the preface in Arnold's speculations upon the remote ancestry of "Presbyter Anglicanus," ancestors from "long before the birth of Puritanism" (p. xii). It is overt in the reference to "an epoch of dissolution and transformation, such as that on which we are now entered" (pp. xv–xvi). And it merges naturally with assertions of the permanence of truth and the transience of lives and fashions.

Mr. Wright, with his concern for the existence of himself and his translation of Homer, reappears, I have said, as the "portly jeweller from Cheapside," a representative of "the great English middle class, [with] their passionate, absorbing, almost blood-thirsty clinging to life" (p. xvii). The Philistines base themselves upon the seemingly solid pragmatism of bank dividends and gravel walks (p. xvii). The edifices they build are the logicians' pyramid of addled eggs with one fresh egg of truth buried in the middle (p. viii), or

[29] Müller, the railway murderer, escaped to America, whence he was brought back to England by Inspector Richard Tanner (*Complete Prose*, III, 484–85, 489). Earlier in the preface Arnold had envisioned the Philistines' "Palatine Library of the future" with volumes expressive of "the healthy natural taste of Inspector Tanner" (p. xiv). Tanner is not mentioned in the paragraph of transcendentalist consolation, and this small thread of coherence in the preface depends, as the implicit association of Wright and the Cheapside jeweller does not, upon an external and topical connection.

"the Palatine Library of the future. A plain edifice, like the British College of Health enlarged" (p. xiii). Their heroes are "Goliath, the great Bentham" (p. xiii) and "that representative man, that Ajax of liberalism, one of our modern leaders of thought, who signs himself 'Presbyter Anglicanus' " (p. xi). Their god is Dagon, their "Palladium of enlightenment, the hare's stomach" (p. xiii), which Bishop Colenso had used to exemplify the scientific inaccuracy of the Bible.[30] Their religious life is exercised in "a pious pilgrimage, to obtain, from Mr. Bentham's executors, a sacred bone of . . . [their] great, dissected Master" (p. xviii). Their literature constitutes a library free "from all the lumber of antiquity," except for Demosthenes, "because he was like Mr. Spurgeon" (p. xiv), and fills "the whole earth" with "the magnificent roaring of the young lions of the *Daily Telegraph*" (pp. xii–xiii). Mr. Wright, that Philistine by unlucky association, would do well to remember that in the Philistine future there will be no place "for his heroic blank verse Homer" (p. xiii). Nor, presumably, will there be any place for the blank verse Homer of the Chancellor of Oxford, despite "its freshness, its manliness, its simplicity" (p. xv).

The wit of the preface, with its grand edifices and strange gods, with its constant writing up of polemical debate into incongruous battle, is mock-heroic. Arnold, the preface reminds us, is not only the most classical, but also the most neoclassical of the Victorians. The imaginative wit which is at times, as the *Pall Mall Gazette* noted, "so whimsical,"[31] the urbane teasing which is at times so facetious, are reminiscent of Swift's *Battle of the Books*. In the counterpoint of Homeric translation and Benthamite jewellers there is even the suggestion of an ancients and moderns controversy.

But if the mock-heroic elevation of his adversaries and their creeds provides Arnold with multiple opportunities for the exercise of urbane wit and through the wit for the establishment of tone and ethos, the elevation also provides those comfortable worldlings of "the great English middle class" (p. xvii) with a religion, a temple, a field of battle, and a cadre of champions to set against the heroic cause of those valiant for truth. The preface begins with an account of Truth as a "mysterious Goddess, whom we shall never see except in outline. . . . He who will do nothing but fight impetuously towards her on his own, one, favourite, particular line, is

[30] *Complete Prose*, III, 487–88.
[31] *Pall Mall Gazette*, I, No. 16, p. 127.

inevitably destined to run his head into the folds of the black robe in which she is wrapped" (p. vii). The religiose transcendentalism of this personification establishes the tone of patience and humility, as well as the images of battle and the feminine patronage of truth.[32] The tone is tested in verbal battle with "a people 'the most logical' " and self-assured "in the whole world" (pp. vii–viii). The Goddess Truth finds an adversary in the Philistine Dagon and a false-semblant in that "Urania, the Goddess of Science herself,"

[32] In these terms the Goddess Truth seems to be Arnold's invention. The immediate source for his personification is probably (Complete Prose, III, 482) Renan's Préface to his Essais de Morale et Critique of 1859 with its opening image for the ineffable reality of existence: "Des voiles impénétrables nous dérobent le secret de ce monde étrange dont la réalité à la fois s'impose à nous et nous accable; la philosophie et la science poursuivront à jamais, sans jamais l'atteindre, la formule de ce Protée qu'aucune raison ne limite, qu'aucun language n'exprime" (Paris, 1924, pp. i–ii). Renan's proceeding to insist that to love good and hate evil "aucun système n'est nécessaire" (p. ii) is paralleled by Arnold's attack on "the elaborate machine-work of my friends the logicians" (p. viii). It is perhaps unnecessary to enquire further, but it should be noted that, if Renan is Arnold's sole source, Arnold has combined Renan's two images of an ineffable formula for truth which changes like the god Proteus and a secret reality shrouded in impenetrable veils into a single image of a "mysterious Goddess" in an enveloping black robe. Plutarch is closer to the attributes of Arnold's deity in his account of Isis in De Iside et Osiride. Principally, Isis is for Plutarch matter and multiplicity to complement the form and unity of Osiris. But several of his points seem relevant to Arnold's preface. Plutarch begins with a philological attempt to connect Isis with knowing, wisdom, and truth, and her adversary, Typhon, with conceit, ignorance, and violent destruction (Moralia, 351 F). He later records that statues of Isis, the moon goddess, are draped in black garments (Moralia, 372 D). Equally of note is his use of one of Isis' shrines to illustrate the way in which Egyptian philosophy "is veiled in myths and in words containing dim reflexions and adumbrations of the truth. . . . In Saïs the statue of Athena, whom they believe to be Isis, bore the inscription: 'I am all that has been, and is, and shall be, and my robe no mortal has yet uncovered' " (Moralia, 354 C, trans. Frank Cole Babbitt, Loeb Library [Cambridge, Mass., 1936], V, 23–25). The robe, or peplos, of Isis-Athena was certainly full and probably included a veil, hence Banier's rendering of the last clause of the inscription at Saïs as "nul entre les mortels n'a encore levé mon voile" (Mythologie [Paris, 1748], II, 296). This is the goddess whom Tennyson used in Maud, Part I, IV, viii, to image the dark "drift of the Maker": "an Isis hid by the veil." And see Bulfinch, The Age of Fable (1855) in Bulfinch's Mythology (New York [1947]), p. 296: "Isis was represented in statuary with the head veiled, a symbol of mystery." There is a curious passage in one of Arnold's early letters to Clough, in which he advances the proposition that a writer should be an "Exhibition" not a "Reformer," should keep pure his "Aesthetics" by not trying to urge it "as doctrine." Such writers will be "fellow worshippers of Isis . . . [believing] in the Universality of Passion as Passion" (Clough Letters, p. 59; [1845?]). In the Oxford lecture on Maurice de Guérin, later included in Essays in Criticism, Arnold praised Guérin for the "natural magic" of his interpretation of nature and for his "sense of what there is adorable and secret in the life of Nature . . . his expression has . . . something mystic, inward, and profound. So he lived like a man possessed; with his eye not on his own career, not on the public, not on fame, but on the Isis whose veil he had uplifted" (Complete Prose, III, 34).

who numbers among her hierophants "Professor Pepper, Professor Anderson, Professor Frickel" (p. xv), conjurors and magicians of the day who adopted the title of Professor,[33] and so, we are assured, convinced Arnold he should not congratulate himself on possessing the Chair of Poetry at Oxford (pp. xiv–xv). The Goddess Truth finds at last her true champion among her own sex in Oxford, the "Queen of Romance," an Oxford which "hast given thyself so prodigally, given thyself to sides and to heroes not mine, only never to the Philistines" (p. xix).

But Oxford is not only a warrior queen engaging herself on behalf of a mysterious goddess. In the final apostrophe's blend of tones and roles unqualified admiration for the "Queen of Romance" is simply the last note. If it were the only note, the praise of Oxford would be, perhaps, rapturous to the point of sentimentality. The drift to idolatry is checked by the note of irony which accompanies the introduction of Oxford in the final paragraph. It is not the irony, teasing to the point of occasional facetiousness to which the Philistines were earlier subjected. The irony now is indulgent and affectionate. But it serves to recall that earlier in the preface there were aspects of Oxford almost as ridiculous, as vulnerable to irony, as Mr. Wright, the *Saturday Review,* and "Presbyter Anglicanus." One of these aspects was the writings of "nebulous professors" pilloried by Disraeli in a speech at Oxford (p. xi). The other, the blank verse translation of Homer by the "illustrious Chancellor" under whom Arnold served, was found, for all its Anglo-Saxon virtues of manliness and simplicity, to be lacking in Homer's "charm" and "play of a divine light" (p. xv). These ironies return at the beginning of the apostrophe to qualify the succeeding admiration:

Beautiful city! so venerable, so lovely, so unravaged by the fierce intellectual life of our century, so serene!
"There are our young barbarians, all at play."
And yet, steeped in sentiment as she lies, spreading her gardens to the moonlight, and whispering from her towers the last enchantments of the Middle Age, who will deny that Oxford, by her ineffable charm, keeps ever calling us near to the true goal of all of us, to the ideal, to perfection,—to beauty, in a word, which is only truth seen from another side. (p. xviii)

[33] *Complete Prose,* III, 484.

The distinction here, focused syntactically by "And yet," is between an earthly Oxford, withdrawn from the age into nostalgia for the past, and a spiritual or, perhaps, essential Oxford, beckoning to a goal which is out of time. The distinction is analogous to that between the Oxford of the nineteenth century and of Duns Scotus in Hopkins' sonnet. Such a distinction serves in the final sentence to resolve the preface's running contrast between passing lives and fashions and eternal verities:

Apparitions of a day, what is our puny warfare against the Philistines, compared with the warfare which this Queen of Romance has been waging against them for centuries, and will wage after we are gone? (p. xix)

The final sentence resolves rather than simply concludes the contrast between permanence and transience because it associates, for the first time in the preface, the battles of the intellectual life with the hitherto unpolemical quest for Truth. A distinction was made in the opening paragraph between those who "try and approach Truth on one side after another" and those who "do nothing but fight impetuously towards her" (p. vii). This contrast between uncombative quest and unproductive battles for opinions runs throughout the preface to be resolved, I say, by making of Oxford in the final apostrophe a quester upon a chivalric errand involving along the way the dispatch of various false gods and champions. As her "unworthy son," fighting in her cause (p. xix), Arnold must try to articulate "her ineffable charm" (p. xviii), must try to glimpse the mysterious goddess, must try to state the charm and "divine light" of Homer, so missing from the Chancellor's translation. He must also—it is an important part of his ethos—apologize, if mockingly, for his undue vivacity to Mr. Wright, and decline, also mockingly, to "raise a finger in self-defence against Mr. Wright's blows" (p. x). For the mockery, the urbane teasing, is the weapon he wields in that busy field of satire which is the preface to *Essays in Criticism*. Corydon has come down from the Cumnor hills, suspending his quest for permanence, in order to renew the battle in the plain, and assault once more the unbreachable, if long-battered fortress of the world, which now interposes its wall between him and the bright vision of truth on mountain tops. The pastoral care of English sheep is no longer restricted to liberating and giving them sustenance; now, it is clear, they must be prodded and goaded to better pastures than those they graze so contentedly.

But Arnold's neoclassicism was not strong enough to dominate his Victorian Romanticism for long. In later editions the preface was extensively cut to remove, especially, the more uncompromisingly topical of his attacks: a procedure Pope would scarcely have comprehended. Also removed were some of the more facetious and whimsical sallies of wit, a cut which suggests that Arnold was not prepared to run for long the risk a good satirist must accept: the risk of bad taste. Gone, too, were many of the false edifices and deities: the logicians' pyramid of eggs, the Palatine Library of the future, the Urania of professorial conjurors. Something of the original effect remains. But with this cutting and knotting of so many of the threads of coherence the reticulation of mood and motif, tone and image, gives place to a strong and familiar regret for a Romantic quest gone astray, the attention distracted from the proper experiencing of truth by a need to decide what must be done with life and the age. Less qualified by ironies than in the original, the elegiac note sounds more clearly in the final version of the preface:

We are all seekers still: seekers often make mistakes.

It is not, after all, a bad epitaph for Arnold's prose; and it is the best of epitaphs for his poems.

Appendix:

Arnold's Volumes of 1849, 1852, 1853, and 1867

Poems are listed in the order in which they appeared in each volume. The titles are those which Arnold eventually gave to each poem. Original titles, where different, are shown in parentheses, together with, in the case of reprinted poems, the date of first publication and the place, when other than a volume of Arnold's poems. The date preceding each title is that of composition as conjectured or established by Kenneth Allott in his edition of the poems; but I have recorded only his question marks, not his other qualifications. The contents of all Arnold's volumes of poems are listed by Russell in *Works*, XV, 343–55. This listing of Arnold's four most important volumes of poetry is offered as a convenient supplement to my discussion at various points of their constitution.

The Strayed Reveller and other Poems (Feb., 1849)

1848?	Quiet Work (Sonnet)
1843–44?	Mycerinus
1848	To a Friend (Sonnet: To a Friend)
1847–48?	The Strayed Reveller
1847–48?	Fragment of an 'Antigone'
1847–48?	The Sick King in Bokhara
	Sonnets:
1844	Shakespeare

1844?	To the Duke of Wellington: On Hearing Him Mispraised
1844	Written in Butler's Sermons
1844	Written in Emerson's Essays
1844–47?	In Harmony with Nature: To a Preacher (To an Independent Preacher, who preached that we should be "In Harmony with Nature")
1847–48	To George Cruikshank: On Seeing, In the Country, His Picture of 'The Bottle' (original title differs only slightly in syntax)
1848	To a Republican Friend, 1848 (originally without the date)
1848	[To a Republican Friend] Continued
1848?	Religious Isolation: To the same Friend
1848–49	A Memory-Picture (To my Friends, who Ridiculed a Tender Leave-taking)
1848–49?	A Modern Sappho
1843–45	The New Sirens (The New Sirens, A Palinode)
1844?	The Voice
1844?	A Question: To Fausta (To Fausta)
1844	Stagirius (Stagyrus)
1843–44	To a Gipsy Child by the Sea-Shore: Douglas, Isle of Man
1843–45	The Hayswater Boat
1847–49?	The Forsaken Merman
1848?	The World and the Quietist
1846	In Utrumque Paratus
1843–48?	Resignation

Empedocles on Etna and other Poems (Oct., 1852)

1849–52	Empedocles on Etna: A Dramatic Poem
1850	Faded Leaves I: The River (The River)
1850?	Urania (Excuse)
1850?	Euphrosyne (Indifference)
1850	Faded Leaves II: Too Late (Too Late)
1850	Faded Leaves IV: On the Rhine (On the Rhine)
1850	Faded Leaves V: Longing (Longing)
1849	Switzerland I: Meeting (The Lake)
1849	Switzerland II: Parting (Parting)
1849–50	Switzerland VI: Absence (Absence)
1849–50?	Destiny

1849	Switzerland V: To Marguerite—Continued (To Marguerite: In Returning a Volume of the Letters of Ortis)
1849–50?	Human Life
1849–52	Despondency
1849–50?	Youth's Agitations (Sonnet)
1849–52	Self-Deception
1849–51	Lines Written by a Death-Bed
1849–52?	Tristram and Iseult
1850	Memorial Verses, April, 1850 (1850: *Fraser's Magazine*)
1849–50?	Courage
1849–50?	Self-Dependence
1849–52	A Summer Night
1849–52	The Buried Life
1849	Switzerland III: A Farewell (A Farewell)
1849	Stanzas in Memory of the Author of 'Obermann': November, 1849 (Originally without the date)
1849–51	Consolation
1849–52	Lines Written in Kensington Gardens
1849–50?	The World's Triumphs (Sonnet)
1849–52	The Second Best
1849–52	Revolutions
1850–52	The Youth of Nature
1852	The Youth of Man
1852?	Morality
1852?	Progress
1852?	The Future

Poems. A New Edition (Nov., 1853)

1853	Preface
1848?	Quiet Work (Sonnet; 1849)
1852–53	Sohrab and Rustum
1843–44?	Mycerinus (1849)
1849–52	Cadmus and Harmonia (1852—from Empedocles on Etna)
1852–53?	Philomela
1847–48?	The Strayed Reveller (1849)
1852–53?	Thekla's Answer
1849–52?	Tristram and Iseult (1852)
1852–53?	The Church of Brou
1852?	The Neckan
1847–49?	The Forsaken Merman (1849)

Switzerland:

1848–49	I	A Memory-Picture (To my Friends, etc.; 1849)
1849	II	Meeting (The Lake; 1852)
1849–53	III	A Dream
1849	IV	Parting (1852)
1849	V	To Marguerite—Continued (To Marguerite; 1852)
1849–50	VI	Absence (1852)

1852 Richmond Hill (1852—from The Youth of Man, ll. 51–60)
1848–49? A Modern Sappho (1849)
1849–53? Requiescat
1852–53 The Scholar-Gipsy

Sonnets:

1848 To a Friend (1849)
1844 Shakespeare (1849)
1844 Written in Emerson's Essays (1849)
1847–48 To George Cruikshank. . . . (1849)
1848 To a Republican Friend, 1848 (1849)
1848 Continued (1849)
1848? Religious Isolation. . . . (1849)
1849–50? The World's Triumphs (1852)
1851 Stanzas in Memory of Edward Quillinan
1852 Power of Youth (1852—from The Youth of Man, ll. 112–18)
1852? Morality (1852)
1849–50? Self-Dependence (1852)
1849–51 Consolation (1852)
1852? The Future (1852)

New Poems (July, 1867)

1867 Persistence of Poetry (No title)
1849–52 Empedocles on Etna (1852)
1864–65 Thyrsis (1866: *Macmillan's Magazine*)
1859–60 St. Brandan (1860: *Fraser's Magazine*)

Sonnets:

1863 A Picture at Newstead
1863 Rachel I
1863 Rachel II
1863 Rachel III
1863 East London
1863? West London

1863	The Better Part (Anti-Desperation)
1863	Immortality
1863	Worldly Place
1863	The Divinity
1864	The Good Shepherd with the Kid
1864?	Austerity of Poetry
1864	East and West
1864	Monica's Last Prayer
1850	Calais Sands
1851	Dover Beach
1863	Switzerland VII: The Terrace at Berne (The Terrace at Berne)
1859	Stanzas from Carnac (Stanzas composed at Carnac, May 6, 1859)
1859	A Southern Night (1861: *Victoria Regia*)
1847–48?	Fragment of Chorus of a 'Dejaneira'
1864–67	Palladium
1849–50?	Human Life (1852)
1855	Early Death and Fame (1855: *Fraser's Magazine*—from Haworth Churchyard following l. 73)
1849–51	Youth and Calm (1852—from Lines . . . by a Death-Bed)
1849–50?	Youth's Agitations (1852)
1864–67	Growing Old
1864–67	The Progress of Poesy : A Variation
1864–67?	A Nameless Epitaph
1864–67?	A Nameless Epitaph (Another)
1864–67	The Last Word
1865	A Wish
1849–52	Lines Written in Kensington Gardens (1852)
1849–52	The Second Best (1852)
–1852	A Caution to Poets
1864–67	Pis-Aller
1864–65	Epilogue to Lessing's Laocoön
1860–67	Bacchanalia; or, The New Age
1852?	Progress (1852)
1857–60?	Rugby Chapel, November, 1857
1858–63	Heine's Grave
1851–55	Stanzas from the Grande Chartreuse (1855: *Fraser's Magazine*)
1865–67	Obermann Once More

The index is of persons and titles, but includes entries for landscape features frequently mentioned. See Landscapes.

THE JOHNS HOPKINS PRESS

Designed by Arlene J. Sheer

Composed in Linotype Baskerville text and ATF Baskerville display by Baltimore Type and Composition Corporation

Printed on 55-lb. Perkins and Squier R by Universal Lithographers, Inc.

Bound in Holliston Roxite Vellum and Lindenmeyr Elephant Hide by L. H. Jenkins Co., Inc.